Grammar and Good Taste

Grammar and Good Taste

Reforming the American Language

DENNIS E. BARON

Yale University Press
New Haven and London

Published with assistance from
the Kingsley Trust Association
Publication Fund established by the
Scroll and Key Society of Yale College.

Designed by Sally Harris
and set in Times Roman type.
Printed in the United States of America by
The Murray Printing Co., Westford, Mass.

Library of Congress Cataloging in Publications Data

Baron, Dennis E.
  Grammar and good taste.
  Bibliography: p.
  Includes index.
  1. English language—United States—History.
2. English language—Reform—History. I. Title.
PE2809.B28   420'.973   82–1873
ISBN 0–300–02799–0   AACR2
    0–300–03080–0 (pbk.)

10 9 8 7 6 5 4 3 2

For Iryce

Contents

Preface

When the nineteenth-century arts critic Richard Grant White undertook to reform the language of his fellow Americans, he brought to the task the bitter memory of being physically punished by a childhood tutor for failure to understand his grammar lessons. Not having always fared well myself in studying grammar or in teaching it, I can understand both White's point of view and that of his instructor. For example, I clearly remember cowering at my desk in a ninth-grade English class while a certain Mrs. B—— rained mysterious objects she called nouns and verbs at us like bombs. I finally mastered the parts of speech in graduate school, or so I thought until I found myself on the other side of the desk, standing before a New York City high school English class, Warriner's grammar book in hand, with instructions from my department head to teach a grammar lesson. The instantaneous Pavlovian glaze in my students' eyes took me back again a dozen years.

White and I reacted in opposite ways to our encounters with grammar. He became a language reformer, joining that band of diehards, now sometimes called pop-grammarians, who fear our language is dying if not already dead, and I became a professor of English linguistics, curious about the reformers of the language who have—to paraphrase the words of Mark Twain—greatly exaggerated the reports of its death.

In my study of American language reform and its failure, I have tried to trace the history both of our present-day concern—or mania—for correctness in speech and writing, and of our continued suspicion—or fear—of formal language regulation. Language critics have lodged the same complaints against English for more than two hundred years, and language reformers have repeatedly advocated the same reforms of our spelling, vocabulary, grammar, and usage. In response to these pressures, the American public has generally agreed that the language is in some need of improvement, yet it has stolidly resisted all attempts at linguistic manipulation, a resistance that only serves to increase the zeal of the reformers.

Many people have assisted me in my work, and I would like to thank them here. My wife, Iryce, has read this manuscript with a tireless critical eye, pointing out inconsistencies and infelicities I would never have nòticed. Professors Frederic G. Cassidy and Brian Wilkie both have been generous with their comments and their encouragement. I would also like to thank Ellen Graham and Sally Serafim, of the Yale University Press, for their faith in my work and their help in getting it before the public; Anne Schmidt, my valuable research assistant; and the various librarians of the University of Illinois who patiently helped me to locate some rare and rather obscure material. Yale University Press and the American Philosophical Society kindly provided the illustrations of Benjamin Franklin's alphabet (figs. 1 and 2). The libraries of the Ohio State University, the University of Illinois, and the Boston Athenaeum furnished the materials from which the illustrations of the alphabets of Amasa D. Sproat (fig. 5), N. E. Dawson (fig. 6), and James Ewing (fig. 4) are drawn. The sample of Jonathan Fisher's reformed alphabet (fig. 3) is reprinted from Alice Winchester's *Versatile Yankee: The Art of Jonathan Fisher, 1768–1847* (Princeton, 1973), by permission of the author. I have tried to follow the suggestions of my friends and colleagues wherever possible; any errors and omissions remain, of course, my own.

1 English Language Planning and Reform

Language planning is the conscious, systematic alteration of a language, or, in the words of sociolinguists Joan Rubin and Björn Jernudd, "*deliberate* language change."[1] It is undertaken for a variety of reasons: political, philosophical, social, economic, literary, and educational. And it is undertaken to improve a given language, to make it a more suitable or a more efficient vehicle of communication. Yet when language planning is discussed we tend to think of it in terms of languages other than English. We may think instead of the obvious triumphs of language planning: the development of modern Hebrew as the national language of Israel; the elevation of the native Norwegian *landsmaal*, or folk-speech, to the status of a literary language in direct competition with the borrowed Danish *bokmaal*, or book-speech, of Norway; the exclusion of Latin and Greek terms from the German vocabulary; and the modernization of Turkish. Or we may think of language planning as a means of encouraging national unity and technological advancement in developing areas of the world, as in the case of Malay. If we are inclined to a historical perspective we may consider such apparent success stories as the deliberate modification and spread of standard French at the expense of the provincial dialects of France, beginning in the mid-seventeenth century with the formation of the French Academy and continuing with great nationalistic fervor during the century after the French Revolution. And we may think of language planning in terms of great projects yet to be undertaken, for example the much anticipated romanization of the Chinese writing system. We may even think of the cross-cultural attempts at language planning, the creation of international auxiliary languages such as Esperanto, Volapük, and Anglic. But we should also realize that for centuries the English language has been the object of deliberate efforts of planning and reform.

Perhaps the earliest such attempt occurred in the thirteenth century, when the monk Ormin devised a system of spelling that employed single and double consonants to indicate the length of preceding vowels. For example, *for* 'went', with long *o*, contrasts with *forr* 'for', with short *o*; *ferd* 'army', contrasts with *ferrde* 'went', *birde* 'lineage, birth' with *birrde* 'becomes', and *cwen* 'queen' with *cwennkenn* 'quench'. While Ormin's manner of spelling was not adopted by any other writers, it does provide us today with important clues to the pronunciation of Middle English. Spelling reforms were again attempted in the sixteenth and seventeenth centuries, and in the eighteenth century there was a flurry of attempts to revise or standardize English grammar, spelling, and usage. In the nineteenth century, particularly in America, the schools joined in the effort to regulate the course of the language, and in the present century it has become apparent that almost every speaker of English has some idea of what should or should not be done with the language in order to improve it.

Yet we do not think of English when we think of language planning and reform because the schemes to direct, reverse, or otherwise alter the course of the language have always fizzled out. Speakers and writers have continually resisted regulation. Even when paying lip service to language reform, they have proved unwilling or unable to modify their usage to fit the newly prescribed molds. This is partly because the language reformers themselves provided poor models for imitation. They have been remarkably inconsistent in their proposals. They have shown a tendency to quarrel among themselves or to get up on soapboxes, urging the adoption of their favorite hobbyhorse while confusing and alienating their audiences. And unlike the scientific language planners of today, they have invariably failed to secure official and popular approval for their endeavors.

Some reformers of English have felt a certain amount of discontent with the state of their language, seeking to rescue it from the advanced stages of decay in which they find it. Others, cheerful optimists and believers in science and rationality, have sought simply to improve an already lively English so that it might take its rightful place among the great languages of the world. Some of the proposals for modifying English have been modest, for example the often repeated call for the strict observance of the subject-verb agreement in the written language. Others have been more complex and even more impractical, such as the suggestion that the Roman alphabet be replaced by a system of phonetic representation similar to that used in shorthand transcription. Some suggestions have been motivated by social prejudice: the argument, for example, that regional peculiarities should be suppressed because they are inappropriate in formal discourse. And others are more blatantly political: the proposal to rename the language of the United States as *American* rather than *English*.

Sterling A. Leonard and Hans Aarsleff have written definitive accounts of the history of language thought and planning in seventeenth- and eighteenth-century England, and the history of the English language in America has been thoroughly discussed in works by George Phillip Krapp, H. L. Mencken, and Allen Walker Read, among others. But in this book we will examine an area that until now has been more or less neglected, the history of language planning and reform in America. Our study will be largely confined to the eighteenth and nineteenth centuries, a period in which the major patterns of American language reform crystallized. We must look to this period if we wish to trace the sources of many of our present ideas about American English and if we wish to evaluate more objectively contemporary proposals for the modification of the language. We will concentrate on the work of American language reformers, but it will often be necessary to consider the influence of British and even French writers, for the planning of language often transcends national boundaries.

The language reforms we will examine largely concern such specific measures as the modification of grammar or spelling to make them more regular; and the resistance to neologism, the formation of new words, or to errors in idiom and pronunciation. Occasionally the plans are more sweeping. Both the purists who wanted to purge all foreign words from English, replacing them with native "Saxon" equivalents, and the spelling reformers, whose phonetic renderings of English words were as visually confusing as they were inconsistent, drew fire from critics for striking at the very essence of English and threatening to supplant our language with a foreign tongue. While most plans aim simply at the restructuring of the English language, implicit in many of them is the assumption that a change in language will produce a corresponding change in the world view of its users: a more rational English language would, it was thought, produce more rational speakers of English. Such notions are reflected in contemporary English reform as well. For example, the movement to promote nonsexist language, which has its linguistic roots in mid-nineteenth century attempts to find a palatable alternative to the generic use of the third person singular pronoun *he*, has as one of its major goals the creation of a nonsexist society.

It is also important to note that those who busied themselves with planning the English language in the eighteenth and nineteenth centuries were not professional linguists, despite the fact that these very centuries were a time of intense activity in comparative and historical linguistics. Concerned with the problem of the linguistic ignorance of language reformers, H. C. G. von Jagemann, in "Philology and Purism" (1899), his presidential address to the Modern Language Association, urges that philologists take a more active role in language planning. He acknowledges the fact that many scholars do not like to interfere with the natural processes of linguistic development, but he notes that amateurs have already meddled with language to such an extent that it is often difficult to know what is natural change and what is not. Von Jagemann warns against the common assumption of the language planners of his day that regularity and simplicity are desirable in language: "What tends to regularity may also tend to destroy variety and euphony, what promotes simplicity may destroy accuracy." Calling for better linguistic education, he decries the general public's view of how language works: "That the weather clerk really makes the weather probably none but infants believe, but that language is made by the compilers of dictionaries and grammars is a conception not confined to the young or ignorant."[2]

The American linguist Charles C. Fries also complained that popular misconceptions about language interfere with the pursuit of linguistic knowledge. Because the publishers of books must cater to the desires and superstitions of the buyers, no dictionary, according to Fries, "even for the sake of scientific truth and language accuracy, could afford to oppose the prejudices and the common beliefs of the school public which buys the dictionaries."[3] And H. C. Wyld, professor of philology at Oxford University, comments, in his inaugural lecture in 1921, on the unwillingness of the public to be educated about the science of language: "The general ignorance concerning it is so profound that it is very difficult to persuade people that there really is a considerable mass of well-ascertained fact, and a definite body of doctrine on linguistic questions."[4]

The statements of Wyld and Fries are certainly as applicable today as they were half a century ago. Despite advances in descriptive and theoretical linguistics in the last one hundred years, the American public still believes in what Fries has called the doctrine of original sin in grammar, and language planning remains in America to a large extent in the hands of the self-styled expert, the untrained pop-grammarian, with predictable results. What H. C. Wyld said in 1921 was as true in 1300 and 1700 as it is today: "The subject-matter of English Philology possesses a strange fascination for the man in the street, but almost everything that he thinks and says about it is incredibly and hopelessly wrong. There is no subject which attracts a larger number of cranks and quacks than English Philology" (p. 10).

While some of the planners and reformers of the American language that we will encounter certainly deserve to be called cranks and quacks, others do not. Yet all are quite serious in their endeavors and all have nothing but the good of the language at heart. Most are optimistic that their plans will succeed, while a few admit candidly that there is little chance that their reforms will be adopted. For those like Noah Webster, planning the American language was a life's work; for others it was a more casual enterprise. But for all, the perfection of the language was a paramount concern, and any personal contribution that they could make to its improvement was worth their effort.

We will begin this study by examining early attitudes toward the English language in the New World, and the development of the concept of Federal English in post-Revolutionary America. A part of the rising tide of federalism, Federal English sprang from a notion that the New World provided a language laboratory in which improvements in the democratically based English language would be made as a matter of course, and it contributed directly to our present-day notion of Standard English. In later chapters we will consider the movements for spelling reform and for the creation of a language academy on the model of the French Academy, ideas which seem perennially to be with us. We will then examine the role of the common schools in directing the course of English through grammar instruction, and finally we will consider the numerous nineteenth-century guides to correct usage, which picked up where the schools left off (or which tried to succeed where the schools had failed) in their mission to create a linguistically orthodox, uniform, and sophisticated American public. We will conclude with a brief look at the state of present-day language reform, which differs very little in form or substance from its precursors.

The following chapters will demonstrate that language reform in America, for all its good intentions, has proved an exercise in futility. Poor or inconsistent planning, the lack of adequate publicity, and the inability to arouse public support have all contributed to this failure, but perhaps the greatest stumbling block for language reformers has been their own misunderstanding of what is involved in deliberate language change. It is true that American language reformers have been able to arouse the linguistic consciousness, or at least the linguistic insecurity, of the nation: most people, if questioned, would probably admit to a concern with correct spelling, good grammar, and good taste in English usage. But these same reformers have not been able to get the American public to alter its linguistic behavior very much in order to achieve these or any other goals. Because language change is not normally a rational and deliberate process, any attempt to make it so must be supported by a mechanism to implement planned change. Such a mechanism does not exist in American society, where there is no language academy and where legal action to regulate language behavior has not been forthcoming. Even in societies where such official direction of language exists, the language tends to exhibit a life of its own, breaking free of artificial constraints and defying the means of planning and control.

The history of the failure of language reform in America should serve as a warning to those who would modify the language of its people. But if past attempts at reform are any indication, some of the specifics may change, but the same complaints about the English language will continue to be made, and planners will continue to make new proposals or revive old ones, all of which are doomed to fail.

2 Language and the New Nation

The Treasure of Our Tongue

The New World originally presented an attractive prospect to the European mind, a vision of Eden where civilization might flourish unchecked. The opportunity it afforded for the transplantation of language and culture, and for the nourishing of the future, is described by Samuel Daniel in 1603 in his poem "Musophilus":

> And who, in time, knowes whither we may vent
> The treasure of our tongue, to what strange shores
> This gaine of our best glory shall be sent,
> T'inrich vnknowing Nations with our stores?
> What worlds in th'yet vnformed Occident
> May come refin'd with th'accents that are ours?[1]

The treasure of the English tongue was planted on the shores of the New World, and what grew from that planting was a crop of a controversial nature. The English language in America has been variously regarded as a new staff of life and a curse. Americans, in general, sought to plan their language, to cultivate, refine, and improve it, to make it more—or less—like the language of Great Britain. The British, on the other hand, generally came to ridicule a dialect of their language that seemed to threaten their political and cultural existence, and they too sought to manipulate the rebellious tongue. In this chapter we will examine the development of the idea of a Federal English, an American language independent of its origins (though not necessarily cut off from them), a language that could be planned to reflect the peculiar American political, social, and cultural genius, a language in which the laws and literature of the new nation could be inscribed. We will trace this idea from its origins, just after the American Revolution, to its twilight in the mid-nineteenth century, examining, at the same time, related ideas on language and language planning, in order to create a picture of what the American language *seemed* like (not necessarily what it *was* like) to contemporary observers, and what they felt it should become. We will look at some attempts to alter American English materially, and we will see that, while attempts to reform the American language usually failed, the ideas and ideals related to that language were not abandoned. In the 1780s, for example, some people feared and others hoped that American English would become a language wholly different from British English. This was equally true in 1860. After the Revolution, many Americans felt their language was destined to become a universal one. And this idea was very much alive in 1900. The term *Federal English*, coined most likely by Noah Webster to represent the linguistic equivalent of political federalism, quickly fell into disuse. But the ideas which it incorporated did not. They exist today, slightly transmuted but only thinly disguised, in the term *Standard American English*: both terms are idealistic, poorly defined—if not incapable of definition—and both serve primarily as rallying cries for language reformers.

An American Language

One of the earliest accounts of English in America finds the language to be thriving. Hugh Jones, clergyman and professor of mathematics at William and Mary College, believed the coming of Europeans to the New World fulfilled an Old Testament prophecy. In *The Present State of Virginia* (1724) he describes a linguistic paradise that should have been the envy of anyone in England: "The *Planters*, and even the *Native Negroes* generally talk good English without *Idiom* or *Tone*, and can discourse handsomly upon *most* common subjects."[2] But on closer examination, the New World proved as postlapsarian as the Old, and while Jones was praising what he found—or what his idealism led him to find—others concentrated on the weeds growing in the new Eden. Francis Moore, who accompanied Oglethorpe in his explorations of the Southeast, complains of the barbarous use of the word *bluff* to indicate a riverbank in Georgia (1735), and as early as 1758 there is a call for the formal regulation of English in America through education. An article in the *American Magazine* advocates English as a school subject, "for as we are so great a mixture of people, from almost all corners of the world, necessarily speaking a variety of languages and dialects, the true pronounciation [*sic*] and writing of our own language might soon be lost among us, without such a previous care to preserve it in the rising generation."[3] Americans took to the idea of teaching English to speakers of English, regarding as major faults the British educational system's neglect of English and its emphasis on classical languages. The traditions of praising and blaming English in America began early, but it was not until the Revolution that the American language became a political issue, and efforts to establish or reform the language of the United States were seen in the same light as those to establish or reform its government and social institutions. An address "To the Literati of America," appearing in the *Royal American Magazine* in 1774 and suspected to have been written by John Adams, paints in optimistic terms the role of the English language in the New World and proposes a means of regulating it:

> As Language is the foundation of science, and medium of communication among mankind, it demands our first attention, and ought to be cultivated with the greatest assiduity in every seminary of learning. The English language has been greatly improved in Britain within a century, but its highest perfection, with every other branch of human knowledge, is perhaps reserved for this Land of light and freedom. As the people through this extensive country will speak English, their advantages for polishing their language will be great, and vastly superior to what the people in England ever enjoyed.

The writer goes on to suggest a "plan for perfecting the English language in America," a group to be known as the Fellows of the American Society of Language, whose task will be to "correct, enrich and refine it until perfection stops their progress and ends their labour."[4]

The proposed society was never organized, although John Adams later suggested more formally the creation of an American Academy to oversee the language, and a bill was introduced into Congress to create such an organization. Private groups, however, did try their hand at language planning. On July 23, 1788, a procession was held in New York City to celebrate the ratification of the new American Constitution by ten states, and to encourage its adoption by the somewhat recalcitrant state of New York. The procession, an homage to federalism, included groups of laborers, tradespeople, and professionals, many carrying elaborate or ingenious symbols showing the support of their group for the new government. Four master bakers, for example, rode in a wagon and held aloft the federal loaf, which measured 10 feet by 27 inches by 8 inches, and which had the names of the ten ratifying states and the initials of the other three inscribed upon it.[5] The playwright, artist, and theater historian William Dunlap, looking back on that event some forty-five years later, recalls the symbolic role language was singled out to play: "In the procession . . . an association of young men, of which the writer was one, called the Philological Society, carried through the streets of New-York a book inscribed *Federal Language*, as if any other than the English language, the language of our fathers, the cotemporaries of Hampden and Milton, could be desirable for their sons and the inheritors of their spirit." Dunlap's retrospective comment suggests that his earlier ardor for an American language, independent of its British roots, had cooled. His principal concern is with the establishment of a national literature, and he states that this can be brought about not by altering the language or writing only about the New World, but by giving American literature "the impress of our republican government" and having our writers "warn mankind of the evils of governments usurped over the people."[6] But for many Americans, the idea of a Federal Language, as vibrant and independent as the new nation itself, was one that did not die.

The result of the kind of linguistic patriotism shown by the members of the Philological Society is to place English in America in the paradoxical position both of being and of having to become a language. It must justify its existence as a valid form of communication in competition with Standard British English and in the face of ridicule from British observers and American anglophiles. At the same time, it must define itself, establishing its own standards to protect it from the internal and external forces of decay that were seen as menaces to all language. We find American English asserted as a given, a fait accompli. Yet many of those who assert and celebrate its existence and independence also go to great pains to establish its links with the old country, or mother country, as England was called. American pronunciations are traced to English locales, and American expressions are shown to be fine, upstanding, if at times antiquated British forms that have survived, or revived, upon transplantation to the New World. We are told, for example, that Noah Webster assured Basil Hall, a British visitor, that "there were not fifty words in all which were used in America and not in England. . . . All these apparent novelties are merely old English words, brought over to America by the early settlers."[7] Stereotypes of the American dialect arise, are ridiculed and defended, even described and explained scientifically. Amateur linguists, more professional ones, travelers, and literary figures comment on the language of the New

World, noting its forms—or what they feel to be its forms, for their descriptions are not altogether reliable. Indeed, it is often difficult to know how much of what is being said is the simple reflex of a language stereotype, copied perhaps from an uncited authority, and how much is the result of direct observation.

Webster, Adams, Franklin, Jefferson, Madison, and other linguistic patriots become the sternest critics of the Federal Language, applying to it prescriptive standards based on their occasionally idiosyncratic ideas of usage, etymology, or reason in order to recreate the language as a perfect reflection of the American character, an idealized vehicle for American letters, and, most boldly, the next universal language. The American language, being somewhat ornery, responded to such patriotic attempts to steer its course by acquiescing and rebelling, justifying the faith placed in it and confirming the deepest fears. Even today Americans exhibit an ambivalent attitude toward their language, taking pride in it and at the same time complaining that it has all but succumbed to the attacks of barbarians.

Noah Webster, who was to become the best known of American dictionary makers, was a leading member if not the moving force behind the Philological Society, and a staunch federalist as well. He exemplifies this dual attitude toward American English, arguing both for its perfection and its need to be perfected. His interest in the language is both idealistic and commercial. Not only does Webster call for a Federal language, he plans and markets it as well, turning the idea of American English into a career, asking any friends, acquaintances, and "respectable characters" he could find to endorse his books. For example, shortly after it was founded the Philological Society publicly commended Webster's *American Spelling Book*.

Webster gives a detailed eyewitness account of the Federal Procession in the New York *Packet* of August 5, 1788. He notes that the society's contingent was headed by "the secretary, bearing a scroll, containing the principles of a *Federal* language."[8] Although the book or scroll that was carried in the procession has not survived, we can be reasonably sure that the principles of the Federal Language were dictated largely—perhaps entirely—by Webster, and we can find in his correspondence and publications some indication of what those principles were. We can be certain, for one thing, that the Philological Society championed a variety of English, and not Hebrew, Greek, or French, languages that had been proposed as replacements for English out of strong anti-British sentiment. The Marquis de Chastellux, a

French soldier and intellectual who aided George Washington and published an account of his travels in North America in the 1780s, discusses the suggestion of Hebrew:

> [The Americans] have carried it even so far, as seriously to propose introducing a new language; and some persons were desirous, for the convenience of the public, that the *Hebrew* should be substituted for the English. The proposal was, that it should be taught in the schools, and made use of in all public acts. We may imagine that this project went no farther; but we may conclude from the mere suggestion, that the Americans could not express in a more energetic manner, their aversion for the English.[9]

In an article sharply critical of everything American, the *Quarterly Review* of London is less neutral on the subject. Speaking of the Americans, it says, "Nor have there been wanting projects among them for getting rid of the English language, not merely by barbarizing it . . . but by abolishing the use of English altogether, and substituting a new language of their own. One person indeed had recommended the adoption of Hebrew, as being ready made to their hands, and considering the Americans, no doubt, as the 'chosen people' of the new world."[10] Defending his country against this charge, and of the charge that Americans planned to substitute the phonetic alphabet devised by William Thornton, a Scot who emigrated to America, for the more traditional one, Charles Jared Ingersoll replies, "ninety-nine, out of a hundred, and more probably nine hundred and ninety-nine, out of a thousand, *Americans*, never heard of either."[11] But Herbert Croft, a British scholar who unsuccessfully proposed a revision of Dr. Johnson's *Dictionary*, indicates in 1797 that such ideas did have some currency among patriots: "During the American revolution, the idea was started of revenging themselves on England, by rejecting its language and adopting that of France."[12] And Charles Astor Bristed, grandson of John Jacob Astor, in an essay explaining, and at times excusing, American English to his British friends (1855), mentions the equally unsuccessful proposal for making Greek the national language of America:

> Dreams of a new or a different tongue did indeed haunt the imagination of some more zealous than wise patriots in the earlier period of American history. It is still on record that a legislator seriously proposed that the young republic should complete its independence by adopting a different language from that of the mother-country,

"the Greek for instance," which proposition was summarily extinguished by a suggestion of a fellow representative [Roger Sherman of Connecticut, delegate to the Continental Congress and a member of the committee that drafted the Declaration of Independence] that "it would be more convenient for us to keep the language as it was, and *make the English speak Greek.*"[13]

American Linguistic Independence

The newly independent Americans were unwilling to give up their language, but many of them were equally unwilling to share it with their former rulers. This linguistic nationalism, which in its extremes has contributed to the twentieth-century stereotype of the "ugly American," is described by the Marquis de Chastellux:

As for the Americans, they testified more surprize than peevishness, at meeting with a foreigner who did not even understand English. But if they are indebted for this opinion to a prejudice of education, a sort of national pride, that pride suffered not a little from the reflection, which frequently occurred, of the language of the country being that of their oppressors. Accordingly they avoided these expressions, *you speak English; you understand English well*; and I have often heard them say—*you speak American well; the American is not difficult to learn.* [*Travels*, 2:265]

Some Americans were reluctant to part ways with the language of the old country, and they expressed their disapproval at the direction things were going, though most patriots were happy to celebrate American English as a new and distinct variety of the language. In 1814 a correspondent signing himself "Lemuel Lengthy" advises the readers of the *Analectic Magazine* that the best way to assure American linguistic independence "would be, to invent an entire new language." This being impractical, Lengthy defends our right to an American language, which "is ours by right of conquest, for when we wrested these states from England, we subdued the language with them, and in acquiring a right to make laws for the land, gained also the power of making laws for the language." Lengthy advises us to shape our language as we would any other branch of our manufacturing system. He resents British criticism of our English as an "attempt to interfere with the privilege of speech, a privilege for which our ancestors left their native country," and he criticizes the American veneration of everything foreign, particularly "the patience with which we listen to the bad English of Englishmen . . . [who] rail at the ideous habsurdity of the Hamerican abit of speaking" (3:404–08).

A few extremists preferred to deny linguistic ties with Britain altogether. As late as 1859 James P. Herron, author of *American Grammar: Adapted to the National Language of the United States*, strongly recommends calling our speech *American Language*. He sees any association of the United States with England as damaging both to our domestic and our international image. American achievements and our status in the world merit "our *language* in our country's *name*, that any desired effect may not be frustrated by prejudice to England and the British Government." We must no longer "keep our tongue clothed in the scarlet garb of a British Isle." Herron regards the American Language as a new one, an independent, melting-pot language derived from many sources, not just English: "We express our own free thoughts in *language* our own, adopted from the tongues of the many nations, of our forefathers. . . . Consequently, language in the United States is *Polyglot*—national with our people—not borrowed from any one distinct tongue."[14] Herron's prefatory comments are more radical than the material he presents in the body of his grammar. There we find simply a recognition of some distinctive American spellings based on the 1847 edition of Webster's *Dictionary*, and by that time Webster's successors had retracted his most extreme orthographic innovations. Fortunately, Herron does not try to prove his claim of philological independence for the American Language, a task that even the most hard-nosed British critic of our tongue would find impossible.

Herron's declaration of linguistic independence, while radical, was by no means a new phenomenon. The terms *American language* and *American grammar* appeared in print often after the Revolution. Sometimes they referred to simple geography. Robert Ross's *American Grammar* (Hartford, 1782) was nothing more than a grammar of English and Latin that was published in America, and *The Compendious American Grammar* that Daniel Humphreys printed in Portsmouth, New Hampshire, in 1792, is entirely silent on the political language controversies of the day. Benjamin Dearborn's *Columbian Grammar* (1795), and *Cramer's United States Spelling Book* (1839) are similarly mute. But it is likely that the following entry, dated July 20, 1778, from the *Secret Journals of the Acts and Proceedings of Congress*, is concerned with a little more than geography. It specifies the manner of communicating with ministers from abroad, avoiding any mention of the taboo word,

English: "All speeches, or communications in writing, may, if the pub-
lick ministers choose it, be in the language of their respective countries.
And all replies, or answers, shall be in the language of the United
States."[15]

The Idealized Character of American English

Often enough the adjective *American*, when applied to language, had
clear political overtones. Early commentators on the language situation
in the New World did not hesitate to take sides.[16] While some simply
noted the appearance of new terms to meet new situations, others were
more critical of what they found. The Marquis de Chastellux, tying his
opinion of the language to his observation of American pragmatism,
finds the innovations of American English to be impoverished. Discussing a blue jay that he has managed to shoot, he says:

> The Americans call it only by the name of the *blue bird*, though it
> is a real jay; but the Americans are far from being successful in
> enriching their native language. On every thing which wanted an
> English name, they have bestowed only a simple descriptive one:
> the jay is the blue bird, the cardinal, the red bird; every water bird
> is a duck, from the teal to the *canard de bois*, and to the large black
> duck which we have not in Europe. They call them, *red ducks,
> black ducks, wood ducks*. It is the same with respect to their trees;
> the pine, the cypresses, the firs, are *all* comprehended under the
> general name of pine-trees; and if the people characterize any par-
> ticular tree, it is from the use to which it is applied, as the *wall-nut*,
> from its serving to the construction of wooden houses. I could cite
> many other examples, but it is sufficient to observe, that this pov-
> erty of language proves how much men's attention has been em-
> ployed in objects of utility, and how much at the same time it has
> been circumscribed by the only prevailing interest, the desire of
> augmenting wealth, rather by dint of labour, than by industry.
> [*Travels*, 1:41–42]

The anonymous English translator of this work takes exception to one
of the marquis's examples: "Here the Author is a little inaccurate respecting the English language, as the same word *wall-nut*, is applied to
the same tree in England, and with no reference whatever to any such
use" (*Travels*, 1:42). Nevertheless, one of the common stereotypes of
American English was its pragmatic nature. The British sailor and nov-

elist Capt. Frederick Marryat, in an account of his American travels published fifty years later, comes to the same conclusion as the Marquis de Chastellux, although he does not necessarily find fault with Americans for their plainness of style: "The Americans are very local in their phrases, and borrow their similes very much from the nature of their occupations and pursuits."[17]

Functional naming may be a sign of language deprivation to the marquis, but the mere hint of Americanism signaled anarchy—both in government and language—to many in Britain. The London *Eclectic Review*'s remarks on the first major collection of Americanisms, John Pickering's *Vocabulary, or Collection of Words and Phrases Which Have Been Supposed to Be Peculiar to the United States of America* (1816), indicate the fear with which Europe could regard the American linguistic wilderness. In an elaborately constructed metaphor, the reviewers represent themselves as the sole forces of social stability: "A democratic insubordination spreads through the republic of letters, which, were it not for the salutary authority of us Reviewers, would speedily terminate in a total disregard of the constituted lexicographical authorities, in the degradation of the literary aristocracy, and, in short, in a kind of literary anarchy" (ser. 2; 13[1820]: 357). But the *Eclectic*'s reviewers had about as much hope of stopping the onslaught of transatlantic English as the redcoats did of getting the colonial armies to speak Greek.

A Democratic Tongue

The comments of the Marquis de Chastellux and of the British reviewers connect language with both society and government. Such connections were common, and they were not always negative. In 1789, Roland de la Platière, who was to become a minister after the French Revolution, expressed the opinion that American English would one day replace French as the world language. To qualify for such a position, a language must have reached a state of perfection, and it must be employed by a sufficiently large number of people. According to Roland, English had the merits of ancient Greek, but was hampered by the insufficiencies of the British. However, the United States, where the same tongue was spoken, offered conditions better suited for the flourishing of the language:

> The inhabitants of the United States, as proud and no less brave than the English, as active and no less industrious, more tempered

by misfortune and more pressed by need, are more human, more generous, more tolerant, all qualities that make one want to share the opinions, adopt the customs, and speak the language of such a people.[18]

Citing the descriptions of American society written by his former compatriot, the naturalized American Michel-Guillaume Jean de Crèvecoeur, Roland praises its social and commercial enlightenment. Americans will be strangers to no one; they will fraternize with the universe, showing the same indulgence to the ignorant savages who are their neighbors and the jealous Europeans who are their allies. Their government creates patriots, and their resources create the most powerful of merchants. In short, everything about America favors the extension of its language:

The very charm of their philosophy, so suited to win people's hearts, seems to pave the way for the triumph of their opinions and must one day convert many to their consoling religion. . . . It seems to me that the language of such a nation will one day be the universal language. [P. 92]

In his remarks, Roland recognized what Americans had already suspected for some time. John Adams, suggesting in 1780 that Congress establish an academy to oversee the language, notes the salutary effects that government and language can have on one another: "It is not to be disputed that the form of government has an influence upon language, and language in its turn influences not only the form of government, but the temper, the sentiments, and manners of the people." Asserting that republics have attained greater "purity, copiousness, and perfection of language than other forms of government," Adams points to Athens and Rome as examples of the connections between liberty, prosperity, glory, eloquence, and language, and he predicts "that eloquence will become the instrument for recommending men to their fellow-citizens, and the principal means of advancement through the various ranks and offices" in American society. He also predicts that within a generation English will replace French as the world language, "because the increasing population in America, and their universal connection and correspondence with all nations will, aided by the influence of England in the world, whether great or small, force their language into general use, in spite of all the obstacles that may be thrown in their way, if any such there should be."[19] As far as Adams is concerned, the influence of England on world matters will in the future be minimal: "England will never have any more honor, excepting now and then that of imitating the Americans,"[20] and he suggests that if Congress establishes a language academy, the British may follow suit. Charles Jared Ingersoll, writing in 1810, is even more pessimistic about the state of the language in England. Seeing a clear danger to the survival of European English posed by the French armies and the French tongue, Ingersoll assures the British that they need not fear for their language: "There is on this side of the Atlantic a nation capable of preserving and transmitting it to future generations."[21] Although the date when English would become universal was put back several times, optimism over its eventual triumph did not wane in America. In 1901, the philologist Brander Matthews predicts "that the world language at the end of the twentieth century—should any one tongue succeed in winning universal acceptance—will be English. If it is not English, then it will not be German or Spanish or French; it will be Russian."[22]

Claims for the universality of American English arise partly from a spirit of national exuberance and partly in reaction to the negative reception of American language and literature in England and, to a lesser extent, elsewhere. They are reasoned hypotheses and defensive stances, and in both cases they serve as the basis for the establishment and formal planning of the American language. It is in the early work of Noah Webster, and to a lesser degree in the work of William Thornton and William S. Cardell, that we find the language of America deliberately planned to fit its politics, and it is to this work that we will ultimately turn to discover the principles of the Federal Language that so caught the spirit of the Federal Philologists as they marched in the New York procession. But first we must examine the linguistic aspect of that procession, and survey some of the ideas about the nature of American English that were current in the eighteenth and early nineteenth centuries.

An American Coat of Arms

William Dunlap, who was an artist as well as a dramatist and theater historian, carried the arms of the Philological Society in the Federal procession of 1788. No doubt he and Noah Webster were responsible for the planning and execution of the elaborate design, which Webster describes and explicates in his account for the New York *Packet*. Here we find an idealized portrait of language, tailored specifically for independence and federalism, making a conscious break with the classical tradition that had dominated English grammar in the eighteenth century. The coat of arms, which has not survived, appeared as follows:

Argent three tongues, gules, in chief; emblematical of *language*, the improvement of which is the object of the institution. Chevron, or, indicating firmness and support; an *eye*, emblematical of *discernment* over a pyramid, or rude monument, sculptured with Gothic, Hebrew, and Greek letters. The Gothic on the *light* side, indicating the *obvious* origin of the American language from the Gothic. The Hebrew and Greek, upon the reverse or *shade*, of the monument, expressing the remoteness and *obscurity* of the connection between those languages and the modern. The *crest*, a cluster of cohering magnets, attracted by a key in the centre; emblematical of *union* among the society, in acquiring *language* the *key* of knowledge; and clinging to their *native* tongue in preference to a *foreign* one. The *shield*, ornamented with a branch of the oak, from which is collected the *gall*,[23] used in making ink, and a sprig of *flax*, from which *paper* is made, supported on the dexter side, by *Cadmus*, in a robe of Tyrian purple, bearing in his right hand, leaves of the rush or flag, *papyrus*, marked with Phoenician characters; representing the introduction of letters into Greece, and the origin of writing. On the sinister side, by Hermes, or Taaut, the inventor of letters, and god of eloquence, grasping his caduceus or wand. Motto—*Concedat Laurea Linguae* ['Yield, honors, to the tongue'—a paraphrase of Cicero]—expressive of the superiority of *civil* over *military* honors. The flag, embellished with the Genius of America, crowned with a wreath of 13 plumes, ten of them starred, representing the ten States which have ratified the *Constitution*. Her right hand pointing to the Philological Society, and in her left, a standard, with a pendant, inscribed with the word, Constitution.[24]

Webster asserts that the American language derives directly from Gothic. His omission of any explicit reference to English surely reflects his patriotic spirit, although Webster spells *centre* in a fashion he would soon repudiate as illogical and anglophilic. Hebrew and Greek are placed in shadows to indicate their irrelevance to the American language of the 1780s, although the arms, their imagery, and the motto of the society certainly owe more to the classics than to Gothic. But these are minor matters, not sufficient to trouble a man like Webster, whose idealism and sense of self-worth allowed him to transcend the mistakes and inconsistencies with which his work abounded, and which his critics were only too pleased to point out. More important are the ideas of federal language that the society's coat of arms expresses. The magnets of the crest signify not just political but linguistic union as well. They are a force for linguistic uniformity, and in so far as they repel foreign influence, they are a statement of linguistic isolationism. The coat of arms as a whole and its motto stress the importance of language and letters, while the Genius of America, holding the Constitution in one hand, points with the other—the right hand—to the Philological Society, a gesture which raises that enthusiastic if immodest group to national prominence. Language is also raised to a level of the greatest importance, where, equated with American independence and with the American state itself, it has remained, at least symbolically, to the present day.

Webster: American for the Americans

Noah Webster was a language planner from the start. As early as 1783, when he was writing a grammar of American English, Webster places language reform in the context of politics. Writing to his friend John Canfield in that year he says, "I am fully of the opinion that the reformation of the language we speak will some time or other be thought an object of legislative importance."[25] Language reform was hardly a new idea in the eighteenth century. It permeated linguistic and literary discussions and led to such influential works as Samuel Johnson's *Dictionary* and Bishop Robert Lowth's *Grammar*.[26] Nor was official language reformation a new idea, although such reform was usually seen as the province of an academy devoted to philological concerns and not of any legislative body.

Webster continues in his letter to Canfield, connecting grammar and literature, and expressing the hope that his grammar "may have some influence in exciting a spirit of literary industry." He echoes a common sentiment of the age: "America must be as independent in *literature* as she is in *politics*, as famous for *arts* as for *arms*." While Webster is mainly thinking about British domination of the English language and its letters, other foreign influences are also to be avoided. In *Sketches of American Policy* (1785), a pamphlet that Webster considered crucial to the framing of the Constitution, we are told that Americans must shun loanwords, and fashionable borrowings from French are singled out as particularly vicious: "America is an independent empire, and ought to assume a national character. Nothing can be more ridiculous than a servile imitation of the manners, the language, and the vices of foreigners. . . . the *belles* and the *beaux*, with tastes too refined for a vulgar language, must, in all their discourse, mingle a spice of *sans souci* and *je ne scai* [sic] *quoi*."[27]

Webster recognized in immigration a second source of negative foreign influence on the language. Writing to the Legislature of New York in 1783, he requests a copyright to sell his new *American Spelling Book and Grammar*, "designed particularly for the youth in the American Empire," in that state. His book is "calculated to extirpate the improprieties and vulgarisms which were necessarily introduced by settlers from various parts of Europe . . . [and] render the pronunciation of [the language] accurate and uniform by demolishing those odious distinctions of provincial dialects which are the subject of reciprocal ridicule in different states" (*Letters*, p. 5).

America Has No Dialects

Webster felt that uniformity in pronunciation should be a major feature of the Federal Language, and he favored a reformation of the spelling as an aid to the attainment of his goal. Observers had noticed at the outset that in America there was much less regional variation in pronunciation than in England. The British conceded this to be a plus for American English, and American observers (as well as some British ones) were quick to remind the English of their own poor showing in this area. Charles Jared Ingersoll cites Samuel Pegge, author of a book on London English: "Bring together two clowns from *Kent* and *Yorkshire*, and I will wager a ducat, that they will not be able to converse, for want of a dialect, common to them both." In America, native speakers can understand one another easily: "nothing like a dialect can be found in this country" (*Remarks*, pp. 143–44). Pickering, who listed Americanisms in his *Vocabulary* (1816) in order to eradicate them, argues that absence of dialect is no insurance that Americans have not strayed from the purity of the language.[28] And James Fenimore Cooper, in his *Notions of the Americans* (1828), a work addressed to a British audience, admits the existence of variation in American English, but denies that it is significant: "In America, while there are provincial, or state peculiarities, in tone, and even in the pronunciation and use of certain words, there is no patois. An American may distinguish between the Georgian and the New-Englandman, but you cannot."[29] Cooper also feels regional variation in the United States to be continually decreasing: "The distinctions in speech between New-England and New-York, or Pennsylvania, or any other State, were far greater twenty years ago than they are now. Emigration alone would produce a large portion of this change." The general absence of dialect is seen by Cooper as a reflection of American character: considering our vast land area, "this resemblance in speech can only be ascribed to the great diffusion of intelligence, and to the inexhaustible activity of the population, which, in a manner, destroys space" (*Notions*, 2:126). Cooper attributes the irregularities of speech that do exist to the want of a capital on the order of London and, despite his general praise of the language situation in America, he states his preference for the English spoken by the descendants of English parents in the Middle States, and of educated Southerners (2:130).

Do Americans Speak Better English?

In addition to absence of dialect, it was also a common opinion, particularly among Americans, that English was spoken better in the New World than in the old. Even some of the British conceded that the average American spoke better than the average Briton. This was attributed to the democratic makeup of American society, where the different classes associated more freely, and commoners could learn from their betters. But the British insisted that, for this very reason, those who spoke the language best in England were far superior to their colonial counterparts, whose language was no doubt pulled down to the level of mediocrity by association with the riffraff. Captain Marryat expresses the common British view of American speech: "If their lower classes are more intelligible than ours, it is equally true that the higher classes do not speak the language so purely or so classically as it is spoken among the well-educated English" (*Diary*, p. 218), and many Americans agreed with this opinion. James Fenimore Cooper, in 1828, says, "the people of the United States . . . speak, as a body, an incomparably better English than the people of the mother country. . . . We speak our language, as a nation, better than any other people speak their language" (*Notions*, 2:125–26). Cooper concludes his outspoken defense: "There is vastly more bad English, and a thousand times more bad grammar spoken in England than in America; and there is much more good English . . . spoken there [i.e., in America] than here" (2: 135–36). Ten years later, having returned to America from an extended residence abroad, Cooper echoes this sentiment, though in a more tempered form: "The great body of the American people use their language more correctly than the mass of any other considerable nation . . . [however]

a smaller proportion than common attain to elegance."[30] And, in 1860, the *North American Review* says simply, "Here the many speak better than in England, the few not so well" (91:515). As we have seen, the *Quarterly Review* of London is harsh on the subject of the American language and of Americans: "They are not very fond of the English language, but so long as they do condescend to employ it, they are determined to maintain that they make a better use of it than we do ourselves" (10:527).

The British traveler Isabella Lucy Bird, in *The Englishwoman in America* (1848), is more charitable than most commentators toward the American upper classes and their speech, although she clearly does not approve of what some Americans have done to their language, or to their culture. Bird defines Americanisms as "peculiarities of dress, manners, and phraseology, and, to some extent, of opinion, [that] may be partly produced by the locomotive life which the American leads, and the way in which all classes are brought into contact in travelling. These peculiarities are not to be found among the highest or the highly-educated classes, but they force themselves upon the tourist to a remarkable, and frequently to a repulsive extent."[31]

One democratizing aspect of American usage that particularly irritated both the British and the linguistic anglophiles in America was the apparent abandonment of the words *master* and *servant* in favor of *boss* and *help*, and the extension of the term *gentleman* to cover those not to the manner born. James Fenimore Cooper was a harsh critic here, charging that *boss* is used instead of *master*, although it "has precisely the same meaning in Dutch!" Of *help*, he says, "A man does not usually hire his cook to *help* him cook his dinner, but to cook it herself," and of *gentleman*: "To call a laborer, one who has neither education, manners, accomplishment, tastes, associations, nor any one of the ordinary requisites, a gentleman, is just as absurd as to call one who is thus qualified, a fellow." Cooper concludes, "in all cases in which the people of America have retained the *things* of their ancestors, they should not be ashamed to keep the *names*" (*Democrat*, p. 122).

While the American language was criticized for being hypocritically democratic and vulgar, it was also attacked for preciosity. Both Cooper and Marryat see an American propensity for affectation, and Marryat attributes this in part to the desire of Americans "to improve upon the Old Country . . . and to be excessively refined in their language and ideas." In doing so, he feels Americans have ignored the danger of veneer: "There are certain words which are never used in America, but an absurd substitute is employed." Although Marryat eschews indelicacy, he finds that Americans are too dependent on euphemisms. He relates an incident in which a woman became offended at his use of the word *leg*, informing him that *limb* was the preferred term, and adding, "I am not so particular as some people are, for I know those who always say limb of a table, or limb of a piano-forte." Marryat then tells of his visit to a seminary for young ladies where, to ensure good taste, a four-limbed pianoforte had had its limbs dressed "in modest little trousers, with frills at the bottom of them!" (*Diary*, pp. 246–47).

The Danger of Divergence: A More Realistic Assessment

Jonathan Boucher, a clergyman and lexicographer whose loyalist sympathies forced him to return to England after the American Revolution, acknowledges the absence of regional dialects in America in the preface to his *Glossary of Archaic and Provincial Words* (ca. 1800), but Boucher sees this as a dangerous linguistic situation. He feels that American English is itself an illiterate dialect in danger of becoming a separate language:

> Thus, the United States of America, too proud, as it would seem, to acknowledge themselves indebted to this country, for their existence, their power, or their language, denying and revolting against the two first, are also making all the haste they conveniently can, to rid themselves of the last. With little or no dialect, they are peculiarly addicted to innovation: but such as need not excite our envy, whether we regard their elegance, or their propriety. The progress may be slow; but if they continue to be a separate government, and a government too so eminently unpropitious to sound learning and virtuous manners, it will be sure: and it is easy to foresee that, in no very distant period, their language will become as independent of England, as they themselves are; and altogether as unlike English, as the Dutch or Flemish is unlike German, or the Norwegian unlike the Danish, or the Portuguese unlike Spanish.[32]

Boucher's ideas on the development of the Indo-European languages may be shaky, and his attitude toward America colored by political bitterness, but his opinions are echoed by some Americans, as well as by the British travelers who wrote of the language situation they encountered during much of the nineteenth century.

The *North American Review*, commenting on the divergence of British and American English, takes a conservative stand, affirming the American right to expand the language but chastising American writers for breaking with tradition in language as well as in letters. Even in this rejection of the notion of a Federal Language, patriotism is invoked:

> Along with much foolish talk about a national American literature, has sprung up among many American writers a disposition to claim that there is, and of right ought to be, full license allowed to this great, free American people to modify the language, as they have modified customs, institutions, and laws. . . . and though we do not find many writers going so far as to insist upon an American language, yet they do insist upon being absolved from all allegiance, and even from any special deference, to English use and authority. [91:507–08]

Captain Marryat agrees in part with Jonathan Boucher in attributing American language problems to educational deprivation: "The upper classes of the Americans do not, however, speak or pronounce English according to our standard; they appear to have no exact rule to guide them, probably from a want of any intimate knowledge of Greek or Latin" (*Diary*, pp. 219–20). He is less severe and more optimistic than Boucher: "The Americans generally improve upon the inventions of others; probably they may have improved upon our language" (ibid.). And John Woods, another British traveler, is almost laudatory, finding fault with only one aspect of American speech: "With regard to the language of this country, I have found no difficulty to understand any of the Americans I have met with, a few words only excepted. I have seen several from England, that came from a distant part from that in which I resided, that I have had far more trouble to understand. Yet the manner of discourse among the true Back-woods-men is rather uncouth to the English ear."[33]

New World Dialects

Backwoodsmen and Yankees draw most of the linguistic fire, though Southerners, blacks, women, and Germans are also subject to criticism. Royall Tyler, author of the first American dramatic box-office success and creator of the stock character known as the stage Yankee, notes in his essay, *The Yankey in London* (1809), an interesting New England peculiarity that in the twentieth century has come to be regarded as an ethnic, rather than a geographical, stereotype. According to Tyler, there is one shibboleth that will "distinguish an Old from a New-England-man. . . . An Englishman puts and answers a question directly, a New-Englandman puts his questions circuitously and always answers a question by asking another."[34] James Fenimore Cooper takes aim at the southern drawl: "In Georgia, you find a positive drawl, among what are called the 'crackers' " (*Notions*, 2:133), and Charles Dickens manages a dig at both women and blacks at the same time: "All the women who have been bred in slave States speak more or less like negroes, from having been constantly in their childhood with black nurses."[35]

During the nineteenth century stereotypes of American language traits solidified, though at times they seemed based on shifting ground. During his absence from America, Cooper praised the speech of women in the Middle States: their voices "are particularly soft and silvery." He felt that English, a harsh language at best, "is made softer by our women" (*Notions*, 2:133). But upon his return to this country his opinion changes dramatically, reflecting an opposite language stereotype: "Contrary to the general law in such matters the women of the country have a less agreeable utterance than the men" (*Democrat*, p. 118). This, he feels, is unfortunate for the language because of the important role the nursery plays in its acquisition.

Immigrants also troubled commentators on the American language. The intrusion of languages in competition with English was a concern in the eighteenth century, although most observers seemed confident that English would survive any attack. Although the English were sometimes referred to as foreigners, it was non-native speakers who posed the greatest problem. Areas of German settlement proved particularly worrisome, both to the British traveler and the English-speaking American. The visiting Englishman Charles Augustus Murray clearly does not admire the dialect of Easton, Pennsylvania: "It would kill a grammatical purist to spend a week in that vicinity. . . . Take of the German spoken by the labourers near Baden, one half; of bad Dutch, one quarter; and of craven Yorkshire, one quarter: mix these thoroughly well, and let the nose have its due share in the pronunciation—then you have the Easton dialect."[36] Even as early as the mid-eighteenth century, Benjamin Franklin, advocating an English rather than a classical education, was particularly concerned with the language situation in Pennsylvania. He writes, in 1751: "Why should Pennsylvania, founded by the English, become a colony of aliens, who will shortly be so numerous as to Germanize us instead of our Anglifying them, and will never adopt our language or customs any more than they can acquire our complexion?"[37] And a century later, Charles Astor Bristed considers German as the only language in the United States that can have the slightest pretension to rival English. Bristed concludes, however, that English is in no serious danger of being usurped.

Nasality, Drawl, and Climate

Despite the recognition of regional and foreign dialects, the common feeling in Britain was that an American accent, transcending regionalism, existed, and that this accent, while rarely unintelligible, was unattractive. The major characteristic of this American accent, according to the British, was its nasality. Even the favorable accounts of the American language mention this. Murray, who reinforces the stereotype that American women do not speak as well as the men, calls it simply "the intonation of voice common to Americans of both sexes: it varies in character in the northern, western, and southern States; but in all it is quite distinct, and may be called a national peculiarity: it has no preference to pronunciation, and is observed by French and German travellers as well as by the British, though of course the latter are more sensible of it from the language being their own. There are many exceptions to this, as to every general statement, and more among the men than among the ladies" (*Travels*, pp. 319–20). Marryat notices a drawl—which he attributes to an aspect of American character—as well as a nasal intonation: "The Americans dwell upon their words when they speak—a custom arising, I presume, from their cautious, calculating habits; and they have always more or less of a nasal twang" (*Diary*, p. 222). Cooper sees a similar cautiousness underlying an expression commonly regarded as a New Englandism: *I guess* (*Notions*, 2:134). Though Marryat is at best neutral about pronunciation, nasality has a history of negative associations among speakers of English, and it is often attributed to speakers of dialects that are regarded as stigmatized or undesirable. In 1833, E. T. Coke expresses his dislike of this feature of the American accent: "I can affirm that the nasal twang, which Americans, of every class, possess in some degree, is very grating and disagreeable to the ears of an Englishman."[38]

The stereotype of the American nasal twang is so widespread that Americans become not simply defensive about this feature of their accent, they attempt to justify it on physiological grounds. The *North American Review* turns nasality into a virtue by pointing out advantages of American speech organs over those of the British: "We are mimicked all over the world by speaking through the nose." An American among the British is "like a goose hissing among tuneful swans." However, "as regards articulation, the Americans, we think, have a natural advantage over the English in a superior delicacy of structure of the vocal organs." The English organs are thick and unmanageable, resulting in the "spluttering and mouthing" so common when they speak. Even the American drawl is explained away scientifically. It comes from "a secondary accent on the penultimate syllable of long words," while the English trip "lightly over all the syllables after the accent" (91:524–25). Cooper earlier explained the New England drawl in a similar fashion, claiming it to be, not a drawl, but a "peculiar pause they make on the last word" (*Notions*, 2:130–31).

An unsigned article appearing in *Godey's Lady's Book* in 1872 carries the scientific explanation into the realm of the ridiculous, attributing the differences between British and American speech to climate:

> The moist atmosphere of the British Islands is said by physiologists to favor what is called, in learned speech, the deposition of adipose matter—, or, in other words, to make people, as well as sheep and cattle, tend to grow fat. By this growth of fat the air passages are liable to become partially clogged, and a thick, wheezy, indistinct pronunciation is the result.
>
> On the Western continent, along the Atlantic seaboard, the air is dry, and not favorable, it seems, to adiposity. The passages of the voice remain clear; and as one of them leads through the nose, the result is apt to be that the pronunciation is not only distinct, but has a nasal twang, which our English friends declare to be even more unpleasant than their wheeziness can be to us. . . . The English thickness of speech becomes, when properly corrected and subdued, a softness and smoothness of utterance, which, in their best speakers, is peculiarly agreeable. The American twang, on the other hand, gives place, in the cultivated voice, to a resonant and often a melodious clearness of utterance, which, for a public speaker, is of great advantage.[39]

While *Godey's* attempts to be fair, it clearly prefers the American twang to the British "wheeze." As additional proof of the climatological hypothesis, the only damp portion of the United States, the Pacific slope, where "the same winds come laden with moisture from the ocean, as in the British Islands," produces linguistic effects similar to those in England: "The Indians of the Oregon coast are said to have a remarkably thick and indistinct utterance, which is probably due to this particular influence of the climate on the human frame." American English is then compared to Chinese. Chinese was often used in popular, nonscientific commentaries in the eighteenth and nineteenth centuries as an example of a language whose written form had degenerated to a point of hopeless complexity. Spelling reformers often cautioned that English would experience a similar fate if their suggestions went unheeded. In *Godey's*, it is the spoken language of China that is of concern. Chinese nasality is not directly criticized, for the point being made is that both Chinese and American English owe their nasality to climate. However, the description of the oriental language is not particularly flattering. In China, where the dry climate resembles that of the eastern portion of the United States, nasality is a prominent linguistic feature: "It is a curious fact that the whole pronunciation, or 'sound system,' of the Chinese language is based upon the mode of utterance which with us is considered so great a defect. Chinese pronunciation is a sort of nasal sing-song, carried on with a perpetual succession of twanging inflections, the strict observance of which is essential to determine the meaning of the words uttered." The author of the *Godey's* article concludes by asserting a relationship between the American climate and another supposed characteristic of American speechways. It is the dryness of the American climate, "the influence of the crisp and bracing atmosphere" that has bred in Americans a love for oratory and has turned America, according to *Godey's*, into "a nation of 'stump-speakers.'"

Another feature of American speech that provoked some comment—perhaps because of its nasality and because it seemed to some to reflect an aspect of the American character—is a usage for which no name could be found. John Woods describes the phenomenon as it appeared among backwoodsmen: "Many of them, instead of saying yes, make a sort of noise, like 'him, him,' or rather like pronouncing 'm, m,' with the mouth shut" (*Two Years' Residence*, p. 83). Captain Marryat is somewhat more descriptive in his account: "There are two syllables—*um, hu*—which are very generally used by the Americans as a sort of reply, intimating that they are attentive, and that the party may proceed with his narrative; but, by inflection and intonation, these two syllables are made to express dissent or assent, surprise, disdain, and (like Lord Burleigh's nod in the play) a great deal more. . . . They can be pronounced without the trouble of opening your mouth, and you may be in

a state of listlessness and repose whilst others talk" (*Diary*, p. 229).
Marryat finds the expressions useful enough, and admits to having gotten into the habit of employing them himself.

The American Self-Image: Love It or Leave It

The negative opinions so frequently expressed by critics of the American language, at home and abroad, do not seem to have dampened the spirits of most Americans, if we are to believe another stereotypical notion of American English. Frances Trollope, a British traveler who satirized everything she could find on her journey to the former colonies, finds American smugness offensive: it is the American opinion,

> that they only, among the sons of men, have wit and wisdom, and that one of their exclusive privileges is that of speaking English *elegantly.* There are two reasons for this latter persuasion; the one is, that the great majority have never heard any English but their own, except from the very lowest of the Irish; and the other, that those who have chanced to find themselves in the society of the few educated English who have visited America, have discovered that there is a marked difference between their phrases and accents and those to which they have been accustomed, whereupon they have of course decided that no Englishman can speak English.[40]

Writing at just about the same time, E. T. Coke reinforces Trollope's remarks, finding an analogy between the situation of French in Canada and English in the United States, and giving us a brief impression of American stereotypes of the British:

> Not an American, let him be Yankee or Southerner, from the banks of the Hudson or the Mississippi, but flatters himself that he speaks more correct English than we illiterate sons of the mother isle. If you ask a Canadian in what part of the globe the purest French is spoken, he will reply, 'upon the shores of the St. Lawrence,' and assign as a reason for such being the case that a *patois* was introduced in the old country when the *canaille* gained the ascendency during the Revolution of 1792, and that the correct language falling, with the princes and nobles, Canada alone, which has not been subject to any such convulsions, retains the language in its original purity. Incredible as it may appear, I was frequently told by casual acquaintance in the States, 'Well, I should have imagined you to be an American, you have not got the *English brogue*, and aspirate

the letter *h*, when speaking.' And once I was actually told, by a
fellow-passenger in the stage coach from Alexandria to Winchester, 'Really I should never have thought you to be from the old
country, you pronounce your words so well, and have not got the
turn-up nose!' [*Furlough*, pp. 154–55]

As we can see, many Americans either ignored or rejected the attacks
that were made upon their language. Charles Henry Wilson, an Englishman, does not like what he regards as the American propensity for
renaming the familiar: "Before I left New York, I found a new vocabulary requisite, for these *reformers* of Sheriden, Walker, Ash, Johnson,
and Bailey, had given a novel reading, not only to things, but re-bap-
tized animals; for a *cock*, I found a *rooster*, a female of the *dog* species,
a *slut*, and other ridiculous Republican innovations. . . . Thus they
'Nick-name God's creatures, and make their wantonness their ignorance.'"[41] But Wilson is told, when he complains too much, what may
be the first recorded instance of a common refrain: "It's a good country,
and let those who don't like it, leave it" (p. 38).

British versus American

Two Americans, at least, took the defense of American English across
the seas. Robert Walsh published *An Appeal from the Judgments of
Great Britain Respecting the United States of America* in London in
1819. The *Eclectic Review* of London, speaking of Walsh's book, deplores the widening gap between England and America, generously
placing the blame squarely with the British: "The community of language between the two people,—a circumstance which seems to proffer
the means of reuniting the hearts which have been so unnaturally divided,—has, in fact, only facilitated and stimulated this 'labour of
hatred'" (13:403). Charles Astor Bristed, writing in 1855 while in residence at Cambridge University, tries to reason with the British. In his
essay, "The English Language in America," Bristed makes some attempt
to convince the British that American English should not be allowed to
stand between the two nations. He claims, for example, that no one
cares about changes in New World Spanish simply because the countries involved are insignificant both politically and in their literature.
He sees Yankeeisms as having replaced Hibernicisms "as a fertile
source of common-place material for cheap wit and vulgar ribaldry"
among the British. A speaker who sarcastically uses these "has flattered
himself with the idea of having thereby, at the same time established his

reputation for humor, and presented an unanswerable argument against democracy." Bristed complains that the treatment of American English has been decidedly unfair: "Anything which was bad English has been passed off for American" ("English in America," pp. 57–58). Bristed then attempts to explain the American language to the English, laboriously describing what he regards as insignificant regional peculiarities that the Americans themselves are not even aware of. He invokes the democratic stereotype of the American language, claiming that, while English provincialisms keep their place, "American provincialisms are more equally distributed through all classes and localities" (p. 62). Bristed allays the fear that English in America may be endangered by other languages, and goes on to placate the British. He assures them that political separation will not lead to linguistic separation, and that the unfortunate ideas of Noah Webster that have come to symbolize American English enjoy their currency only because of the commercial success of his work (Bristed points out that Webster himself recanted many of his proposals before his death): "They have obtained a temporary circulation among a certain class of writers and publishers, but have always failed to obtain a footing in the best quarters." Even in the unlikely event that "Webster's vagaries"—Bristed no doubt means his spellings—were to become universally adopted in America, "they would be no more to the whole body and structure of the language than an unsightly wart on a man's hand, or pimple on his face, is to his whole physical frame" (p. 76).

Bristed's essay, though critical of British reaction to American English, is conciliatory in tone. He ultimately rejects the American language that he has so carefully described, as nothing more than a blemish to be covered up or ignored. It is insignificant; certainly not a Federal Language. But his dismissal of Webster's ideas as temporary, harmless, and insignificant reflects a feeling that was common in some American intellectual circles in the mid-nineteenth century. Webster's dictionaries and spellers were highly successful, but he did have competition. Joseph Worcester published a *Dictionary of the English Language* that followed more conservative, British spellings, and held London pronunciation as the model for Americans to imitate. An intense rivalry was stirred up between Webster and Worcester, fueled by charges of plagiarism—Webster accused Worcester of stealing his definitions— and by geographical partisanship: Yale favored the work of Webster, the Hartford lexicographer, while Harvard permitted only the dictionary of Worcester, a Bostonian, to be used by its students. Arbitrating the spelling controversy that had arisen, the *Atlantic Monthly* in 1860 declares Worcester to have won the battle of the dictionaries. Webster's mistake, we are told, "was in attempting to force his peculiar notions upon the world in his Dictionary, instead of confining them to his Preface." Although the *Atlantic* concedes that many of the changes proposed by Webster will eventually be adopted, it criticizes Webster's prescriptivism and his support of an American language. Webster, we are told, "calls the result of his labors an '*American* Dictionary of the English Language,' as if provincialism were a merit. He evidently thought the business of a lexicographer was to *regulate*, not to *record*." On the other hand, native son Worcester is praised because he "has aimed to give us a true view of English as it is, and not as he himself may have wished it should be or thought it ought to be."[42] It is ironic that two descendants of Webster's work, *Webster's International Dictionary* (1890) and *Webster's Third New International Dictionary* (1961), were generally faulted for attempting to be just what the *Atlantic* called for in 1860, dictionaries of record, not guides to approved usage. For example, Gilbert M. Tucker attacks the permissiveness of *Webster's International* in *Our Common Speech* (New York, 1895): "The recognition, in a book like Webster's dictionary, of pretty nearly every sort of erroneous use of common words that the editors have observed, without warning the reader of the impropriety of such use, naturally induces the supposition that the lexicographer not only explains the error, but lends it his authority as correct, thus aiding and abetting in the process of depraving the tongue" (p. 132), and reactions to *Webster's Third* were, in some quarters, even stronger. But what is important in the *Atlantic*'s discussion of the Webster-Worcester contest is its labeling of the American language as provincial.

One Language or Two?

The question of one English or two pervaded discussions of language in America in the eighteenth and nineteenth century, and almost every observer had some recommendation or warning to offer. John Pickering argues that commerce, religion, and law all move us to keep a common tongue, cautioning Americans that their language must not stray too far from its origins: "If [our countrymen] are ambitious of having their works read by Englishmen as well as by Americans, they must write in a language that Englishmen can read with pleasure." Similarly, he warns that we must preserve the language so that we can read the great literature of the past. Imagine if Americans could no longer understand Milton, "without the aid of a *translation* into a language, that is to be called at some future day the *American* tongue!" (*Vocabulary*, pp. 9–10). The preservation of one English must be a conscious effort, for circumstances will work against it: "That a radical change in the language of a people, so remote from the source of it, as we are from England, is not an imaginary supposition, will be apparent from the alterations which have taken place among the nations of Europe; of which no instance, perhaps, is more striking, than the gradual change and final separation of the languages of Spain and Portugal, not withstanding the vicinity and frequent intercourse of the people of those two countries" (p. 20).

The lawyer and author Samuel Lorenzo Knapp, in his *Lectures on American Literature* (1829), also favors a continuity of language with Britain: "We have wisely followed the public taste of the mother country, nor vainly thought that it would be wisdom to struggle for an independency in letters, as far as they regarded the use of our vernacular." Knapp generally approves of the forms the language has taken in the New World. Of the Americans, he says,

> Their language alone is theirs by inheritance. They received it from their progenitors, and have kept it unpolluted and unchanged. It has been in different ages here a little modified, as in England, to be a more explicit medium of thought; and taste and euphony have, at times, made some exertions to drop one class of words and assume another; but they have destroyed none; and as occasion requires, those left out of fashionable use, for a season, have, after a while, been called up and restored to their former places in good company.[43]

In its article on the *English language*, the *Encyclopedia Americana* (1834) claims "the orthography of our language has undergone no material change in the U. States." The article on *Americanism* goes on to stress the sameness of the British and American tongues, arguing that most expressions considered under that heading are of limited occurrence: "A great proportion of the words are of local use, technical, mere vulgarisms, or used only by individual writers, whose caprice and affectation of style are not followed by the nation at large." The article stresses the unity between British and American English, noting that the greatest areas of difference are in pronunciation, and these have little impact on the language itself. But the *Encyclopedia*, while optimistic about the continued unity of English, adopts a wait and see attitude toward the outcome of what it regards as a great experiment: "England and the U. States of America offer the first instance in history of two great, independent and active nations daily developing new and characteristic features, situated at a great distance from each other, and having a common language and literature. . . . Authority, in regard to language, will go far, but never can withstand for a long time the energies and wants of a free, industrious and thinking people." Citing the frequently mentioned example of the divergent languages of Spain and Portugal, the article hints at the eventual separation of the two Englishes unless there is a slowdown in the centrifugal forces at work: "The contest of language will be more languid, in proportion as there is less energy and activity in the mother countries, and less progress in the arts and sciences, as well as less political advancement, in the states which have lately shaken off the yoke."[44]

Jacob A. Cummings, author of a number of popular educational works, recognizes in his *Pronouncing Spelling Book* (1819) that dialects are detrimental to the new nation: "If we consider the great importance of preserving uniformity in our country, and of avoiding what already begins to be called northern and southern pronunciation, no attempt to preserve harmony in the republic of letters will be regarded as too minute." He fears that America's unique geographical situation can lead to the formulation of local dialects: "As we become more extended, the greater is the probability that our language may be broken into a variety of provincialisms."[45] Rather than allow this to happen, Cummings advises following British authority in linguistic matters.

James Fenimore Cooper too warns that language in America must be reduced to rule, "or else we shall have a dialect distinct from that of the mother country," but he also reassures us that this separation is not likely to occur, for in twenty years England will be imitating us as we once did them. Responding to fears that American regionalism would ultimately disrupt the Union, Cooper feels that, at the most, three new nations could be created. Even if that were to happen, we would still retain a single language and, in a century and a half, 200 million Americans would be exerting their linguistic as well as political influence on the world (*Notions*, 2:128–29). Royall Tyler, on the other hand, is suspicious of attempts to regulate the language. Regarding languages as evolutionary in nature, Tyler sees English as being in its decline. Furthermore, he feels that "the perfectibility of language is as ridiculous as the perfectibility of man" (*Yankey*, p. 175). And John Pickering, who is all for perfectibility but is suspicious of perfectionists, traces linguistic decline in part to attempts to regulate language: "In this country, as in the case in England, we have thirsty reformers and presumptuous sciolists, who would unsettle the whole of our admirable language for the purpose of making it conform to their whimsical notions of propriety. Some of our corruptions have originated with such people" (*Vocabulary*, p. vi). Apparently regarding himself as one of the reformers and sciolists that Pickering referred to, Noah Webster, who had been a friend of Timothy Pickering, father of the author of the *Vocabulary*, fired off a fifty-page review-letter pointing out errors and disagreeing step by step with the young Pickering's opinions on the state of the language.

One Englishman who recognized and approved of the language of the United States was lexicographer Herbert Croft. As early as 1788 Croft discussed, in the *Gentleman's Magazine* of London, his proposal for revising Samuel Johnson's *Dictionary*, which he regarded as both riddled with errors and obsolete. Croft assured his readers that the American language would not be overlooked in his new work, and that he had already consulted with the American ambassador on the inclusion of American terms. Croft's proposed *English and American Dictionary* never got off the ground, but in 1797 some of his opinions about language were published, including the following, which shows him to be one of the few English commentators who felt that language was perfectible in America, and that the New World could exert a positive linguistic influence on the mother country:

> The future history of the other three quarters of the world will, probably, be much affected by America's speaking the language of England. Its natives write the language particularly well; considering they have no dictionary yet. . . . Perhaps we are, just now, not very far distant from the precise moment, for making some grand attempt, with regard to fixing the *standard* of our language (no *language* can be fixed) in America. Such an attempt would, I think, succeed in America, for the same reasons that would make it fail in England; whither, however, it would communicate its good effects. [*Letter*, p. 2n.]

Despite the optimism shown by Croft, antagonism toward American English has remained the rule in England rather than the exception, as many an American traveler will attest. In *The American Language* H. L. Mencken chronicles modern British opposition to our speech, and Gilbert M. Tucker devotes much of his book *American English* (New York, 1925) to a demonstration that many supposed Americanisms, vulgar and otherwise, are actually British in origin. In an astonishing reversal of the stereotype of a uniform American speech contrasted with a diverse British one, London *Times* writer Philip Howard has recently claimed that American English is fragmented, while British English is not: "Ethnic minorities in the United States tend to preserve the languages, accents, and idiosyncratic uses of the lands that their immigrant forefathers came from, and to campaign vigorously for these immigrant dialects to be brought into the educational system and officially recognized in other ways. . . . As a consequence the central core of American English is breaking up into dialects. . . . Fortunately in Britain we manage to integrate our immigrants quite successfully, linguistically." Howard does not document either his claims about American speech or those about Britain, but it is clear that he, like many of his forebears, equates dialectal diversity with language disintegration, and that he regards American English as a prime example of the "danger that the universal ocean of English may be split and parcelled into a number of mutually incomprehensible dialects."[46]

Fixing the Standard

There was no lack of advice concerning the regulation of the American language, and its ultimate perfectibility. Cooper, discussing the setting of linguistic standards, points out the differences between England and America. In England, and in the British Empire, London's "better company" are the arbiters of taste in language. According to Cooper, in England "fashion is far more imperious than even the laws of the schools" (*Notions*, 2:123–24). This might have been true in America, as well, but we have no great capital, like London, "to produce any great effect on the language." Instead, each American town sets its own standards, and none desires to imitate any of the others. For this reason, Cooper feels that "an entirely different standard for the language must be established in the United States, from that which governs so absolutely in England" (p. 125). We have no elite society, no established church, and no dramatic stage that can provide language standards (Cooper disqualifies the American theater because its actors are all "foreigners"). Congress cannot do so, "for that does not represent the fashion and education of the nation," and the Court cannot, for America has no equivalent of this Royalist institution. Here, "there is none but the President." We cannot imitate English fashions, "for we often find as much fault with them as we do with our own." All these failing us, we must base our language standards on reason, authority, analogy, and all the known laws of language. Cooper is not as optimistic as Croft about the effects that the American dependence on reason will have on the language of Great Britain: "In another generation or two, far more *reasonable* English will be used in this country than exists here now. How far this melioration or purification of our language will affect the mother country, is another question" (p. 127).

John Pickering is more specific in his comments on the American language, finding three types of corruption in it: the formation of new words, the giving of new significance to old words, and the retention of words that have become obsolete in England. Pickering cites unfavorable comments on American English in the British reviews, but he is not altogether damning in his own opinions. He asserts our right to coin new words, adding that our passion for neologism is cooling. According to Pickering, the greatest danger to our language is the continued use of antiquated words, brought here nearly two hundred years ago, "some of which were at that day *provincial* words in England" (*Vocabulary*, p. 20). Charles Jared Ingersoll, taking the offensive, accuses the English of practicing what they preach against: "We *retain some words, which you have dropped*; and you retain some, which we have dropped. We *have made a small number of new ones.* You have made ten times more" (*Remarks*, pp. 139–40). Ingersoll turns the tables and criticizes London speech, taking his examples from Samuel Pegge's *Anecdotes of the English Language* (1803), an ironic defense of London Cockney, and concluding, "How great a part of the *English* nation must speak miserable English" (p. 144). And James K. Paulding, an American writer and politician who carried on a lively debate with the English reviews, actually accused the British of fraud in their attacks on the American language: "Travellers have been sent out to this country who . . . were paid by England for the degrading work of collecting materials for misrepresenting our national character and manners."[47]

Despite the vigor both of the defenders and reformers of language in America, and although only seventy years had passed between the Federal Procession of 1789 and the *Atlantic Monthly*'s belittling of the American dialect—which had indeed diverged from its British parent to a considerable extent—as provincial, the idea of a Federal Language was still just that, an idea. The plans that Webster and the other language patriots formulated, although they influenced attitudes toward the American language, and even altered its course to some extent, remained plans that never received formal implementation. Shirley Brice

Heath, discussing the debate over proposals like that of John Adams for a language academy, sees the failure of the proposals as an aspect of government policy: "In rejecting a national language academy, the founding fathers made clear their choice *not* to designate a national tongue. . . . Instead, national political leaders and state and local agencies promoted respect for diversity of languages."[48] In fact, although some attempts had always been made to communicate with American language minorities in their own tongues, there was never any doubt that Standard American English (whether or not it resembled Standard British English) was to be the national language. What the founding fathers did do, as Heath acknowledges, was decline to set up a federal mechanism to define the language that they all agreed must exist. Others did attempt to define the language. Most notable among these is Noah Webster, who actually sought but failed to obtain government support for his definition.

Language by Legislation

In fact, government action has proved to be the least effective way to deal with language regulation in the United States. As recently as 1923 Washington Jay McCormick, a Republican representative from Montana, introduced in Congress a "Bill to define the national and official language of the Government and people of the United States of America, including the Territories and dependencies thereof." In his bill, McCormick establishes the official name of the language of the United States as "the American language" and orders all Congressional acts and government regulations to be amended "to the extent of substituting in the text for the word 'English' the word 'American.'" The bill, which was to take effect six months after its passage and approval, makes no attempt to deal with the specifics of American English, although it does foresee Congressional action that would: "Until Congress shall make specific provision for the official and more particular standardization of the American language, words and phrases generally accepted as being in good use by the people of the United States of America shall constitute a part of the American language for all legal purposes."[49]

McCormick's anglophobia is reminiscent of the young Noah Webster. Not only does he wish to drop all references to English, he wishes to do away with any usage that suggests British influence. McCormick is quoted in *The Nation*, elaborating on the intentions of his bill:

I might say I would supplement the political emancipation of '76 by the mental emancipation of '23. America has lost much in literature by not thinking its own thoughts and speaking them boldly in a language unadorned with gold braid. It was only when Cooper, Irving, Mark Twain, Whitman, and O. Henry dropped the Order of the Garter and began to write American that their wings of immortality sprouted. Had Noah Webster, instead of styling his monumental work "The American Dictionary of the English Language," written a "Dictionary of the American Language," he would have become a founder instead of a compiler. Let our writers drop their top-coats, spats, and swagger-sticks, and assume occasionally their buckskin, moccasins, and tomahawks.[50]

McCormick's bill was referred to the House Judiciary Committee and died there, but a similar bill, proposed by State Senator Frank Ryan of Illinois, was passed by the legislature of that state and signed into law in 1923. The law as passed was a toned-down version of the generally anti-British original, but its intent was clearly unaltered: "Be it enacted by the people of the State of Illinois, represented in the General Assembly: The official language of the State of Illinois shall be known hereafter as the 'American' language, and not as the 'English' language."[51] Ryan's law produced no sweeping changes in usage in the state of Illinois, where English, not American, continues to be taught in the public schools and universities.

3 Webster and Federal English

Noah Webster was certainly the most vocal and perhaps, in the long run, the most influential commentator on the state of language in America. But language was not his sole concern. He was a trained lawyer, made his living as a teacher, and fought against Burgoyne during the Revolutionary War. In addition to his spelling books, his grammar, his dictionaries, and his language commentaries, Webster wrote on politics, medicine, and religion, advocating federal union, investigating the causes of yellow fever, and expurgating the Bible. Eager to protect the income from his publications, Webster was instrumental in the passage of state and federal copyright laws. He was also greatly interested in the American educational system. He saw his role primarily as that of an educator, and one of his projects was to provide American schools with all the textbooks they required, linguistic and otherwise. Writing in 1807 to his former Yale classmate, the poet Joel Barlow, Webster says, "My plan has been to furnish our schools with a tolerably complete system of elementary knowledge in books of my own, gradually substituting American books for English and weaning our people from their prejudices and from their confidence in English authority."[1]

From the outset Webster devoted himself both to the description and the reformation of American English, and, while he did not always make himself popular in this task, partly because of the radical nature of some of his ideas and partly because of his flinty personality, his spelling books and dictionaries generally outsold the competition in the nineteenth century. Some 20 million copies of his spellers were sold before Webster's death in 1843, and more than a million were sold annually for some time thereafter. In the twentieth century his spellers have fallen into disuse, but his name has become synonymous with the word *dictionary*, a reference work often considered by the general public to be the last and most authoritative statement on the language.

The Federal School Book

Webster's earliest major work, the first part of his *Grammatical Institute of the English Language* (1783; reissued in 1787 as the *American*

Spelling Book), is a spelling text intended for use in the schools, and in his introduction to the work Webster makes clear his rejection of British authority in language, and of the British system of education in general. Referring repeatedly to changes in American attitudes toward Great Britain that followed the Revolution, he sees an opportunity for the new nation to reform its language in the same way that it has begun to reform its customs and its social and governmental institutions: "It is the business of *Americans* to select the wisdom of all nations, as the basis of her constitutions,—to avoid their errours,—to prevent the introduction of foreign vices and corruptions and check the career of her own,—to promote virtue and patriotism,—to embellish and improve the sciences,—to diffuse an uniformity and purity of *language*,—to add superiour dignity to this infant Empire and to human nature." [2] In his first speller, Webster was concerned with establishing uniformity of speech in the United States through education. He openly rejects orthographical reform, and while he spells *music* and *comic* without a final *k*, he retains the *u* in words like *honour* and *rigour*, the extra *g* in *waggon*, and the *re* of *metre* and *mitre*, spellings he rejects in later, more radical editions of his spelling books. Instead, Webster is concerned with expounding rules of pronunciation in order to purify the language of social or regional dialects. What gives his book an American flavor is the introduction, full of patriotic zeal, and the list of geographical names, the majority of which are American, not British.

In a letter to his publishers, Hudson and Goodwin, in 1788, Webster suggests that his *Grammatical Institute* should be advertised as essential for the nation's linguistic unity:

> It may be useful to notify the public that it is the wish of many leading men in America that all the children in the different States should learn the language in the same book, that all may speak alike. The Philological Society in New York recommend this work with a view to make it the *Federal school book*. The University of Georgia [chartered in 1785], preferring this to Dilworth, Perry, Fenning, or any other, have determined that this alone shall be used in all the schools in that state. The publishers flatter themselves that the northern states will heartily concur in the design of a *federal language*. [*Letters*, pp. 79–80]

Webster felt that the adoption of a single textbook—his textbook—could produce uniformity in speech and serve the cause of federalism, and he felt that the time was right for such an enterprise. In his *Disser-*

tations on the English Language (1789), Webster urges Americans to seize the opportunity afforded by the Revolution and accept his suggestions: "We have . . . the fairest opportunity of establishing a national language and of giving it uniformity and perspicuity, in North America, that ever presented itself to mankind. Now is the time to begin the plan. The minds of the Americans are roused by the events of a revolution . . . the danger of losing the benefits of independence, has disposed every man to embrace any scheme that shall tend, in its future operation, to reconcile the people of America to each other."[3] A uniform language, according to Webster, will prove a cohesive force, helping to amalgamate what were in 1789 thirteen independent states not yet unified under a federal constitution. For Webster such a language was, therefore, an imperative: "*A national language* is a band of *national union*. Every engine should be employed to render the people of this country *national*" (p. 397). In the appendix to his *Dissertations*, an essay on reforming the spelling of English so that it will conform more closely to the pronunciation of the language, Webster repeats his theme: "NOW is the time, and *this* the country, in which we may expect success, in attempting changes favorable to language, science and government. . . . Let us then seize the present moment, and establish a *national language*, as well as a national government. . . . our reputation abroad demands that, in all things, we should be federal; be *national*" (p. 406).

Although he strongly believed in the necessity of a uniform language, Webster felt himself to be a descriptive rather than a prescriptive grammarian. In a letter written in 1798 to the "Governors, Instructors and Trustees of the Universities" he attacks those ignorant grammarians who would have language conform to rules rather than allow rules to be derived from language. Webster feels that a language must be not only formed but perfected before its grammar can be constructed, adding, "Grammars are made to show the student what a language *is*, not how it *ought to be*" (*Letters*, p. 175), an echo of a similar statement in the *Dissertations* some years earlier: "It is our business to find what the English language *is*, and not, how it *might have been made*" (*Dissertations*, p. ix). Webster does give a rather detailed description of the varieties of American speech that can be found in the northern, southern, and middle states in the *Dissertations*. But he makes it clear that his aim in describing the American language is always either to praise its superiority over British varieties or condemn particular forms as local or illogical. Webster modifies Horace's *usus est jus et norma lo-*

quendi, 'usage is the law and rule of speech', to fit his federalism: "If Horace's maxim is ever just, it is only when custom is national, when the practice of a nation is uniform or general. In this case it becomes the common law of the land, and no one will dispute its propriety" (p. 166). In effect Webster is a prescriber more than a describer. He records dialects for the purpose of eradicating them. An idealist, Webster sees faulty education at the root of the dialect problem, and he is ready to supply the necessary standard that has previously been unavailable: "The want of some standard in schools has occasioned a great variety of dialects in Great-Britain and of course, in America. Every county in England, every State in America and almost every town in each State, has some peculiarities in pronunciation which are equally erroneous and disagreeable to its neighbors." Webster complains that the teaching of pronunciation "is *left* to parents and nurses—to ignorance and caprice—to custom, accident, or nothing—Nay, to something worse, to coxcombs who have a large share in directing the polite taste" (*American Speller*, p. 5). He condemns fashionable speech in a manner most puritanical, and criticizes Americans for abandoning the doctrine of usage: "The truth is, *usus est Norma Loquendi*, general custom is the rule of speaking, and every deviation from this must be wrong. The dialect of one State is as ridiculous as that of another; each is authorised by local custom; and neither is supported by any superior excellence" (p. 7).

Webster rejects the class distinctions of England as being inappropriate for American society, but, a schoolmaster at heart, he maintains a distinction between the learned and the common people: "The intercourse among the learned of the different States, which the revolution has begun, and an American Court will perpetuate, must gradually destroy the differences of dialect which our ancestors brought from their native countries." On the other hand, dialect will be perpetuated among the "body of the people." Only the educational system, properly organized and furnished with the right materials, can eradicate localisms. Unless they have schools and the proper books, the common people will "fall into many inaccuracies, which, incorporating with the language of the state where they live, may imperceptibly corrupt the national language." In addition to the linguistic corruption that dialects may produce, they can prove detrimental to the body politic: "A sameness of pronunciation is of considerable consequence in a political view; for provincial accents are disagreeable to strangers and sometimes have an unhappy effect upon the social affections. . . . Our political harmony is therefore concerned in a uniformity of language" (*Dissertations*, pp. 19–20).

Americans Must Not Be Imitators

Uniformity of language is necessary, but not sufficient, for Webster. It must be an American uniformity. Webster rejects British authorities out of hand. Arguing that the subjunctive mood does not exist in English, he attacks Robert Lowth's treatment of the subject and appeals to American nationalism: "It would be little honorable to the founders of a great empire to be hurried prematurely into errors and corruptions, by the mere force of authority. Yet what but the mere authority of names could lead Americans into such barbarisms in speech, as shuperstition, constitshution, keind, gyuide, advertise, if he do, and many others? Where shall we rest, if we are to be led from change to change, by the caprice of any foreign stage-player, who chooses to be singular, or any compiler of a dictionary or grammar, who sets his own opinions in opposition to the established practice of a nation?" Webster argues that when we make a linguistic choice, when we adopt a particular standard, we must take into account its nationalistic implications: "It will be honorable to us as a nation, and more useful to our native tongue and science, that we examin the grounds of all rules and changes before we adopt them, and reject all such as have not obvious propriety for their foundation, or utility for their object" (*Letters*, p. 177).

Webster recognizes that Americans owe their language to the mother country. But inheritance does not preclude change, and change must be calculated according to principles of reason and nation: "This language is the inheritance which the Americans have received from their British parents. To cultivate and adorn it, is a task reserved for men who shall understand the connection between language and logic, and form an adequate idea of the influence which a uniformity of speech may have on national attachments" (*Dissertations*, p. 18). It is clear to Webster, as it was to many other Americans, that the inherited language had already been improved on: "The people of America, in particular the English descendants, speak the most *pure English* now known in the world. There is hardly a foreign idiom in their language." Furthermore, comparisons between American farmers and their British counterparts are inappropriate: "The American yeomanry . . . are not to be compared to the illiterate peasantry of [England]. . . . These men have considerable education. . . . The people of distant counties in England can hardly understand one another, so various are their dialects; but in the extent of twelve hundred miles in America, there are very few, I question whether a hundred words, except such as are used in employments wholly local, which are not universally intelligible" (pp. 288–89).

According to Webster, the differences between British and American English will only increase with time, and ultimately two separate and distinct languages will emerge. Because British and American English are subject to different influences, there will be produced, "in a course of time, a language in North America, as different from the future language of England, as the modern Dutch, Danish, and Swedish are from the German, or from one another" (pp. 22–23). And Webster opposes any attempt to bridge the growing gap between the two tongues, his nationalism getting the better of his linguistic rationalism: "As a nation, we have a very great interest in opposing the introduction of any plan of uniformity with the British language, even were the plan proposed perfectly unexceptionable" (p. 171).

Holding an opposing view is Joseph Worcester, compiler of the other great nineteenth-century American dictionary. Worcester has no qualms about urging Americans to imitate the British whenever possible, and he chooses for his standard of pronunciation the speech of London: "It is advisable for American writers and speakers to conform substantially to the best models, wherever they may be found. . . . There is no one city in the United States which holds a corresponding rank as a centre of intelligence and fashion." Worcester feels that most Americans already speak London English, and that the dialect is in fact more popular in America than it is in England: "Pronunciation in the United States is, indeed, now substantially conformed to the usage of London. . . . there is, undoubtedly, a more general conformity to London usage in pronunciation throughout the United States, than there is throughout Great Britain."[4] But Webster reinforces his rejection of a British standard for America by rejecting localism of any sort, whether of London or of Boston. According to him, the attempt to set a standard based on local practice "must keep the language in perpetual fluctuation, and the learner in uncertainty." Instead, a standard should be based on what Webster vaguely terms "*the rules of the language itself*, and the *general practice of the nation*" (*Dissertations*, p. 27).

Although later in the *Dissertations* Webster rejects a comparison between British and American agricultural society, there is one common linguistic feature shared by the two that feeds his xenophobic soul: a core vocabulary of "Saxon" origin, free from improvements, that is, borrowings from French and the classical languages:

> Language is the effect of necessity, and when a nation has a language which is competent to all their purposes of communicating

ideas, they will not embrace new words and phrases. This is the reason why the yeomanry of the English nation have never adopted the improvements of the English tongue. The Saxon was competent to most of the purposes of an agricultural people; and the class of men who have not advanced beyond that state, which in fact makes the body of the nation, at least in America, seldom use any words except those of Saxon original. [Pp. 57–58]

And despite his constant warnings against localisms, Webster finds time to praise New Englanders for what he feels is their adherence to the true, or Saxon genius of the language:

Altho the country people in New England, sometimes drawl their words in speaking, and, like their brethren, often make false concord, yet their idiom is purely Saxon or English; and in a vast number of instances, they have adhered to the true phrases, where people, who despise their plain manners, have run into error. Thus they say, "a man is going *by*," and not *going past*, which is nonsense. They say, "I *purpose* to go," and not *propose* to go, which is not good English. . . . whatever improprieties may have crept into their practice of speaking, they actually preserve more of the genuin idiom of the English tongue, than many of the modern fine speakers who set up for standards. [P. 389]

Spelling and Pronunciation

Although his most monumental contributions to American English are the dictionaries that he spent so much time writing and revising, Webster in the early part of his career was chiefly concerned with the pronunciation and spelling of the language rather than with its definition. He apparently considered these to be the areas of English in which the clearest distinctions between British and American usage could be made. Webster finds that the English and the Americans choose their language standards differently. In England, pronunciation is set by the upper classes, and, as a result, general or national usage is altered to conform to localism, for the aristocracy center around London and the Royal Court. In modern linguistic terms, one might say that this situation could produce hypercorrection as nonaristocratic speakers try to imitate an unfamiliar norm. Webster comes to a similar conclusion:

"Whatever has been the effect of these attempts in Great Britain, the result of them in the United States, has been to multiply greatly the diversities of pronunciation." Complicating the situation, Webster feels that Americans take their standards from the written rather than the spoken language: "In this country, where the people resort chiefly to books for rules of pronunciation, a false notation of sounds operates as a deception and misleads the inquirer."[5] Webster is quick to attack local dialects, but a New-Englandman himself, he often sees New England language characteristics as common throughout the United States or recommends them to his readers as most correct. Like Webster, James Fenimore Cooper notes the American dependence on books for language standards, but Cooper finds this dependence localized to New England. He attributes the New England accent to the intelligence of the inhabitants and to their stay-at-home nature: "They all read and write; but the New-Englandman, at home, is a man of exceedingly domestic habits. He has a theoretical knowledge of the language, without its practice" (*Notions*, 2:132). According to Cooper, the New England accent, then, is a result of spelling pronunciation, and Webster feels that, in order to avoid the dangers of incorrect spelling pronunciations, American orthography must be reformed.

Webster argues that spelling and pronunciation must go hand in hand, and to that end he would have the spelling of English made appropriately phonetic, serving as a brake on pronunciation changes: "It is important that the same *written words* and the same *oral sounds* to express the same ideas, should be used by the whole nation." He implies that if this is not done, English may go the way of French, losing what Webster regards as its basic virility: "The English language, when pronounced according to the genuine composition of its words, is a nervous, masculine language. . . . The French language, by the loss of imperfect use of articulations, though rendered easy in utterance, has become so feeble in sound as to be unfit for bold, impressive eloquence" (1828 *Dictionary*, n.p.).

Webster must decide which spelling and which pronunciation should be promoted as authoritative. Despite an obvious preference for his native New England dialect, he repeatedly claims to reject localism. Similarly he rejects the efforts of other reformers, colleagues whom he prefers to regard as competitors, except when they are correcting errors and producing uniformity. And he acknowledges that his own task is a thankless one: "To attack established customs is always hazardous; for mankind, even when they see and acknowledge their errors, are seldom obliged to the man who exposes them" (*Dissertations*, p. 147). The complexity of the task and the inconsistency of some of Webster's own attitudes account for some of the contradictions that can be found in his work. One example, on the national scale, is striking. Webster generally advocated a separation of British and American English. In the *Dissertations*, he says, "As an independent nation, our honor requires us to have a system of our own, in language as well as government" (p. 20). An anecdote has it that on tours through the states to promote sales of his textbooks, Webster visited local printing offices, trying to persuade printers to spell as he did, and handing out tracts describing his spelling system. But by the 1820s, Webster's position had softened. As early as 1809 Webster showed signs of being worn down by his critics. Writing to his brother-in-law, Thomas Dawes, in that year, he speaks wistfully of a spelling reform, "a plan so simple as not to require an hour's attention to be perfectly master of it; and it might be introduced in a tenth part of the time required to render general the practice of reckoning money by dollars and cents. But I shall not attempt it" (*Letters*, p. 332).

Webster blames for his decision to abandon the field of spelling reform not the general population, whom he sees as favorably disposed to his proposals, but the critics, who are stuck in their ways and will not be reformed. After the publication of the *Compendious Dictionary* in 1806, when word got out that Webster was planning the two-volume folio dictionary that was finally published in 1828, criticism of his work forced him to take a defensive stance. In a circular entitled "To the Friends of Literature" (1807), to which is attached a statement of support by the faculty of Yale College, Webster assures his audience that his position on language reform is not as radical as they might have assumed. He states that orthography, where it is already settled, should remain unaltered. Where spelling and pronunciation are in dispute, respectable usage ought to be followed. He claims to favor the pronunciation of England as it had been during the first two-thirds of the eighteenth century.[6]

Noah's Ark: The Reaction to Webster

Two early examples of the strong reaction against Webster's ideas reveal what he was up against. The *Monthly Magazine and American Review* published an anonymous article, "On the Scheme of an American Language," in its issue of July 1800. While Webster is not specifically named, the article argues against the ideas he had been advocating at the time. It praises patriotism, but only when it is strictly disciplined and limited. Language patriots, however, are not to be tolerated: "Some of those among us who devote themselves to letters, are extremely anxious that, as we are politically independent and distinct from other nations, we should likewise be so in literature and language. They are ambitious of obtaining, not only a national individuality in policy and jurisdiction, not only a government that shall be American, but likewise an American *language*. For this end, they think grammars and dictionaries should be compiled by natives of the country, not of the British or English, but of the American tongue. Whatever may be said in favour of fostering the spirit of jealousy and animosity to foreign nations in a political sense, seems totally out of place in relation to science" (3:1).

The writer urges that we strive to lessen the differences between languages, not increase them, reminding readers of the story of the tower of Babel. He longs for a return to a pre-Babel state, with a universal language that is not mutable, like our present-day varieties. Claiming that books are the only adequate authorities for the use of words, and pointing out that comparatively few English books have been written in America, the writer notes that any American dictionary must necessarily draw all of its material from British literature. As for the notion of an *American* tongue, he reminds us that the name of a language is not dependent on the place where it is spoken. Greek was still Greek when it was spoken in Asia Minor. If the "petty and puerile" distinction must be made, *American* is certainly an improper term: it is only the language of the northeast corner of the northern American continent, and it derives from the name of an Italian who was not even the first visitor to, and never set foot on, what is now the United States. If the language must be renamed, the writer goes on, the most suitable name would be New English. American place-names and the like may be admitted to the dictionary, but "any other species of American words, are manifest corruptions; and, to embalm these by the lexicographic process, would only be waste of time and abuse of talents" (p. 4).

In "Remarks on American Criticism," in the same volume of the *Monthly Magazine*, another reference is made to American English: "There is an *American language*, which can only be criticised upon American principles." But the writer of these remarks is hardly defending its existence, as the following characterization of American English as artificial and eccentric indicates: "We wish to be *independent* of all the world, in a *literary* as well as in a *political* sense. Such independence cannot be secured but by our adopting many peculiarities" (p.

185). Finally, in an article on a supposed Americanism, "The Trial and Condemnation of Lengthy," by one A. B., the development of an American language is condemned on the grounds that it will antagonize foreigners. *Lengthy* was a word of relatively recent origin that provoked much opposition. Although it was found in reputable British writing, particularly in the critical reviews, it was often felt to be a New World corruption and as such those who did not like it refused to be able to understand it. A. B. sees such examples of corruption as stumbling blocks to understanding not just at home but in the international community: "This, by the way, is an insuperable obstruction to the scheme of an American language; for who *will* or *ought* to adopt a language which will make him unintelligible to the *foreign* readers of English, or which will lessen his elegance or perspicuity in their eyes? especially as there *is* a language by the use of which he will be in danger of offending *nobody*" (p. 173).

A second series of attacks, more directly aimed at Noah Webster, began in October of the following year in the *New-England Palladium*, under the rubric, The Restorator. Purporting to be a review of Webster's proposed dictionary, the Restorator begins with a mock defense of American English:

> The advantage of a distinct language must strike every unprejudiced person. It will prove the best *palladium* of our independence, and tend more than any other circumstance, to lessen that *British Influence* which continues to endanger our freedom. . . . If we can once become unintelligible to foreigners, one great source of corruption will be dried up. Whilst we retain the language of *Britain*, we cannot forget that we were once a colony. . . . To coin new words, or to use them in a new sense, is, uncontrovertibly, one of the unalienable rights of freemen.

One of the Americanisms mentioned in the article, the use of *Miss* to refer to married as well as single women, was found both in England and America in the late eighteenth and early nineteenth centuries, and is an interesting precursor of the modern *Ms.* Like some present-day purists, the writer of this diatribe holds the usage up to ridicule. Twisting the argument of language reformers that spelling simplification will facilitate language learning, he says, "*Miss*, applied equally to married and single ladies; may sometimes lead foreigners into an error, but then by simplifying the language it facilitates its acquisition." Concluding with a reference to Frances Grose's *Classical Dictionary of the Vulgar*

Tongue (1785), a compilation of British slang and low-life argot, the writer suggests a new name for Webster's tome, a name more suited to its geographic bias toward New England: "As his dictionary, I understand, is to be the dictionary of the vulgar tongue in New-England, would it not be better to prefix to it the epithet Cabotian, instead of Columbian?"[7]

The following month, a letter signed by a certain Aristarchus replies to the tongue-in-cheek approval of American English. Referring to Webster as a "hypercritic," Aristarchus describes the purpose of his own letter: "I shall endeavour to show the absurdity of establishing a *Columbian* language, and point out some strong objections against innovations in the established orthography." Another reference to Webster allies him with a group of "new-light" religious revivalists then popular in New England in order to demonstrate the lexicographer's ineffectuality: "The *new-light* grammarian of Connecticut has made but few converts to his absurd orthographical doctrines." Aristarchus turns in his letter from argument to personal vilification:

> A language, arrived at its zenith, like ours, and copious and expressive, in the extreme, requires no introduction of new words. . . . The decline of taste, in a nation, always commences, when the language of its classical authors is no longer considered an authority. . . . Now in what can a *Columbian* dictionary differ from an *English* one, but in these [colloquial] barbarisms?
>
> If the *Connecticut* Lexicographer considers the retaining of the *English* language as a badge of slavery, let him not give us a *Babylonish* dialect in its stead, but adopt at once the language of the aborigines. . . . The *Connecticut* Lexicographer tells us, that we must spell as we pronounce. But where, in this country, is there a standard of pronunciation?

Aristarchus concludes his attack with the hope that, should Webster's proposals be adopted, he will at least allow us "to study English as a *dead* language." His final statement shows the antagonism that is generated in those who regard themselves as language purists: "Let, then, the projected volume of *foul* and *unclean* things bear his own Christian name, and be called—Noah's Ark" (18[Nov. 6]:1).

An article entitled "American Literature" in the *Palladium* a week later similarly rejects an American dialect: America will not come into her own culturally "by compiling *Columbian* dictionaries, or by inventing a jargon called the *Columbian* language. All such attempts will retard the progress of literature, and must tend, as far as they have influence, to carry us back to the dark ages" (18[Nov. 13]:1). Webster's outraged protest against the personal attacks appearing in the *Palladium* is printed in the November 20 issue, along with an editorial disclaimer of responsibility, and on December 18 a closing attack on Webster is found under the title, "On the Vanity of Authors": "Sometimes vanity appears among us in the shape of a new spelling-book. . . . Sometimes it appears in proposals for publishing a *Columbian* dictionary, in which the vulgar provincialisms of uneducated *Americans* are to be quoted as authorities for language" (18[Dec. 18]:1).

Even after Webster had abandoned some of his early and more controversial opinions on language, he could not live down the reputation he had acquired as a linguistic anarchist. An anonymous critic writes in the *New York Mirror* in 1835, "I see no prospect of our ever again attaining to the uniformity in spelling, which existed before [Webster's] labours" (12[Apr. 25]:33g). And as late as 1875, in an advertisement for Worcester's *Dictionary* that rebuts the claim of the G. and C. Merriam Company, publishers of Webster's *Dictionary*, that Webster's was the standard in the United States Government Printing Office, A. R. Spofford, Librarian of Congress, writes, "whenever proofs from the Congressional Printing Office embody the innovations upon English orthography which Webster introduced, they are invariably returned with corrections restoring the established spelling, as represented by Worcester and the usage of all great English writers."[8]

Webster's Later Opinions

Although Webster gave in on individual points, he remained convinced that his spellers were effective textbooks. Never averse to praising his own work in signed or anonymous printed reviews, Webster writes in a brief article, "History of Spelling Books," that his *Speller* "has been the chief instrument of correcting a multitude of errors in pronunciation, & of forming, in some measure, our national language. Most of the members of Congress & of all classes of public men have received the rudiments of instruction in that book. This is admitted by gentlemen from Maine to New Orleans."[9] Webster engaged his critics more directly in letters to various periodicals, supporting his position and never backing down in the face of direct attack. But he did publish modifications of his ideas. The most notable of these is his reversal on the question of one language or two.

In 1824, during a stay in England while researching his *Dictionary* of 1828, Webster wrote to Dr. Samuel Lee, a professor of Arabic and Hebrew at Cambridge University, proposing a meeting with a delegation from Oxford and Cambridge, an informal language summit to resolve differences between British and American English. Webster saw such a meeting as an opportunity for him to explain his ideas on orthography to British intellectuals. In his letter, Webster speaks of British and American English as being virtually identical, and he notes the desire of his countrymen to assure the continuation of this uniformity: "In regard to the great body of the language, its principles are now settled by usage, and are uniform in this country and the United States. But there are many points in which respectable men are not agreed, and it is the sincere desire of my fellow citizens that such a diversity may no longer exist" (*Letters*, p. 412).

The meeting Webster sought never took place. Those Englishmen who commented on his proposal generally felt no agreement could be reached on issues as complex as the points of language to be considered. But Webster persisted in speaking of British and American English as one language. His 1828 *Dictionary* reflects this new position. Discussing the spread of the pronunciation *yu* for *oo* in words like *suit*, Webster implies that his goal has become more universal. He is concerned with establishing a standard not simply for American but for world English (this softened position may be accounted for in part by the fact that Webster now sold his dictionaries in England as well as in the United States): "The zeal manifested in this country, to make this pronunciation a standard, is absolute infatuation, and if adopted in its full extent, it would introduce many differences in the pronunciation of words in the two countries, where sameness now exists; and even the attempt, should it not be successful, must multiply discordances and distract opinions, and thus place the desired uniformity at a greater distance than ever" (1828 *Dictionary*, n.p.).

In his *Elementary Spelling Book* (1829), a revision of the *American Spelling Book* which Webster commissioned Aaron Ely to write in order to bring the spellers into accord with the more conservative stand Webster took in his 1828 *Dictionary*, Webster speaks of one English language, not two: "The pronunciation, with few exceptions, is in exact accordance with the best usage both in England and the United States" and again, "the pronunciation here given, is that which is sanctioned by the most general usage of well-bred people both in the United States and in England." In matters of spelling, Webster has also silently doffed his crusading garb. Declaring, in an uncharacteristic show of humility—

although he often silently reverses a position, he seldom admits a mistake openly—that "no lexicographer is consistent with himself" in matters of spelling, Webster says, "I have adopted, both in this work, and in my dictionary, that orthography which is most simple, and which is now the best authorized." While Webster still adheres to some spellings that he had earlier labeled as characteristically American, he resorts to the use of diacritical marks, not orthographical revisions, as a means of "remedying, in some measure, the evils of a very irregular orthography, which cannot be reformed."[10]

Writing to the editor of the *Westminster Review* in response to an article in that journal on Webster's revised *Dictionary* of 1831, Webster takes a temperate stand on the two language question though he still defends American English from attack: "Our language is English—it is as well understood & as well spoken on the west side of the Atlantic, as it is in England. It is desirable that the language on both sides of the Atlantic should remain the same, as far as circumstances & the nature of things will admit, but some differences must necessarily exist; & when new words are formed & become generally used in the United States, they are not to be condemned by Englishmen. It is improper as it is illiteral. Very few words however have been coined in America. In this respect, our writers are far more cautious than the English, whose licentiousness, in this kind of coinage, especially in their periodicals, is deeply to be regretted."[11]

In an undated, and otherwise unidentified, clipping in the Webster Collection of the New York Public Library, Webster asserts, somewhat paradoxically, both the sameness and difference of British and American English. The article presumably was written during or shortly after Webster's visit to England, and it is quite likely that Webster's interlocutors would have disagreed with his final statement:

> The six or seven authors who have given us dictionaries to regulate pronunciation differ in more than a thousand words; yet in conversation both in England & the United States, the differences in pronunciation almost wholly disappear; they occur in a very few words. I have repeatedly conversed with English gentlemen in London, Cambridge, & Oxford, for half an hour or an hour, without hearing or using a single word which would distinguish an Englishman from an American.

Webster then turns about and discusses the differences between British usage and American, returning to his perennial argument that it is inappropriate to try to impose transatlantic standards on Americans. He asserts that no uniformity of language can be expected in England because of the strength of provincial dialects and the dearth of common schools, and he warns against American linguistic insecurity:

> In regard to the language, we are subjected to one great evil; which is, the opinion that the English understand it better than any of our citizens, & that their usages are to be adopted in this country. This opinion had a laudable and a natural origin in our descent from Great Britain; but my researches have proved that our confidence, in this respect, is misplaced.

Webster concludes with a brief paean to New Englanders: "We are genuine English men born on the west of the Atlantic. . . . We are less infected with various dialects, the remains of the languages of the different conquerors of the English nation, than the inhabitants of England."

Webster's later opinions contrast, sometimes sharply, with those expressed in the *Dissertations* some forty years earlier. But even when he is advocating a common language for Britain and America, Webster's anti-British sentiment cannot stay long submerged. In the *Dissertations*, discussing the imitation by Americans of the British *woond* for *wound* (Webster prefers to rhyme this with *sound*), the English are seen as having as insidious an effect on our language as the French or the Germans: "Will not the Atlantic ocean, the total separation of America from Great Britain, the pride of an independent nation, the rules of the language, the melody of English poetry, restrain our rage for imitating the errors of foreigners?" (*Dissertations*, p. 135).

Webster as Purist and New Englandman

Rejecting British fashion and foreign influence, Webster is concerned in the *Dissertations* and other early work with establishing the true genius of the language. He finds this genius most manifest in the common people. The educated, on the other hand, can be forces of decay. Many purists and language reformers have agreed with Webster's claim that "the principal corruptions of our language, within the last five hundred years, are the work, not of the vulgar, as is commonly supposed, but of authors and writers, pretending to purify and refine the language."[12] But despite sops to the common people, Webster was himself an educated literary purifier who found errors to be corrected in everybody's language. Discussing, in the *Dissertations*, some of the regional pronunciations of the United States, we find the following:

"Another very common error, among the yeomanry of America, and particularly in New England, is the pronouncing of *e* before *r*, like *a*; as *marcy* for mercy." This pronunciation, dating in the south of England from at least the fifteenth century, is attributed by Webster to an incorrect notion which he would remedy by renaming a letter of the alphabet: "This mistake must have originated principally in the name of the letter *r*, which, in most of our school books, is called *ar*. This single mistake has spread a false pronunciation of several hundred words, among millions of people.* (*To remedy the evil . . . this letter is named *er*, in the *Institute*)" [*Dissertations*, p. 105].

Webster also objects to Southern r-lessness, the omission in speech of an *r* that appears in print, attributing it to carelessness, and to unaspirated initial *wh* (causing, for example, *which* to be pronounced like *witch*), seeing this as a foreign corruption, "for in America, it is not known among the unmixed descendants of the English" (p. 121). On the other hand he approves of *yelk* for *yolk* as representing a historically correct spelling and pronunciation: "*Yelk* is the most correct orthography, from the Saxon *gealkwe*; and in this country, it is the general pronunciation" (p. 123). Perhaps Webster's most celebrated attack, based on supposedly historical principles, is his proposed reformation of the word *bridegroom*. In the *Dictionary* of 1828 he argues the following: *bridegoom* is "a compound of *bride*, and *gum, guma*, a man, which, by our ancestors was pronounced *goom*. This word, by a mispronouncing of the last syllable, has been corrupted into *bridegroom*, which signifies a *bride's hostler*; groom being a Persian word, signifying a man who has the care of horses. Such a gross corruption or blunder ought not to remain a reproach to philology." Webster stuck to his etymology, although his proposed spelling was retracted in the 1847 edition of the *Dictionary*. By 1864 his editorial successors had eliminated the Persian connection, commenting succinctly that the *r* in the modern word was a corruption. *Webster's Third* makes no reference to the *r*, while the *Oxford English Dictionary* attributes it to the Middle English *grome* 'lad', a replacement for the obsolete Old English *guma*.

Other pronunciations that Webster favored but which did not become established are the Eastern *deef* (rhyming with *leaf*), rather than *def*, for *deaf*, and the New England pronunciation of *beard* rhyming with *bird*. Cooper, in *Notions of the Americans*, tells a related anecdote about American regional accents. Leaving the Middle States to be educated in New England, he was laughed at for his strange pronunciation. Returning home, he was similarly teased for the New Englandisms he had acquired, among which was his pronunciation of *beard* as *bird* (*Notions*, 2:131–32). But Webster sees this localism as a standard pronunciation on both sides of the Atlantic: "General practice, both in England and America, requires that *e* should be pronounced as in *were*" (*Dissertations*, p. 128).

Webster sees his task as the purification of American English, but he is also quite favorably disposed to the dialect he is out to purify. In the *Dictionary* of 1806 he makes clear his optimism regarding the future of the American language: "In each of the countries peopled by Englishmen, a distinct dialect of the language will gradually be formed; the principal of which will be that of the United States. In fifty years from this time, the *American-English* will be spoken by more people, than all the other dialects of the language" (pp. xxii–xxiii). One characteristic of this American English that Webster approves of is the way in which it reflects American political and social organization: "I should ascribe the manner of speaking among a people, to the nature of their government and a distribution of their property. Yet it is an undoubted fact that the drawling nasal manner of speaking in New England arises almost solely from these causes." According to Webster, the rich "possess a certain boldness, dignity and independence in their manners. . . . Those who are accustomed to command slaves, form a habit of expressing themselves with the tone of authority and decision." The inhabitants of New England, however (the commercial towns excepted), where there are few slaves and servants, have a different manner:

> The people are accustomed to address each other with that diffidence, or attention to the opinion of others, which marks a state of equality. Instead of commanding, they advise; instead of saying, with an air of decision, *you must*; they ask with an air of doubtfulness, *is it not best?* or give their opinions with an indecisive tone; *you had better, I believe*. Not possessing that pride and consciousness of superiority which attend birth and fortune, their intercourse with each other is all conducted on the idea of equality, which gives a singular tone to their language and complexion to their manners. [P. 107]

The peculiarities of New Englanders may cause their speech to be ridiculed by others, but Webster feels they also reflect the earlier, purer stages of the English language and are therefore more representative of its true genius. New Englanders, particularly those not living in the large commercial towns, do not travel, nor are they "tempted by an intercourse with foreigners, to quit their own habits." This accounts for

the surprising similarity between the idioms of the New England people and those of Chaucer, Shakespear, Congreve, &c. who wrote in the true English stile. It is remarked by a certain author, that the inhabitants of islands best preserve their native tongue. New England has been in the situation of an island; during 160 years, the people except in a few commercial towns, have not been exposed to any of the causes which effect great changes in language and manners. [P. 108n]

Despite this plus, there is still the problem of drawl and nasality in the pronunciation of New Englanders, and it is to this that Webster eventually returns, implying that it derives from their diffidence of speech: "The great error in their manner of speaking proceeds immediately from not opening the mouth sufficiently. Hence words are drawled out in a careless lazy manner, or the sound finds a passage thro the nose" (p. 108).

When it comes to the question of new word formation, an aspect of American English that drew heavy fire from its critics, Webster is not particularly helpful. In a letter written in 1789 to Webster praising the *Dissertations*, Benjamin Franklin asks Webster to reprobate a number of new terms that had been introduced into legislative circles during Franklin's absence in France, but Webster does not respond.[13] Writing to his brother-in-law, Thomas Dawes, in 1809, Webster says that the threat to the English language does not come from Americanisms, that in fact Americanisms are very rare: "The objection [to Webster's *Dictionary* of 1806 and his proposed *Dictionary* of 1828] which has been often made that I am about to give currency to vulgarisms and Americanisms has no foundation. We have very few Americanisms in use— most of those which are called so are Anglicisms." He also assures Dawes that "established orthography will not be disturbed" in his new *Dictionary* (*Letters*, p. 324). In another letter to Dawes a week later, Webster denies the charge that he is attempting to alter the language. He claims only to want to restore it to a state of purity, and correct the errors of others (pp. 325–26). And in a letter to John Pickering, whose glossary of Americanisms was published in 1816, Webster protests against Pickering's criticism of American new words, taking the rather startling position that root creation is impossible: "No new words have been introduced either into the English or into any other language since the dispersion of men" (p. 343). Somewhat later in the letter Webster returns to the theme of the American preservation of the Saxon genius of the language, and he tempers his stand on neology, claiming that it is not Americans, but the British, who are guilty of innovation (by innovation Webster may be talking about loanwords and analogical formations rather than root creations). Americans have done no more than conserve the purity of English:

> Let it be observed, by the way, that so far as a difference between the language of Englishmen and of Americans consists in our use of words obsolete in the higher circles in Great Britain, the change is not in *our* practice but in that of Englishmen. The fault, if any, is *theirs*. When they declaim with vehemence against *innovations*, let them not censure our adherence to old words and phrases, manifesting a disposition *not* to innovate. [P. 390]

In the introduction to his *American Dictionary of the English Language* (1828), Webster sums up his stand with a flourish, a declaration of linguistic independence from the corrupt influence of England coupled with a return to a classical form of English, stable, principled, and free from dialectal variation:

> The common usage of a great and respectable portion of the people of this country accords with the analogies of the language, but not with the modern notion of English orthoepists. . . . When we have principle on our side, let us adhere to it. The time cannot be distant, when the population of this vast country will throw off their leading strings, and walk in their own strength; and the more we can raise the credit and authority of principle over the caprices of fashion and innovation, the nearer we approach to uniformity and stability in practice. [N.p.]

Webster's Federal Spelling

Webster does not comment, in any of his writing, on the work of J. G. Chambers, James Ewing, or James Carrol, nor does he react to William Thornton's widely known proposal for a new alphabet, which was first put before the American Philosophical Society in 1788 (see below, chapter 4). And although Webster was enthusiastic about Benjamin Franklin's ideas on spelling, he felt the major drawback to Franklin's reform and others like it was the introduction of new characters to the alphabet. This would require not only a complete overhaul of the educational system, but a retooling of the presses, and while Webster favored a phonetic spelling, he felt Franklin's proposals were too radical and too cumbersome to succeed. But Franklin's efforts fueled Webster's desire to reform the American language. In 1786 he wrote to Franklin that he had been encouraged, both by Franklin and by the late chairman of Congress, Dr. David Ramsay, to believe "the reformation of our alphabet still possible." Webster's plan calls for "reducing the orthography of the language to perfect regularity, with as few new characters and alterations of the old ones as possible. It is probable that a great number of new and unusual characters would defeat the attempt." He concludes by enlisting Franklin's support: "Should this or any other plan be adopted, it is desired that your Excellency would lay it before Congress for their critical consideration. The advantages of adopting a reformation in this country, whether political or literary, will readily occur to an attentive mind." Webster also reminds Franklin that action must be taken now, while the revolutionary spirit prevails and the nation is of a mind to declare its linguistic independence from England: "The minds of people are in a ferment, and consequently disposed to receive improvements. Once let the ferment subside, and the succeeding lethargy will bar every great and rapid amendment. The favorable reception my lectures have met with encourages me to hope that most of the Americans may be detached from an implicit adherence to the language and manners of the British nation" (*Letters*, pp. 50–51).

Webster's position represents a substantial change from the one he had originally taken in the *Grammatical Institute* of 1783, his first spelling book. There he calmly accepts Samuel Johnson as his guide for spelling and pronunciation, and expresses his suspicion of efforts at spelling reform:

> There seems to be an inclination in some writers to alter the spelling of words, by expunging the superfluous letters. This appears to arise from the same pedantic fondness for singularity that prompts to new fashions of pronunciation. Thus they write the words *favour, honour,* &c. without *u*. But . . . they have dropped the wrong letter . . . for the words are pronounced *onur, favur*. . . . Thus *e* is omitted in *judgment*; which is the most necessary letter in the word; it being that alone which softens *g*. [P. 11]

Webster admits the disparity between spelling and pronunciation in English, and acknowledges that it is regrettable, but he feels in the *Grammatical Institute* that attempts to change this are idle. Spelling reform "will keep the language in perpetual fluctuation without an effectual amendment," while a sudden, total change "would render the language unintelligible" (pp. 11–12).

In the *Dissertations* Webster recants his earlier mistake in another uncharacteristic burst of humility: "I once believed that a reformation of our orthography would be unnecessary and impracticable. This opinion was hasty; being the result of a slight examination of the subject" (p. xi). While he opposes the introduction of new letters, he does propose naming the combinations *th*, *sh*, *ng*, and *si* or *su* as *eth*, *esh*, *eng*, and *ezh*, respectively, and distinguishing the voiced *th* from the voiceless by means of a small mark drawn through *th* (p. 89). In the appendix to his *Dissertations*, an essay "On the Necessity, advantages and practicability of reforming the Mode of Spelling, and of Rendering the Orthography of words correspondent to the pronunciation," Webster characterizes two types of language change that are responsible for the inconsistency between spelling and pronunciation: change due to the "progress of science and civilization" and change due to "the mixture of different languages, occasioned by revolutions in England, or by a predilection of the learned, for words of foreign growth and ancient origin" (p. 391).

To the first of these causés Webster attributes the difference between the spelling and pronunciation of Saxon words: "As savages proceed in forming languages, they lose the guttural sounds, in some measure, and adopt the use of labials, and the more open vowels. The ease of speaking facilitates this progress, and the pronunciation of words is softened, in proportion to a national refinement of manners." Webster notes as proof of his theory the number of aspirates and gutturals remaining in the orthography of Germanic words, and the contrast between the soft pronunciations of France, Spain, and Italy and "the more harsh and guttural pronunciation of the northern inhabitants of Europe." As for the second cause of disparity, linguistic borrowing, Webster asserts, "when words have been introduced from a foreign language into the English, they have generally retained the orthography of the original, however ill adapted to express the English pronunciation" (pp. 392–93). This problem, the proper spelling and pronunciation of loan words, has been of continual concern to reformers of the language, and it continues to defy resolution.

According to Webster, there are three steps required to make the spelling of English both regular and easy. The first is the "omission of all superfluous or silent letters; as *a* in *bread*. Thus *bread*, *head*, *give*, *breast*, *built*, *meant*, *realm*, *friend*, would be spelt, *bred*, *hed*, *giv*, *brest*, *bilt*, *ment*, *relm*, *frend*." This would make writing easier, facilitate the learning of the language, "reduce the true pronunciation to a certainty" and "render the pronunciation uniform, in different parts of the country, and almost prevent the possibility of changes" (pp. 394–95). The second step is the replacement of letters with vague or indeterminate sounds by ones that have a certain, definite sound: "Thus, by putting *ee* instead of *ea* or *ie*, the words *mean*, *near*, *speak*, *grieve*, *zeal*, would become *meen*, *neer*, *speek*, *greev*, *zeel*." To facilitate the principle of one spelling, one sound, Webster would also substitute "*laf* for *laugh*; *dawter* for *daughter*; *plow* for *plough*; *tuf* for *tough*; *proov* for *prove*; *blud* for *blood*; and *draft* for *draught*. In this manner *ch* in Greek derivatives, should be changed into *k*; for the English *ch* has a soft sound, as in *cherish*; but *k* always a hard sound. Therefore *character*, *chorus*, *cholic*, *architecture*, should be written *karacter*, *korus*, *kolic*, *arkitecture*; and were they thus written, no person could mistake their true pronunciation." Webster recommends that the *ch* in words derived from French be changed to *sh*, hence *machine* would be spelled *masheen*, but for some reason—perhaps the inconsistency that plagues all systems of spelling reform—he neglects to change the hard *c* of words like *karacter* and *arkitecture* to a *k*; and elsewhere he argues for the simplification of final *ck* to *c*, rather than *k*, preferring *music* to *musick* and *public* to *publick*. Webster's third suggestion concerns the pointing or alteration of characters to distinguish different sounds: "Thus a very small stroke across *th* would distinguish its two sounds. A point over a vowel, in this manner, *ȧ*, or *ȯ*, or *ī*, might answer all the purposes of different letters" (p. 395). He would also write *ow* as a digraph, or fusion of two letters, *ꝏ*.

Webster feels that his proposals will make it easier for children and foreigners to learn how to spell and pronounce the language. Furthermore, the tendency to pronounce words as they are spelled would now be rewarded, assuring a uniform and regular pronunciation, and, as Franklin observed, making good spellers out of those who were once considered bad spellers because they spelled phonetically: "It would . . . be as difficult to spell wrong, as it is now to spell *right*" (p. 396). Spelling, for Webster, becomes a means of assuring a democratically based society: "All persons, of every rank, would speak with some degree of precision and uniformity. Such a uniformity in these states is very desirable; it would remove prejudice, and conciliate mutual affection and respect." There is also an economic advantage: Webster's revisions would reduce the alphabet, the size of books, and the cost of printing them, by about one eighteenth. More important, a reformed spelling would establish a unique American orthographical system, different from that of Great Britain. This would require the printing, or reprinting, of all books in America—for "the English would never copy our orthography for their own use; and consequently the same impressions of books would not answer for both countries"—and America would no longer be dependent on, or influenced by, British imports.

Perhaps the most important consequence of the spelling reform, for Webster, is not educational, social, or economic, but political: "A capital advantage of this reform in these states would be, that it would make a difference between the English orthography and the American" (p. 397). Underlying all Webster's efforts is a concern for the establishment of a Federal English that would mark America as unique and allow it to take its proper place among nations as a literary as well as a political power. The spelling reform would serve as a prod to Americans to develop their own literature written in their own language:

> However they may boast of Independence, and the freedom of their government, yet their *opinions* are not sufficiently independent; an astonishing respect for the arts and literature of their parent country, and a blind imitation of its manners, are still prevalent among the Americans. Thus an habitual respect for another country, deserved indeed and once laudable, turns their attention from their own interests, and prevents their respecting themselves. [P. 398]

The political aim of the spelling reform requires, according to Webster, a political implementation. As mentioned earlier, Webster hoped Benjamin Franklin would put the spelling reform before Congress. In the *Dissertations* he states, optimistically, that all that is required for the success of his proposals is a resolution in Congress "ordering all their acts to be engrossed in the new orthography, and recommending the plan to the several universities in America; and also a resolution of the universities to encourage and support it" (p. 399). But Congressional action on the proposal was not forthcoming. In fact, although spelling reform was actively urged throughout the nineteenth century, no government action was attempted on any large scale until President Theodore Roosevelt issued a proclamation in 1906 ordering the adoption of simplified spellings. Roosevelt's order promptly backfired, signaling the end of a minor and temporary spelling revolution.

Webster does not follow his own prescription for spelling—except for the occasional omission of a final *e*—in the *Dissertations*, but in his *Collection of Essays and Fugitiv Writings on Moral, Historical, Political and Literary Subjects*, published in Boston in 1790, he includes some attempts at illustrating his scheme. He comments on these in the introduction to the collection:

> In the essays, ritten within the last yeer, a considerable change of spelling iz introduced by way of experiment. This liberty waz taken by the writers before the age of queen Elizabeth, and to this we are indeted for the preference of modern spelling over that of Gower and Chaucer. The man who admits that the change of *housbonde, mynde, ygone, moneth* into *husband, mind, gone, month,* iz an improovment, must acknowlege also the riting of *helth, breth, rong, tung, munth,* to be an improovment. There iz no alternativ. Every possible reezon that could ever be offered for altering the spelling of *wurds,* stil exists in full force; and if a gradual reform should not be made in our language, it wil proov that we are less under the influence of reezon than our ancestors. [P. xi]

Most of Webster's spelling innovations did not catch on. Those that have become part of standard American spelling achieved that status only partly because of Webster's efforts. Endings in *-or, -er,* and *c* had for some time alternated with *-our, -re,* and *ck(e)*. Examination of records from the Colonial and Revolutionary eras shows that spelling was highly idiosyncratic, and the evolution of a standard spelling, while partly attributable to the effects of such authorities as Johnson, Ash, Webster, and Worcester, also owed something to a kind of natural selection process that singled out variants such as *plow* and *ax* in America. Webster himself was fairly inconsistent in implementing his reforms, as an examination of the passage cited above shows. In it we find *writers* alongside *ritten*; a number of final *-e*'s that have no phonetic value (*are, influence, force*); *s* and *z* for the same sound (*writers, reezon*); *s* and *c* for the same sound (*this, force*); single and double consonants (*stil* and *wil,* but *full*). In these essays Webster omits silent letters in some words (*altho, thot*) but retains them elsewhere (*might*), and his phonetic spelling often reflects either New England pronunciation (*heard* becomes *heerd*) or Webster's own idiosyncrasy (*islands* is spelled *ilans*). And Webster varied his spelling from book to book—tending to become more conservative in later years. Lyman Cobb, an American educational writer who published his own speller at the age of nineteen, reviewed Webster's *Elementary Spelling Book*, a revision of the *American Spelling Book* published in 1829. Cobb surveys Webster's spelling in the two spellers and the dictionaries of 1806, 1817, 1828, and 1831, calling Webster's various proposals a "contradictory system of innovations, neither warranted by usage nor analogy, and calculated to 'abolish the superstructure, and bring it back to the confusion in orthography, from which Johnson extricated it.'"[14]

While Webster was assertive in his recommendations and was as harsh with his critics as they were with him, he did counsel moderation in linguistic change, and always maintained that the spelling reform should be gradual and not sudden; progressive and not categorical. Although in the conservative *Institute* he rejects both progressive and sudden change, in the preface to the 1806 *Dictionary* he warns that our language is being reduced "to the barbarism of Chinese characters instead of letters," advocating as a remedy a slow change that would not create inconvenience, violate established principles, or obliterate the "radicals of the language." Gradual changes will "purify words from corruptions, improve the regular analogies of a language and illustrate etymology" (pp. vi–vii). In the preface to the 1821 edition of the *American Spelling Book*, published in Brattleborough, Vermont, Webster makes a similarly toned-down appeal to reform, warning against a multiplicity of standards and texts, and offering his own work as the answer:

> Although perfect uniformity in speaking, is not probably attainable in any living language, yet it is to be wished, that the youth of our country may be, as little as possible, perplexed with various differing systems and standards. . . . the general interest of education requires, that a disposition to multiply books and systems for teaching the language of the country, should not be indulged to an unlimited extent. [P. vi]

Toward the end of his career, Webster became pessimistic about the success of his linguistic efforts, but he never found himself without a scheme of some sort. In 1837 he wrote to the American statesman Daniel Webster, who was no relation, of his latest project, a bowdlerization of the Bible, issued in 1833: "Having nearly lost all hope of benefiting my country by correcting the disorders of our language, but unwilling to believe that the labors of my life must all be fruitless, I still indulge a hope that my efforts to render the language of our English Bible less exceptionable and, in many passages, more intelligible may not be wholly unsuccessful" (*Letters*, p. 459). Webster's pessimism, though strongly expressed, never distracted him from his basic goals, and he continued to revise his *Dictionary*.

Both establishing the uniformity of American English and selling his books were concerns that occupied Webster from the beginning to the end of his career. He saw his first work, the *Grammatical Institute*, as a tool for standardizing pronunciation, and he felt that his greatest work, the *American Dictionary of the English Language*, was to serve the same end. Writing to his wife, Rebecca Greenleaf Webster, in 1831, he tells of yet another attempt to involve the nation's legislators in his scheme: "I . . . drew a paper recommending the *American Dictionary* as a standard to prevent the formation of dialects in this extensive country, and requesting gentlemen who are disposed to favor this design to subscribe it. This paper has been circulated in both houses of Congress, and is subscribed by more than a hundred of the Senators and Representatives. . . . the signatures of such a respectable number of gentlemen from every state in the Union will be of no inconsiderable use to me" (*Letters*, p. 426). The subscription referred to is printed in the *Elementary Spelling Book* (1840). The following excerpt shows that although Webster backed down on the spelling issue, his basic ideas about Federal English and his concern with promoting the sale of his own publications had never changed:

It is very desirable that one standard dictionary should be used by the numerous millions of people who are to inhabit the vast extent of territory belonging to the United States; as the use of such a standard may prevent the formation of dialects in states remote from each other, and impress upon the language uniformity and stability. . . . The public is informed, that the engrossing committees of Congress use the author's dictionaries as their guides in orthography. [P. 4]

4 The Spelling Reform Movement

Federal Spelling: Webster's Competitors

Noah Webster was not the only spelling patriot of the post-Revolutionary period, although he was certainly the best known. In 1785 Robert Ross, a Congregational clergyman who was violently anti-British, produced a *New American Spelling Book* designed, like Webster's work, to replace the traditional British speller of Thomas Dilworth. But unlike Webster, Ross did not attempt to revolutionize orthography; he simply felt that, for reasons of economy and state security, American students should use American texts: "*Dilworth's* Spelling Book recommending Subjection to a foreign Power has a Tendency to promote Disaffection to the present Government, and must therefore be very improper for the Instruction of the *Freeborn* Youth of *America*, since we have become an Independent Nation. . . . And if our own Productions and Manufactures are as good as those of other Nations, why should we import from Great-Britain?" Ross touts his book, which proved fairly popular, as cheaper than European imports and as very useful for the instruction of non-English speakers and those whose English is not standard, particularly the Irish, "who, though they speak English, it is with such a different Accent and Tone in many Instances, as is very disagreeable to an English Ear, and mars the Usefulness of some of their public Speakers." Ross also feels that his text is a suitable vehicle for the education and conversion of the American heathen population: "And if the *Indians* and *Negroes* would employ their leisure Hours, especially the Lord's Day, in this Book, as many of them are not destitute of Genius," they will learn to read and understand the Gospels, "which would be the greatest Priviledge they can enjoy."[1]

Aside from his political and evangelical motivation, Ross's spelling book was not remarkable. Webster, on the other hand, was a true language planner. According to Webster, the key to achieving a uniform, *American* English was to be found in a reformation of the spelling system. Spelling reform was not new to the English language, and the attempts of the seventeenth and eighteenth centuries to regulate orthography were known to Webster and to some of his contemporaries. In America, this reform was given added impetus by nationalism, and Webster and his colleagues capitalized on nationalistic feeling to recommend their own systems of spelling. For example, writing to George Washington in 1786 Webster conceives of his role as spelling reformer as a patriotic one: "I am encouraged, by the prospect of rendering my country some service, to proceed in my design of refining the language and improving our general system of education. Dr. Franklin has extended my views to a very simple plan of reducing the language to perfect regularity" (*Letters*, p. 46).

It was a commonly held assumption that a system of phonetic spelling could ascertain the sounds of a language and prevent their mutation. The actor, orator, and lexicographer Thomas Sheridan (father of the playwright Richard Brinsley Sheridan) states, in his "Dissertation on the Causes of the Difficulties, Which Occur, in Learning the English Tongue" (1762), that spelling should be able, like musical notation, to *fix* a sound.[2] But there was some debate as to whether or not phonetic spelling required the introduction of a reformed alphabet.

Benjamin Franklin's New Alphabet

In 1768 Benjamin Franklin proposed a scheme for a new alphabet and a reformed mode of spelling. His new alphabet contained twenty-six letters, including six new ones of his own devising (see fig. 1).[3] It was structured in "a more natural Order," beginning with the vowels and aspirate *h*, which Franklin renamed *huh*, "the simple sounds formed by the breath, with none or very little help of tongue, teeth, and lips, and produced chiefly in the windpipe." Then come the consonants: first those formed in the back of the mouth, the velar stops *g* and *k*, which Franklin calls *gi* and *ki*; next the palatals and dentals; and finally the front-most sound, *m*, the bilabial nasal formed by "the shutting up of the mouth, or closing the lips, while any vowel is sounding" (*Papers*, 15:177). Franklin pairs voiceless and voiced consonants, changing their names when necessary to link them more clearly in our minds: thus *s* and *z* are to be called *es* and *ez*; *f* and *v* will bear the names *ef* and *ev*.

Franklin's alphabet is designed to provide a single sound for each letter. There will be no more silent letters to take up space: every letter in the printed form of a word is to be pronounced. To accomplish this, Franklin employs seven vowel symbols. Vowel length is to be indicated by reduplication: *mend* will continue to be written *mend*, but *remain'd*,

Characters.	Sounded as now in	Names of the Letters expressed in the reformed Sounds and Characters
o	old	o
a [a]	John, Folly	a
a	man, can	a
e	mane, lane	e
i	een, seen	i
u	tool, fool	u
ɥ [ɥ; Ɏ]	um, un, as in umbrage, unto, &c.	ɥ
h	hunter, happy, high	huh
g	give, gather	gi
k	keep, kick	ki
s [s]	sh, ship, wish	ish
ŋ [ŋ]	ng, ing, reaping, among	ing
n	end	en
r	art	ar
t	teeth	ti
d	deed	di
l	ell, tell	el
ħ [ħ]	th, think	eħ
dh [dh; Ð]	dh, thy	edh
s	essence	es
z	ez, wages	ez
f	effect	ef
v	ever	ev
b	bees	bi
p	peep	pi
m	ember	em

Figure 1. Benjamin Franklin's reformed-spelling alphabet. Reprinted from *The Papers of Benjamin Franklin*, vol. 15, ed. William B. Willcox (New Haven, 1972), facing p. 176.

with a long vowel, is to become *remeen'd*. And some new consonants are required. The single letter Franklin calls *ing* will stand for the sounds now represented by the combined letters *n* and *g*, and two separate letters, *edth* and *eth*, are to be used for the voiced and voiceless *th* of *this* and *think*. Franklin also creates the letter *ish* to replace the conventional alphabetic pair, *sh*. *Ish* can be used after *d* to transcribe the initial sound, or pair of sounds, in *James*, *January*, *giant*, and *gentle*, or after *t* to indicate the initial sounds of *cherry* and *chip*. *Ish* after *ez* gives us the French *j* of *jamais*.

Franklin unfortunately does not provide many explanatory comments about his new alphabet, but he does give some examples in an exchange of letters with his friend Mary (Polly) Stevenson, the daughter of his London landlady. Writing in Franklin's phonetic alphabet, Miss Stevenson complains that it is difficult to use, that it obscures the etymology of words, and that it cannot hope to standardize a pronunciation that is constantly changing. Replying, Franklin maintains that all these difficulties can be surmounted. He feels that his system of letters will actually prove easier than the standard alphabet for poor spellers, who always tend to spell phonetically. Franklin protests that etymologies are uncertain anyway, and we need not worry about their preservation. And he warns that unless a phonetic alphabet is used to stabilize our spelling and pronunciation, books will become obsolete as English changes over the centuries, and "our writing will become the same with the Chinese as to the difficulty of learning and using it" (p. 303). (See fig. 2.)

J. G. Chambers: Phonetics and the Genius of America

In 1791 J. G. Chambers proposed another phonetic alphabet to renovate our orthography. Writing a series of articles in *The Columbian Magazine*, Chambers challenges the popular assumption that the languages of the ancients were truly phonetic, arguing that we cannot be sure of the values represented by the letters of their alphabets, and that we can only guess at the correct pronunciation of their words. According to Chambers, an ancient Roman would puzzle at our Latin: "If Cicero and Demosthenes could be introduced, to hear some of our best modern linguists pronounce the Latin and Greek, they would be at a loss to determine what language was intended to be spoken. The English and Germans cannot understand one another, speaking the Latin and Greek; yet they both learn from the same alphabets."[4]

Chambers sees spelling reform as a particularly appropriate New World enterprise: "Perhaps this is a task reserved for the liberal and

Diir Pali,   Ritsmƴnd, Dsulƴi 20.-68
Ɣii intended to hev sent iu dhiz Pepers sunƴr, bƴt biiŋ bizi fargat it.

Mr Kolman hez mended deeli: bƴt iur gud Mƴdhƴr hez bin indispoz'd uiħ e slƴit Fivƴr, atended uiħ mƴts fiibilnes and uirines. Si uiuld nat allau mi to send iu uƴrd av it at dhi tƴim, and iz nau beter.

Ɣii uis iu to kansider dhis Alfabet, and giv mi Instanses af sƴts Iŋlis Uƴrds and Saunds az iu mee ħink kannat perfektlƴi bi eksprest bƴi it. Ɣii am persueeded it mee bi kamplited bƴi iur help. Ði greeter difikƴlti uil bi to briŋ it into ius. Hauevƴr, if Amendments eer nevƴr atemted, and ħiŋs kantinu to gro uƴrs and uƴrs, dhee mƴst kƴm to bi in a retsed Kandisƴn at last; sƴts indiid ƴi ħink aur Alfabet and Rƴitiŋ alredi in; bƴt if ui go an az ui hev dƴn e fiu Senturiz langer, aur uƴrds uil graduali siis to ekspres Saunds, dhee uil onli stand far ħiŋs, az dhi rittin uƴrds du in dhi Tsuiniiz Languads, huits ƴi sƴspekt mƴit oridsinali hev bin e litiral Rƴitiŋ lƴik dhat af Iurop, bƴt ħru dhi Tseendsez in Pronƴsiesƴn braat an bƴi dhi Kors af Eedses, and ħru dhi abstinet Adhirens af dhat Pipil to old Kƴstƴms and amƴŋ ƴdhƴrs to dheer old manƴr ov Rƴitiŋ, dhi oridsinal Saunds af Leters and Uƴrds eer last, and no langƴr kansidered. Ɣii am, mƴi diir Frend, Iurz afeksƴnetli,

                                                    B. FRANKLIN

Figure 2. Letter from Benjamin Franklin to Mary (Polly) Stevenson: dateline, Richmond, July 20, 1768. Reprinted from *The Papers of Benjamin Franklin*, vol. 15, ed. William B. Willcox (New Haven, 1972), p. 174.

enterprising genius of America" (August 1791, p. 114), and he defines his goals explicitly: "To investigate, critically, all the distinct radical sounds, or powers, of the language. To devise, or adopt, a set of characters, which shall severally represent them" so that one sound is represented by one character, and vice versa; and, to name the sounds and letters suitably (July 1791, p. 36). The Roman alphabet is insufficient for the task, and Chambers's suggestions include digraphs for *ti* and *sh*, the use of a cedilla to mark a sibilant *c*, and the introduction of two new consonantal characters. Vowels will be marked with diacritics to indicate their exact pronunciations. Voiced *s* and *f* will be respelled *z* and *v*: for example, *as* becomes *az*, and *of* changes to *ov*. *Are* is to be respelled phonetically as *er*.

Chambers feels that his new method of spelling will allow mothers to teach their children to read at home, "with less trouble than they usually have to put up their victuals and send them to school" (October 1791, p. 228). In fact, according to Chambers, anything that keeps children away from school may be beneficial:

> Let us take a compassionate view of several millions, the youth of our whole nation, from six to twelve years old and upwards, at school; thirty or forty together shut up in little wretched hovels, like criminals, or prisoners of war! and this at a time of life when they should acquire useful and noble habits, health, activity of body, and vivacity of mind. Here their constitutions are injured, and often destroyed, for the want of free air, exercise, and suitable diet! Their spirits depressed, and faculties stupified [*sic*], under the stern countenance, and hard hand of tyranny. For it is but too generally found, that nothing less than despotic sway can compel recoiling nature to the preposterous task [of learning to read and spell]. [Ibid.]

Jonathan Fisher, Yankee Phonetician

Another early American spelling reformer was Jonathan Fisher, a clergyman and artist who designed a "philosophical alphabet" in 1793 while he was a student at the Harvard Divinity School.[5] Fisher apparently did not attempt to convert others to his method of writing, reserving it for his own use as a shorthand system in his notebooks where, he estimated, it had saved him some fifty dollars worth of paper over a fifty-year period. He also used it occasionally in the English text accompanying his illustrations of plant and animal life, adding a French or Latin "translation" written in conventional alphabetic symbols. (See fig. 3.)

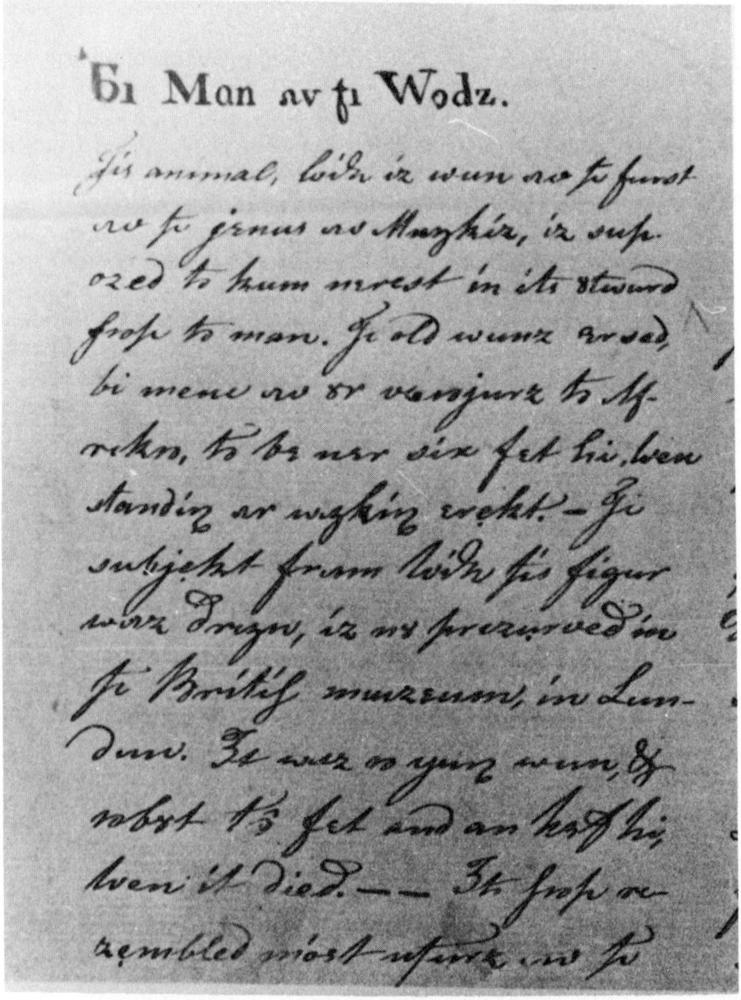

Figure 3. "The Man of the Woods," a description of an orangutan, copied from George Edwards, *Gleanings of Natural History* (London, 1758), vol. 1, and reprinted from Alice Winchester's *Versatile Yankee* (Princeton, N.J., 1973) by permission of the author. Fisher transcribed Edwards's English text, with some modifications, into his own phonetic alphabet but presented the French translation in conventional letters. The English text reads: "This animal, which is one of the first of the genus of Monkeys, is supposed to come nearest in its outward shape to man. The old ones are said, by many of our voyagers to Africa, to be near six feet high, when standing or walking erect. The subject from which this figure was drawn, is now preserved in the British museum, in London. It was a young one & about two feet and a half high, when it died."

Like Franklin, Fisher uses single letters, mostly of his own devising, for the phonemes represented in the English alphabet by combinations of letters such as *sh*, *ti*, *ch*, and *ng*. These new letters often resemble what they are designed to replace: the voiced *th* of *that* is realized by an elongated *t*, descending below the line, and *ch* becomes a digraph combining *c* and *h*. The *ng* symbol, like Franklin's, merges *n* with the tail of *g*, and the voiceless *th* of *throne* is replaced by a letter resembling the Greek theta, Θ. The letters *q* and *x* are used for the sounds of *kw* and *ks*. Fisher also used a variety of symbols to transcribe the vowels of English, including a combination of *i* and *u* for the vowel in *your*; undotted, dotted, and accented *i*'s; Roman and Greek *a*'s and *e*'s; inverted *e* before *r*; and reversed *c* with or without a circumflex accent or a dot.

The Scottish Cadmus

In the same year that Jonathan Fisher developed his philosophical alphabet, 1793, William Thornton, a Scottish physician living in America, published his *Cadmus, or a Treatise on the Elements of Written Language*, advising the citizens of North America to reform their orthography in nationalistic tones reminiscent of Webster: "You have corrected the dangerous doctrines of European powers, correct now the languages you have imported, for the oppressed of various nations knock at your gates, and desire to be received as your brethren." Fisher did not seek to popularize his writing system, but Thornton, who received the prize of the American Philosophical Society for his work, recommends his universal phonetic alphabet as suitable for use in translation and, more important, urges its adoption as a symbol of American independence: "The *American Language* will thus be as distinct as the government, free from all the follies of unphilosophical fashion, and resting upon truth as its only regulator.[6] Thornton does not feel that artificially created alphabets pose any problem: he regards Hebrew as an artificial language that was created only after its alphabet had been devised, and he clearly has visions of a resurrected English to be based on his own orthographical scheme.

Thornton's notions of linguistics are uncertain, as his reference to Hebrew suggests. For example, he sees language as originating in the imitation of certain natural sounds: "The sounds of the *common* vowels, with *l*, *m*, *n*, *ŋ*, we hear daily among cattle and domestic beasts; the *y*, *z*, *j*, *v*, *D*, are like the buzzing of beetles; *ʃ*, *f*, *ə*, *s*, like the hissing of serpents. . . . the English contains so many of these buzzing and hissing sounds, that some Foreigners have called it the language of snakes." Thornton also derives the Greek *s*, as it is pronounced in English, from the hissing of the goose. He finds that the gutturals imitate the croaking of frogs or toads, and he concludes that *r* is the linguistic representation of the snarling of dogs. As proof of this last claim he adds, "and we find nations where there are no dogs that have not the letter *r* in their languages" (pp. 68–69). Despite these shaky foundations, Thornton is certain that his plan will fix American spelling and pronunciation and lead to the disappearance of dialects, both among foreigners and peasants, and he feels that Americans should adopt it even if the British do not: "The best English authors would be reprinted in America, and every stranger to the language, *even in Europe*, who thinks it of more consequence to speak the English correctly, than to write it with the present errors, would purchase American editions, and would be *ashamed* to spell incorrectly" (p. 27).

In Thornton's alphabet, which consists of thirty symbols, capitals differ from lowercase letters only in size, but not in shape. Thornton uses the terms *vowel* and *vocalic sound* to include glides and many sounds now considered consonants. There are seven symbols that serve as vowels in the modern sense of the term, and as in Franklin's system, they can be doubled to indicate length, for example, SOT 'sot', and YOOK 'yoke'. Thornton uses a barred D, Đ, for the voiced, and a theta for the voiceless *th* sound: ĐAT 'that', and θEEN 'thane'. He employs an inverted J for *sh*, and a barred O, distinguished from theta by the fact that the bar does not touch the sides of the O, for *wh*: ϴAIL 'while'.

Thornton's examples are not always consistent. He sometimes omits an unstressed vowel, as in AKSNT 'accent', and he occasionally gives two transcriptions for the same word, for example S ☐ W and S ☐☐ W 'saw'. He is concerned with the pedagogical applications of his alphabet, and he demonstrates how transcriptions using his alphabet can identify and cure pronunciation defects, removing from speakers of the American language any trace of dialect or foreign accent. According to Thornton, the Welsh aspirate their words, producing "a strange effect in speech." The Irish are guilty of this too, and they also exhibit a tendency to place the substantive before the adjective rather than after it. In fact, Thornton has little sympathy for the pronunciation of these more barbarous Celts: "The lower class of the saxons are so inattentive to the difference of the *p* and *b*, the *t* and *d*, the *f* and *v*, &c. that in English they rarely speak without misplacing them" (p. 66). In the following pair of examples, the first line represents the sentence spelled conventionally; the second line shows the correct transcription in Thornton's system; and the third line shows a transcription, again in Thornton's alphabet, of the deviant Welsh pronunciation:

> I vow, by G——d, that Jenkin is a wizzard.
> Ai vou, bai G——d, Ðat Djeŋkin iz a uizzard.
> Ai fou, pai K——t, θat ʃeŋkin iʃs a uiʃʃart.
>
> Boy bring both Pails to the pond.
> Boi briŋ boθ Peelz tu Ð] pond.
> Poi priŋ poth Beels tu d] Pont.

[Pp. 65–66]

Thornton concludes his prize-winning dissertation with a discussion of methods for teaching the deaf to read and write, methods that do not involve the use of his phonetic writing system. Although his alphabet was not generally adopted, Thornton's work was widely read and frequently cited both by opponents and defenders of reformed spelling. As late as 1814 the *Quarterly Review* of London lumps Thornton's ideas together with other plans to abolish English in the New World, calling his work "a project of a more Babylonish kind. . . . a barbarous murder of English orthography" (10:528).

Ewing's Columbian Alphabet

James Ewing, businessman and quite possibly the Revolutionary general of the same name who served with Washington at the battle of Trenton, proposed his *Columbian Alphabet*, "being an attempt to new model the English alphabet," in 1798.[7] Ewing considered the present alphabet an arbitrary construct in which "z might as well mark the sound of a, of y or b, as otherwise, if custom and our teachers had so directed" (p. 4). Furthermore he felt that the Roman alphabet was not suited to the expression of English sounds, and that attempts to write our words in it had led to the present deficiencies and redundancies of our spelling system. The creation of a totally new alphabet, while desirable, was not seen by Ewing as practical. Instead he proposed a modification of the present system that employed diacritics or accent marks, inverted letters, and the assigning of new sounds to old letters that were redundant or ambiguous.

In creating his alphabet, Ewing adheres to four basic principles put forth by lexicographer Thomas Sheridan:

1st No character should be set down, in any word, which is not pronounced.

2d. Every distinct simple sound should have a distinct character to mark it, for which it should uniformly stand.

3d. The same character should never be set down as the representative of two different sounds.

4th. All compound sounds should be marked only by such characters as will naturally and necessarily produce those sounds upon their being pronounced according to their names in the alphabet. [Pp. 10–11]

Ewing regarded *c* as a superfluous letter that could be replaced either by *k* or *s*. He therefore assigned it the sound of *ch*. Since *q* never occurs alone in English, and can be replaced by *k*, Ewing uses it for the velar nasal, *ng*. The letter *w* takes on the functions of *oo*, and *x*, which can be replaced by *ks* or *gz*, is freed to assume the duties of *si* or *zi*, as in *osier* and *brazier*. Ewing uses the long *s*, *ʃ*, to stand for *sh*, and he employs inverted *k* and *y* for the voiceless and voiced *th*. Short vowels are marked with a circumflex: *hat* 'hate', *hât* 'hat', *be* 'be', *bêt* 'bet', and diphthongs by dieresis: *kïnd* 'kind', *fü* 'few'. Ewing felt that, far from posing any problem for learners of the new system, the diacritics would become as much a part of a letter as the dot over the *i*.

Ewing's purpose in introducing his alphabet was twofold: to make the learning of reading easier and to teach correct pronunciation by means of the written word. He thought that the pronunciation guides found in Walker's and Sheridan's dictionaries were inadequate, and that only his new alphabet could remedy the situation: "Few, very few, even of the best educated natives, ever attain to an accurate knowledge of the pronunciation of their mother tongue, and it is wholly impossible for foreigners ever to acquire it from any assistance hitherto offered" (p. 10).

After a description of how each of the thirty-three letters and three diphthongs in his system is produced by the organs of speech, Ewing presents an alphabetical list of respelled words, and a sample of prose. In the following selection, the left column contains the standard form of the word, as spelled by Ewing, and the right column contains the word as he spells it in his Columbian alphabet:

abbreviation	â-bre-ve-a-ʃun
boisterously	bʌest-rus-le
bombasin	bum-ba-zen

cauliflower	kôl-e-flö-ur
charity	câr-i-te
cipher	sy-fur
ear	er
hush-money	huʃ-mun-e
them	ʎêm
theme	ɟem
warning	wʌrn-iq

The portion of the prose passage given by Ewing, which concerns the development of writing, and which contains quite a few inconsistencies, some of which are marked, is followed by a transcription in modern, conventional spelling (see fig. 4).

A Conservative Speller

One eighteenth-century American writer who opposed spelling reform was James Carrol. In *The American Criterion of the English Language* (1795) Carrol recommends a set of pronunciation rules designed to regularize American speech and abolish the regional dialects that he regards as defects plaguing even the most educated of our citizens: "The pronunciation of the southern states of English America is almost as different from that of the New-England states, even among the learned, as any two dialects of the language of any illiterate nation can be supposed to be: and yet both those parts of America abound with men of bright genius, large mental capacities and profound learning."[8]

Carrol notes that, in addition to their regional peculiarities, users of English pronounce their words differently when they are speaking and when they are reading aloud from a written text: "In the latter case [a listener] would have the tympanum of his ear assaulted, almost incessantly, by the impertinent noise of a parcel of letters, which, in the former case, from respect to the speaker, were politely silent" (p. iii). Carrol clearly does not approve of spelling pronunciation, a feature of the New England dialect that he otherwise sets up as his standard: "The reader pronounce[s] that talk, which an extemporary speaker would pronounce tauk; (the same may be observed of a great number of other words, in which an English reader generally sounds letters which ought to be silent)." Similarly, readers pronounce the final -ed of a past tense verb as a separate syllable, while orators do not: "The word which the extemporary speaker pronounces tauk'd, the reader pronounces

I ſhall proceed, by way of illustration, to give a Specimen of the manner of writing with the Columbian
Alphabet ; for which purpoſe I ſhall make uſe of the
introductory obſervations to this publicatien, which will
then appear in the following form, viz.

ᛘe dezyr ᴧv kômünikatiq. ꝺᴧt tu pêrsunz ât a distâns
ând tu pᴧstêrite, undötêdle, gav ryz tu ᛘe ârt ᴧv rytiq.

mân dezyrus ᴧv êkstêndiq his nᴧlêj ând diskuveriz be-
ônd ᛘe nâro kumpâs ᴧv hiz fâkulte ᴧv spec, w̄wd nâtürâle hâv rekors tu sum mêꝺud ᴧv giviq pêrmânêns to hiz
ydeâz.

ᛘe furst âttêmts ât rytiq wêr prᴧbabli vêre r̄wd ând im-
pêrfêkt—neſeſite ᴧlꝺo justle styld ᛘe muᛘêr ᴧv invênſun
kânôt be kᴧld ᛘe muᛘêr vᴧ pêrfêkſun—frᴧm ᛘe prinsipl ᴧv
imitaſun implântêd in mân ând frᴧm hwᴧt haz bin ᴧbzêrvd
ᴧv ᛘe prâktis ᴧv mêne unsivilyzd naſunz, we âr indw̄ɀd

tu supoz ᛘât pikturz wêr ᛘe furst êsᴂ toârdz rytiq—
frᴧm ᛘez tu hyeroglifikz, ᴧr êmblemâtikâl rêpresêntaſunz
ᴧf ᴧbjêkts, ᛘe transixun w̄wd be nâturâl ând eze—ᛘez
hyeroglifikz w̄wd höêvur be but inkômpetênt vᴇhiklz fᴧr
êkstêndiq kômünikaſun—ᛘar vêre natür âtâcd tu ᛘêm
kônfüxun ând danjur ᴧv misintêrpretaſuu.

ᛘe âmbigüite ând difikultez âtêndiq ᛘis mod ᴧv rytiq
w̄wd nâtürâle sugjêst tu sum hâpe jeneus ᛘe âdvântajêz
ᴧv rêprezêntiq w̄urdz by kârâkturz nôt depêndânt ᴧn
ᴧbjêktz—ᛘis wâz ᛘe furst âdvâns frᴧm hyeroglifik êx-
prêſun—ᴧbzêrviq ᛘât nôtwiꝺstândiq ᛘe numbur ᴧv w̄urdz
in üs wêr mêne eit ᛘe numbur ᴧv ârtikülat söndz kum-
poziq ᛘoz w̄urdz wêr kumpârativle fü, synz wêr insti-
twtêd fᴧr ᛘoz ârtikülat söndz—a grat ând impᴧrtânt im-
pruvv̄mênt—difikultez, höêvêr, w̄wd stil ᴧpoz ᛘis infânt
ârt—ᛘe numbur ᴧv ᛘe silâbik synz ᴧr mârks nêsesâre fᴧr
rytiq must be grat ând ᛘe labur ᴧv âkwyriq a kômpetênt

talked. . . . The Greek word, gramma, and the English word, letter, are not more different, as to absolute identity of sound, than such words as tauk'd, tal-ked, chauk'd, chal-ked, lov'd, lov-ed, &c" (p. iv).

Carrol concludes that spoken English differs as much from written English as our language does from Greek, but unlike Webster and Thornton, he prefers not to tamper with our spelling. He would leave silent letters and syllables in our words—to remove them would destroy their "identity to the eye." Instead he proposes to teach Americans how to recognize the sounds and silences signaled by various combinations of letters and how to accent words properly. Carrol admits that disagreements as to proper pronunciation may exist, but he attributes these to "the innovations of sciolists, or fops in learning; the ignorance of the first instructors of youth; and the consequent evil habits established." The heart of the problem is the lack of "a pronouncing and an accenting system of rules in the English language," and Carrol presents us with such a system, for which he claims indebtedness to no other writer,

---

Figure 4. A passage from James Ewing's *The Columbian Alphabet, Being an Attempt to New Model the English Alphabet* (Trenton, N.J., 1798), pp. 26–27, courtesy of the Boston Athenaeum library. Transcribed into conventional spelling this reads,

"The desire of communicating thought to persons at a distance and to posterity, undoubtedly, gave rise to the art of writing.

"Man desirous of extending his knowledge and discoveries beyond the narrow compass of his faculty of speech, would naturally have recourse to some method of giving permanence to his ideas.

"The first attempts at writing were probably very rude and imperfect—necessity although justly styled the mother of invention cannot be called the mother of [Ewing writes *va* instead of *av*] perfection—from the principle of imitation implanted in man and from what has been observed of the practice of many uncivilized nations, we are induced to suppose that pictures were the first essays towards writing—from these to hieroglyphics, or emblematic representations of [Ewing writes *af*] objects, the transition would be natural and easy—these hieroglyphics would however be but incompetent vehicles for extending communication—their very nature attached to them confusion and danger of misinterpretation.

"The ambiguity and difficulties attending this mode of writing would naturally suggest to some happy genius the advantages of representing words by characters not dependent on objects—this was the first advance from hieroglyphic expression—observing that notwithstanding the number of words in use were many yet the number of articulate sounds composing those words were comparatively few, signs were instituted for those articulate sounds—a great and important improvement—difficulties, however, would still oppose this infant art—the number of the syllabic signs or marks necessary for writing must be great and the labor of acquiring a competent"

recommending it as "more infallible,—or rather, more general, than any, or all the systems which I have seen, are, or can be maintained to be" (p. vi).

The Nineteenth Century

The movement for spelling reform picked up momentum in the nineteenth century until, during the period between 1870 and World War I, it had become a large-scale operation in America. Even today, over sixty years after organized spelling reform fizzled out in this country, many people will single out spelling rather than grammar, vocabulary, or usage as the one aspect of the English language that is most in need of reformation (interestingly, the use of obscenity and profanity runs a close second as an aspect of present-day English that is seen to be in need of regulation).

Despite Noah Webster's warnings against changing the alphabet, early nineteenth-century spelling theorists, spurred by developments in phonetic writing, continued to propose new or modified alphabets. Actually, *theorists* may be too strong a word in this context. With some notable exceptions, for example Webster himself and his pupil Francis A. March, the spelling reformers were not philologists. A few were clergymen or teachers, and some had more than a rudimentary knowledge of the classical languages, but most knew little of the history of English, and none was devoted to full-fledged theorizing in any scientific sense. By and large the spelling reformers of the early nineteenth century were unaware of previous spelling reforms or their failures, and they tended to think of their own work as both inspired and unique. Mentions of Franklin's phonetic alphabet, or the more widely publicized and controversial spelling reforms of Webster, are notably absent from their writing, and they even seem unaware of the orthographic reforms being proposed by their close contemporaries.

Spelling *in Vacuo*

Abner Kneeland, one of these early spelling reformers, was a scholar as well as a minister. A Baptist who became a Universalist and then, ultimately, a freethinker—he was once sentenced to sixty days in prison for "scandalous, impious, obscure, blasphemous and profane libel"— Kneeland published a number of studies on the Greek New Testament. In his one venture into the mire of English spelling, his *Brief Sketch of a New System of Orthography* (Walpole, New Hampshire, 1807), Kneeland dismissed the common objection that spelling revisions would obscure the etymology of words, claiming, as did many of his colleagues, that the average person had no need for etymology.

Kneeland proposed an alphabet that required all new type to be made up because he felt that a system which simply modified or added new symbols to the conventional letters would blend too easily with the standard manner of spelling and thus be confusing and ineffective. In contrast, Thomas Embree, in his *Orthography Corrected; or a Plan Proposed for Improving the English Language by Uniting Orthography with Pronunciation* (Philadelphia, 1813), suggested a semiphonetic alphabet employing inversions and digraphs and requiring a minimum of typographical revision: a, ɐ, b, d, e, ɘ, f, g, h, i, ɹ̣, j, k, l, m, n, o, θ, p, r, s, t, u, v, w, y, z, ʃh, tb, bɿ (the last three letters standing for *sh* and for the voiceless and voiced *th*, respectively).

Michael H. Barton, Quaker educator and avid spelling reformer, published a newspaper, *Something New*, in Boston between 1830 and 1833, advocating and in part written in his "new and perfect alphabet" of forty newly designed characters. Barton even goes so far as to redesign our punctuation marks. A dash will replace the comma, a longer dash the colon, and a still longer dash the period. The period will be used for the question mark, and the asterisk for the exclamation point. Barton is apparently unaware of, or unwilling to acknowledge, earlier spelling schemes, for he claims to be the first spelling reformer. He tells the readers of his newspaper that he originally introduced his new alphabet around 1821, when he opened a school in Montreal in order to test his claim that the uneducated could learn to read and write French or English in thirty days using his new method.

As Webster did before him, Barton ties spelling reform in America to its political history: "Like the revolution that made our nation free and independent, it may occasion some inconvenience for a few years, but the blessings resulting from it will extend to all future generations that may speak the English tongue."[9]

Recommending his alphabet to President Andrew Jackson, Barton offers to demonstrate its effectiveness with a money-back guarantee: "Shouldst thou doubt this, I am ready to prove it. Furnish me at Washington, the ensuing winter, twenty bright, active Indians, between 16 and 25 years of age, and if I do not qualify them, as before stated, to read and write, in thirty days, I will give my time and trouble, in going to Washington, and attending upon them" (July 1831, p. 48). Apparently Jackson did not take him up on this offer, for we hear no more of Barton and his ideas.

Benajah Jay Antrim advocated the introduction of a modified phonetic alphabet in his *Pantography*, published in Philadelphia in 1843. Arguing against alphabetic conservatives and their nostalgia for the old ways, Antrim belittles those opponents of phonetic schemes who do not want to see the standard alphabet abandoned: "Some would lead us to believe that their letters or characters came crawling through the nation on the backs of turtles; after which they slowly follow, and when once their tongues and teeth are set to the marks of the beast, they, according to their moving type, hold on as such would in their cases of life and death, and to these, as roots, their letters correspond" (p. 159n). While such prose may not inspire reform, Antrim's alphabet proved even more forbidding. Considering the frequently expressed resentment of French linguistic influence upon English, Antrim's suggestion that if France were to lead the world in phonetic reform, all other nations would follow may also have helped to drive support away from his plan. Antrim acknowledges the influence of Chambers and Ewing. Like his predecessors, he would "discharge" the useless letters *c*, *q*, *w*, and *x* from their duty and use them as single signs for *sh*, *ch*, and the two sounds of *th*. Antrim claims that his system will ensure uniformity in pronunciation and prevent the formation of dialects. It will also facilitate our return to a lost and idealized Golden Age, pre-Babel world, for as its name suggests, pantography will advance "that day of peace, when all nations may have learned to speak one tongue, and one method" (p. 160).

Amasa D. Sproat was perhaps one of the least typical of the spelling reformers. Born in Vermont in 1802, he walked to Chillicothe, Ohio, at the age of sixteen and became a druggist. He grew interested in spelling and published on the subject as early as 1834. In 1857 he proposed his "American Alphabet," consisting of a completely new set of letters designed to show the relationships between similar sounds, with the additional "advantages" that no letter contained descenders (strokes extending below the printed line), and all vowels contained ascenders (strokes extending above it), so that they could be more easily distinguished from the consonants (see fig. 5). Like many of the early language planners Sproat worked in a vacuum. He initially thought himself to be the first to propose an alphabetic reform, and when he did discover the phonetic pioneering of Isaac Pitman and Alexander Ellis in Great Britain, he continued to maintain that his own system was, if not perfect, at least "nearer the truth than any heretofore proposed" (Sproat remains silent about the work of his American colleagues, or competitors).[10]

Sproat argued that since it was natural for all languages to undergo change, no one should object to his own proposals for the revision of English. In addition to spelling reform he suggested that our language be modeled more closely on the classical tongues, often regarded as models of rationality: "The regularity, beauty, and power of the Greek and Latin languages, [and] their grammatical construction . . . prove that they were set in order by men of science. . . . No chance convention of children, or ignorant barbarians, could have produced the harmony and order we see reigning there" (p. 8). Sproat wanted to reform our pronunciation as well as our spelling, and he used Latin, not English, as his standard, hoping to replace the English "soft" *c* and *g*, and monophthongized *ae* and *oe*, with Roman "hard" consonants and diphthongs. Sproat also felt that English could use a new system of suffixes to supplement our poorly marked systems of case and tense representation: "We do not want the machinery of Greek or Latin conjugations and declinations, but we think that short terminals to verbs to note their moods and tenses, and to substantives for their numbers and genders, might be employed with considerable advantage. Endings might be arranged so as to show the parts of speech" (pp. 7–8).

Organized Spelling Reform

Several attempts to involve Congress in the spelling reform proved ineffective. Rev. Ezekiel Rich, of Troy, New Hampshire, presented a rather detailed memorial (that is, a memorandum or report) in 1844 entitled "New Project for Reforming the English Alphabet and Orthography," which was read in Congress and promptly tabled. Rich's reasons for reform are both patriotic and economic. He feels that English is at a disadvantage compared to alphabets of other nations, citing in particular the Cherokee and the Sandwich Islanders. It is up to America to take the lead in spelling reform: "If Old England, from whom we derived our existence and our mother tongue, will not reform, or take the lead in this object, let this young nation, her vigorous and enterprising child, set her a good example, and avail ourselves of the natural advantages of her delinquency. Here truly is an exciting national argument."[11] Besides the elimination of redundant letters, Rich calls for an alphabetic representation of eighteen additional English sounds. His scheme is to take effect in two stages. First, he proposes an interim alphabet composed of twenty-two of the standard letters, to which are added eighteen new ones: inverted letters, uppercase letters, and arabic numerals. Rich renders the sentence "Without delay send the news throughout the country,"

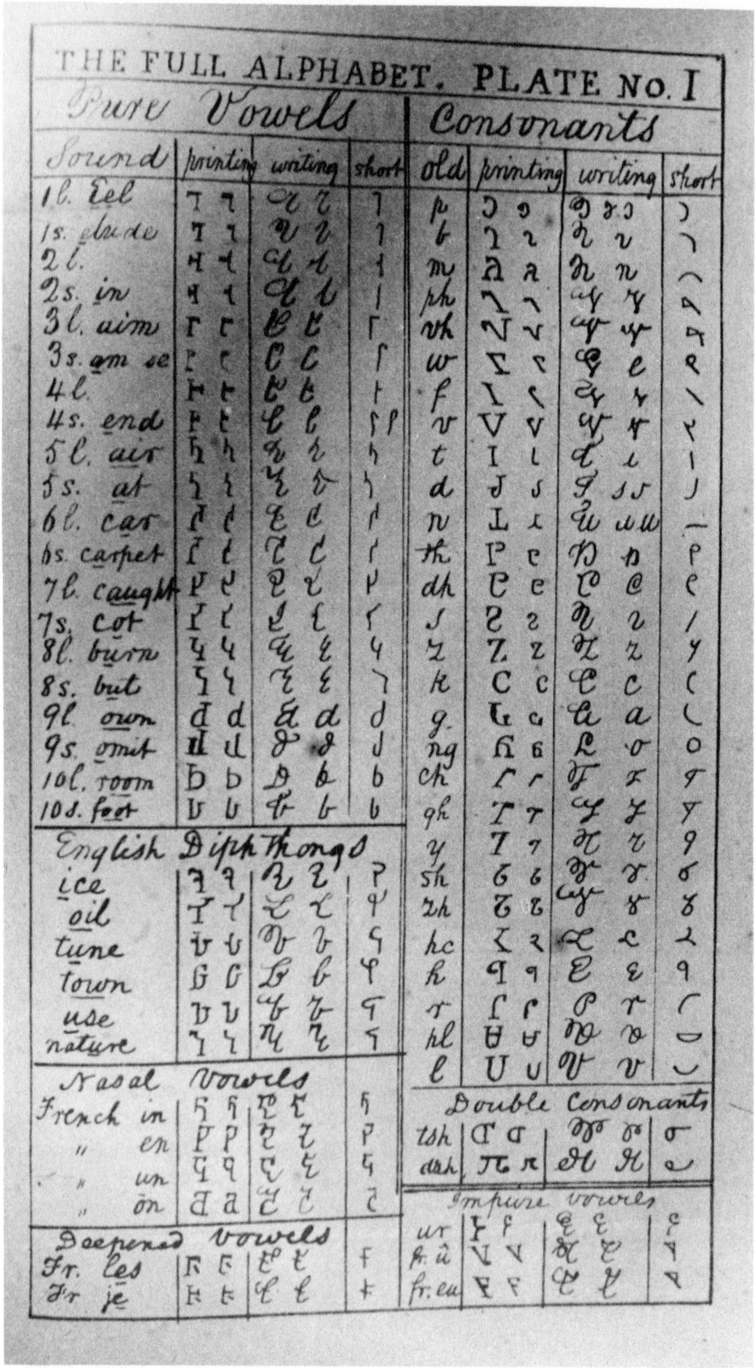

Figure 5. The alphabet of Amasa D. Sproat. Reprinted from *An Endeavor Towards a Universal Alphabet* (Chillicothe, Ohio, 1857).

which contains forty-three letters, as "W4!8t dela snd ɪ nuz Rrr8t ɪ kəntr4," which contains only twenty-eight (p. 20). If this initial alphabet proves successful, Rich will then have a committee of artists and designers create "new letters, the most pleasant and convenient *that can be devised, and then framed* from new type-moulds" as a more permanent system (p. 10). In terms of economics, Rich feels that his alphabet will represent a one-third savings in the cost of reading, writing, and printing, because fewer letters will be used per word. The alphabet itself can be mastered in only six hours. Three years of primary schooling will be rendered unnecessary—in fact, schooling could be undertaken entirely in the home. Students would not be forced to the study of literature until they have reached sufficient maturity. (Rich, like many of his fellow reformers, felt that the common schools were stagnant and stultifying. We shall encounter similar sentiments when we examine grammar and usage reform in later chapters.) In short, Rich's new spelling would double the worth of time in childhood and early youth, speed the coming of the Golden Age, and aid in the spread of Christianity through the world (pp. 7–8). Congress, however, was unconvinced, and Rich was forced to take his appeal directly to the American public in his *Easy Instructions for the General Education of Children and Youth* (Rochester, New York, 1848), a spelling and grammar text that only incidentally recommends the new alphabet and concentrates instead on moral advice for youngsters.

N. E. Dawson, of Burlington, Iowa, presented another memorial to Congress in 1878. It was referred to the Committee on Education and Labor, where it died. Congress was not prepared to take on the massive task of changing the written language. Dawson is an ardent advocate of the spelling reform which, by that time, was in full swing. The American Philological Association had called for such a reform in 1874, and the Spelling Reform Association (SRA) had been formed in 1876. Dawson's memorial cites the major economical, educational, and social arguments adopted in one form or another by the various supporters of the spelling reform movement. He has a sense of the history of reform, attributing the phonetic spelling movement directly to the inspiration of Isaac Pitman, who had devised a means of phonetic transcription for use in shorthand in 1837. Although the SRA favored retention of the traditional alphabet, Dawson feels that all attempts at reform that rely on the standard Roman letters are doomed to failure because they require us to obliterate from our memories all but one phonetic equivalent of each letter. Dawson then cites a large portion of Ezekiel Rich's memorial as support for his own position, although he feels that Rich's alphabet cannot succeed because it is too closely based on the standard Roman one. Dawson also quotes a speech by William T. Harris, superintendent of the Saint Louis public schools—he was later to become United States Commissioner of Education—which in 1866 had adopted a spelling reform proposed by the Saint Louis physician and educator Edwin Leigh. In his speech, Harris refers to our present mode of spelling as *heterography* (some reformers have also used the term *cacography*, on the model of *cacophony*, to describe the chaos and lack of reason they perceive in English spelling). Harris claims that the adoption of Leigh's system saved students one year out of the three it normally took them to learn to read. It also facilitated the process of Americanization, producing in students' speech "distinct articulation, the removal of foreign accent and of local and peculiar intonations." [12] Harris allays fears that respelled English will appear foreign: "As to the peculiar dread which lies under the proposed change of orthography, the introduction of a new language, there would not be so much difference between phonetic print and that ordinarily used now, as there is between the English used now and that of Spenser, and we can read them without much difficulty" (p. 15). Another common argument of spelling reformers that is reiterated by Harris and approved by Dawson is that the "disuse of silent letters will reduce the bulk of books one-tenth part, and save in the item of books millions of dollars per annum" (p. 16). Dawson, in conclusion, presents the Congress with an alphabet in which Roman letters give way to "phonographic" (that is, phonetic) ones. He feels that it is both suited to the practical requirements of English and that "it should also present the basis of a universal or missionary alphabet." Realizing that the transition to a new form of writing cannot be sudden and complete, Dawson proposes a gradual reform:

> The present orthography is not likely to become obsolete at once, and therefore the desirability of a phonetic alphabet from which the transition to the ordinary orthography may be as easy as possible. The child having commenced his education by learning this alphabet and acquiring some idea of the true theoretical relation between the written and the spoken language, the design is to provide a text-book printed in a compound character or type, in which the Roman letter is united with the phonographic, the latter being the more prominent in letters that should be sounded, and omitted from silent letters in words of the ordinary spelling; thus distinctly

presenting both the correct pronunciation and the current authorized orthography. [Pp. 16–17]

Dawson's phonographic alphabet consists of forty-five characters. Similar sounds are paired, thus *k*, the voiceless velar stop, is to be written as a dash,——, while *g*, the voiced velar stop, is to be represented by a somewhat thicker dash (see fig. 6).

The Spelling Reform Association

Francis A. March, born in 1825, had attended Noah Webster's lectures at Amherst College. A schoolteacher and lawyer, in 1857 March accepted a post at Lafayette College in Pennsylvania, and became the first professor of English language and comparative philology in the United States or England. His *Comparative Grammar of the Anglo-Saxon Language* (1870) was a pioneer work that showed the relationship between English and the other Indo-European languages. Interested in orthographic reform, March, who was president of the Spelling Reform Association, took a practical approach to the subject, if indeed any approach can be considered practical. March preferred spelling simplification to the introduction of a new alphabet. In his pamphlet, *The Spelling Reform* (1893), which is written in the simplified spelling that he favored, March recounts the history of the movement. He stresses the usefulness of a simplified spelling for the assimilation of foreign-born non-English speakers into American society. He too feels that the reform will save both time and money in printing and in education. It will shorten learning time by two years and it will reduce the undue emphasis placed on memory work in our schools. It was thought that American youth were at a disadvantage compared to pupils in Spain, France, Italy, and Germany, who did not have to memorize lists of spelling words because their languages seemed more phonetic. March finds that one-sixth of all cost and effort would be saved by simplified spelling. A six-dollar book would sell for only five dollars. Of the time spent on spelling, reading, and dictation, 32.2 percent (some 2,320 hours) would be rendered superfluous.

March notes that in 1881 the Spelling Reform League circulated a pledge asking signers to honor some or all of the recommendations of the Spelling Reform Association, and he assures his readers that the adoption of simplified spelling would not force Americans to speak like Englishmen, despite the fact that "[Londoners] take for granted that with a few examples of the compound letter:

The powers of these characters are as follows:

1. The sound of *p* in *pay* or *cap*.
2. The sound of *b* in *bay*, or *bb* in *ebb*.
3. The sound of *t* in *tame*, or *ed* in *looked*.
4. The sound of *d* in *dame*, or *ed* in *loved*.
5. The sound of *ch* in *chest*, or *tch* in *watch*.
6. The sound of *j* in *jest*, or *g* in *gem*.
7. The sound of *k* in *kelt*, or *c* in *can*.
8. The sound of *g* in *gilt*, or *gue* in *league*.
9. The sound of *f* in *fan*, or *ph* in *phase*.
10. The sound of *r* in *van*, or *f* in *of*.
11. The sound of *th* in *pith*, or in *think*.
12. The sound of *th* in *thy*, or *the* in *breathe*.
13. The sound of *s* in *seal*, or *c* in *icy*.

Figure 6. The phonetic alphabet of N. E. Dawson. Reprinted from "Reformed Alphabet and Orthography," in *U.S. Serials* 1815 (February 5, 1878).

natural unsofisticated Londonese, the speech of the gentleman and scolar of the metropolis, is what is ment by standard English; that if it can only be set forth in print with all its glides and finishes, all its runs of unaccented, indistinguishabl murmurs, and varied droppings and insertions, the rest of the world wil accept and try to imitate." [13]

A set of ten simplified spelling rules was adopted jointly by the American Philological Association (APA), and the Philological Society of England in 1883. Silent *e* was to be dropped when it was "fonetically useless," and *-er* was to replace *-re*, thus *live, single, eaten*, and *theatre* would become *liv, singl, eatn*, and *theater*. *Ea* in *feather* would become *e, fether*. When *o* had the sound of *u* it would be so spelled: *tung, abuv*. Double consonants were to be simplified when phonetically unimportant. A final *d* or *ed* would become *t* when pronounced as a *t*. And *gh* and *ph* would be respelled as *f* when so pronounced, producing *lafter, enuf*, and *fonetic*. A voiced *s* would be spelled as a *z*, and the *t* in *tch* would be omitted (p. 63). In 1886 the two societies recommended a list of over three thousand words respelled according to these principles and urged its adoption by all writers of English.

Examples of the APA list of 1886 (from March, pp. 64–84)

abashed	abasht
above	abuv
accommodative	accomodativ
ache	ake
add	ad
analogue	analog
angle	angl
asphalt	asfalt
axle	axl
bailiff	balif
become	becum
befriend	befrend
bodyguard	bodygard
castle	castl
cattle	catl
crushed	crusht
decked	deckd
heaven	heven
kettle	ketl

knuckle	knuckl
monkey	munkey
phase	fase
pheasant	fezant
riven	rivn
sapphire	saffire
scratch	scrach
shall	shal
striven	strivn
thanked	thankt
though	tho
through	thru
tinkle	tinkl

A number of states, including Connecticut and Wisconsin, had begun to study the possibility of legislating a spelling reform, and in 1888 Charles B. Voorhees, lawyer and Democratic representative from the Washington Territory, was asked by spelling pressure groups to introduce legislation in Congress imposing the amended spelling of the American Philological Association in schools run by the Federal government: "In the common or public schools throughout the Territories and in the District of Columbia, in the Military and Naval Academies of the United States, and in all Indian and colored schools in the territories."[14] Anticipating resistance, drafters of the bill spelled out the stiff consequences that would accompany noncompliance with the new law: "Any . . . officer, school director, committee, superintendent, or teacher who shall refuse or neglect to comply with the requirements of this act, or shall neglect or fail to make proper provisions for the instruction required for all pupils in each and every school under his jurisdiction shall be removed from office." Despite the optimism shown by Professor March and the reform groups that backed and no doubt helped to draft the measure, Voorhees's bill was never approved.

Although legal action was not forthcoming, the spelling reform movement was recognized and often actively supported by the educational establishment. In 1893 the Modern Language Association endorsed the APA list. In 1898 the National Education Association, preferring to begin more slowly, limited its initial plunge into spelling reform to twelve words: *altho, catalog, decalog, demagog, pedagog, prolog, program, tho, thoro, thorofare, thru,* and *thruout.*[15] Webster's dictionaries, to no one's surprise, included many of the amended spellings supported by March, first in the *International Dictionary* (1890) in a separate list, and later in the *New International Dictionary* (1909) in the text itself. Funk and Wagnalls's *Standard Dictionary* (1903) and William Dwight Whitney's *Century Dictionary* (1889–91) also included March's spellings, and Worcester's *Dictionary*, which had been a bastion of orthographic conservatism before the 1870s, printed some reformed spellings in its 1881 edition.

The *Tribune*'s Lonely Battle

According to March, the Chicago *Tribune* began using some simplified spellings as early as 1879. Joseph Medill, a lawyer and one of the founders of the Republican party, had bought the paper some years earlier and turned it from an obscure and virtually bankrupt publication into a profitable antislavery journal and one of America's leading newspapers. Medill, who served a term as mayor of Chicago and also helped to establish the Chicago Public Library, was opposed to the system of conventional spelling. He felt that it was "a monster cruelty to perpetuate the tyranny of absurdities and irregularities that fill our schoolhouses with misery, and keep millions of English-speaking people in lifelong bondage to the unabridged dictionary," and he saw spelling reform as a means of combatting the tyranny of language: "Our written words ought to be, not whimsical, law-defying and troublesome oppressors, but loyal and obedient servants, falling nimbly and aptly into their places without the help of a search-warrant."[16] Medill's grandson and successor, Col. Robert R. McCormick, forced the newspaper to continue the fight for spelling reform long after it had been abandoned by other crusaders. In 1934 he had the *Tribune* adopt more than eighty simplified spellings including *dialog, fantom, hocky, crum, herse, rime, iland, lether,* and *jaz.* In 1949 *sheriff* became *sherif, tariff* became *tarif,* and *sophomore, sofomore.*

The *Tribune* printed an editorial in 1946 explaining its simplified spelling policy in even more simplified English to a child named Phyllis, a sixth grader who had written to ask why *freight* was spelled *frate* in the *Tribune:* "We think that the spelling of words in our language is very disorderly and we are trying to clean up the mess, a little at a time. . . . Ever since there has been an English language, spelling has been changing and most of the changes have been simplifications. All we are trying to do is to carry along the work." The editors refer Phyllis to the *Oxford English Dictionary* for an occurrence of *frate* as early as

1538, and they assure her that their efforts have the support of many prominent Americans: "You will find that the movement for simplified spelling had the approval of Benjamin Franklin, Theodore Roosevelt, and a lot of other distinguished men. You will learn, also, how much Noah Webster, the dictionary man, did to improve spelling when this country was young. You will find that the same kind of people who today fuss about *frate* used to throw fits about *honor* and *labor*, which, they thought, must be spelled *honour* and *labour*. Maybe in a few years, people will think *freight* is a silly way to spell the word."[17]

The Simplified Spelling Board

The Simplified Spelling Board was organized in 1906 to coordinate the efforts of the movement. It issued a series of twenty-six circulars over the next few years, proposing spellings for adoption and reminding the public of its proposals. Supported almost entirely by funds from Andrew Carnegie, the Board offered a basic list of three hundred words. The principles of simplification are similar to those discussed above, and in order to put its proposals in historical perspective the board lists authorities for its spellings which include the dictionaries of Webster, Worcester, and Isaac Funk, and the writings of Shakespeare, Milton, Tennyson, Burns, Addison, Austen (one of the few times a woman was cited as a linguistic authority), and the National Education Association. The three hundred words include forms which were not unfamiliar at the time and which are common enough now: *ax, dike, develop, defense, checker, mama, septet, primeval, tenor*, and *theater*. The list also included words that did not prove successful: *snapt, tho, wisht, winkt, tipt, gazel, gript, droopt, domicil, cutlas*, and *apothem*. The tone of the circulars published by the Board is not only optimistic, it is revolutionary. In "Simplified Spelling and the Universities," Francis James Child, the folklorist and ballad collector, says, "At present I don't much care how anybody spells, so he spells different from what is established. Any particular individual spelling is likely to be more rational than the ordinary."[18]

The Simplified Spelling Board numbered among its members some of the great linguists and lexicographers of the day: Isaac K. Funk, of the *Standard Dictionary*, James A. H. Murray of the *Oxford English Dictionary*, Frederick J. Furnivall, leading member of the London Philological Society and founder of the Early English Text Society, William T. Harris, U.S. commissioner of education, Walter W. Skeat, author of the *Etymological Dictionary*, and Joseph Wright, professor of philology at Oxford. Thomas Wentworth Higginson and Samuel Clemens, as well as the publisher Henry Holt, represented the literary world, and President Theodore Roosevelt represented the political one.

In fact, Theodore Roosevelt favored simplified spelling so much that on August 27, 1906, he issued an executive order directing the Government Printing Office to adopt the three hundred new spellings suggested by the Simplified Spelling Board. He assured the government printer that "there is not the slightest intention to do anything revolutionary or initiate any far-reaching policy" in his decision. If the suggested changes prove popular they will be adopted without government intervention, and if they fail, the president indicates he will back down: "If they do not ultimately meet with popular approval they will be dropt, and that is all there is about it." Roosevelt repeatedly plays down the significance of his order: "It is not an attempt to do anything far-reaching or sudden or violent; or indeed anything very great at all. It is merely an attempt to cast what slight weight can properly be cast on the side of the popular forces which are endeavoring to make our spelling a little less foolish and fantastic."[19] Despite his assurances to the contrary, Roosevelt's order was regarded as extremely radical and it was met by stiff opposition. It was eventually withdrawn, although Roosevelt himself continued to be convinced of the rightness of the spelling movement.

Samuel Clemens was also interested in spelling reform. Simplified Spelling Board Circular 9 (1906) contains a speech in which Mark Twain urges the Associated Press to adopt simplified spellings, and an essay entitled "Simplified Spelling" dated about 1906 puts forth Clemens's arguments for alphabetic reform. In the latter essay Clemens speaks of a "Simplified Spelling epidemic" that he claims to have witnessed in Egypt several thousand years ago, a revolt against hieroglyphics. Cadmus, the leader of the supposed revolt, demonstrates the clumsiness and inefficiency of the old system of writing by rendering the Lord's Prayer in hieroglyphs (Cadmus blithely ignores the anachronism): "He drew in outline a slender Egyptian in a short skirt, with slim legs and an eagle's head in place of a proper head, and he was carrying a couple of dinner pails, one in each hand. In front of this figure he drew a toothed line like an excerpt from a saw; in front of this he drew three skeleton birds." This effort goes on for forty-five minutes, after which Cadmus dashes off the same text in Roman script in one-tenth the time. Clemens adds an argument that is a direct borrowing from the simplified spellers of his own day: "One of the objections to the hieroglyphics is that it takes the brightest pupil nine years to get the forms and their meanings by heart; it takes the average pupil sixteen years; it takes the rest of the nation all their days to accomplish it—it is a life sentence. This cost of time is much too expensive. It could be employed more usefully in other industries, and with better results." And Clemens, satirizing opponents of modern spelling reform, cites the opposition's sentimental but ineffective argument: "That they had always been used to the hieroglyphics; that the hieroglyphics had dear and sacred associations for them; that they loved to sit on a barrel under an umbrella in the brilliant sun of Egypt and spell out the owls and eagles and alligators and saw teeth . . . and weep with romantic emotion at the thought that they had, at most, but eight or ten years between themselves and the grave for the enjoyment of this ecstasy."[20]

In a third essay, "A Simplified Alphabet," Clemens expresses his approval of simplified spelling but indicates his preference for alphabetic reform: "Simplified Spelling makes valuable reductions in the case of several hundred words, but the new spelling must be *learned*. You can't spell them by the sound; you must get them out of the book."[21] A phonographic alphabet, on the other hand, is both time and effort saving. It employs fewer strokes. Clemens says, "I could do three years' copying in one year." He is pessimistic about the success of simplified spelling: "It has taken five hundred years to simplify some of Chaucer's rotten spelling . . . and it will take five hundred more to get our exasperating new Simplified Corruptions accepted and running smoothly" (pp. 261–62). Furthermore Clemens feels that simplified spelling takes the thrill out of words, and that the phonographic alphabet is more pleasing aesthetically.

The Decline of the Reform Movement

Ardent spelling reformers refused to believe that after fifty years of pushing, the movement was ready to be declared dead. Thomas R. Lounsbury, in *English Spelling and Spelling Reform* (1909), announces that the spelling reform movement is finally becoming successful. This despite Lounsbury's recognition of the strong opposition to the movement on the part of the American public, which is not simply indifferent, "it is largely hostile. To many men a strange spelling is offensive; by the ill-informed it is regarded as portending ruin to the language."[22] Lounsbury sees the American and British spelling movements, paralleled by similar developments in France, as "simply part of a world-wide movement in the interests of law and order" (p. 48). He rejects the notion that changed spellings will change the language: "A new spelling meaning a new language! Fancy a boy refusing to wash his face, on the ground that if the dirt were removed he would not be the same boy" (p. 82). Lounsbury also dismisses the opposition of women to the movement. He contends that for women, it is a question not of logic but of taste: "It is their sensibilities that are outraged, not their reason," and he further belittles their opposition by declaring that he finds their irrationality charming (p. 84). Lounsbury rejects the claim by some opponents of reform that etymology will be obliterated by simplified spellings: "A language does not exist for the sake of imparting joyful emotions to the members of a particular group who are familiar with its sources" (p. 286). He notes that those who argue on the grounds of etymology usually refer only to the preservation of traces of Latin or Greek in our language. There are no advocates who favor restoring *back* to its original Saxon *bac*, or *quick* to *cwic*. Lounsbury, like his predecessors, is certain that a reformed spelling will bring about a standard pronunciation and will serve as a brake on linguistic change.

Despite arguments from educators, philologists, lexicographers, literary men, and even presidents, the spelling reform movement failed to get any broadly based support. When Andrew Carnegie died, financial aid to the Simplified Spelling Board ceased. The National Education Association withdrew its endorsement of spelling reform in 1921. H. L. Mencken, who has written one of the most complete accounts of the history of American English, notes that when Taft succeeded Roosevelt as president in 1909, "the New York *Sun* announced the doom of the movement in an editorial of one word: *thru*."[23]

The Chicago *Tribune* did not abandon its crusade for new spellings for many years, but its battle was a lonely one. In 1955 it relaxed somewhat, restoring the *ph* in *sophomore*, the double *f* of *tariff*, and changing *sodder* back to *solder*. In 1975 the *Tribune* all but gave up on spelling simplification. In an editorial entitled "Thru Is Through and So Is Tho," the *Tribune* acknowledged that "*thru, tho*, and *thoro* . . . have not made the grade in spelling class." Some simplified forms were retained by the newspaper because the editors felt that they had come into common use, for example, *archeology, dialog*, and *cigaret* (this last spelling is not common enough, however, for it to be used on cigarette packages or in cigarette advertising, even in the *Tribune*). The main reason given for the abandonment of reformed spelling was the confusion it created in the classroom: "When Johnny spelled Tribune style,.

teacher sat him down." The editors are hopeful that orthography will eventually respond to the demands of logic, but for now they will spell according to *Webster's Third*: "Sanity some day may come to spelling, but we do not want to make any more trouble between Johnny and his teacher."[24] A week later John T. Arima wrote to the *Tribune* complaining that he had found a wayward *thruout* in the editorial directly following the announcement of the resumption of standard spelling (October 26, sec. 2, p.2).

In *The American Language* H. L. Mencken cites several reasons for the failure of the simplified spelling movement. Simplified spelling was associated in America with comic dialect literature, and it was therefore difficult for people to accept such spelling in serious writing. Many Americans resented Theodore Roosevelt's big-stick spelling reform, and Mencken feels that they were suspicious of anything funded by the "diabolical" Andrew Carnegie (Supplement 2, 1948, pp. 304–05). But perhaps the most important reasons for the movement's failure were its inability to agree on one consistent system of orthography—or even to choose a single alphabet for its representation—and the impossibility of imposing such a monumental reform on the largely literate and linguistically rambunctious American public.

5 The American Language and the American Academy

The various American spelling reform groups served functions that in other countries have been delegated to officially constituted language academies. The movement for the foundation of an American language academy has sputtered for over two hundred years, and even today there is still interest in founding such a group. For example, in *What's Happening to American English?* (1978), Arn and Charlene Tibbetts see the formation of a private language academy, independent of both government and the universities, as one means of combatting the linguistic decay they feel is threatening our society: "We propose creating an organization for civilized Americans who would prefer a civilized tongue. This might be called the American Society for Good English. . . . The purpose of the Society would be to make English more precise for reading, writing, and speaking. . . . to note and discuss the good and bad uses of English."[1]

But as Allen Walker Read and Shirley Brice Heath have shown, American attempts to deal with language in an academic or committee setting have not fared well.[2] Two twentieth-century ventures proved ineffective. In 1916, the artist and writer Evangeline Wilbour Blashfield gave $3,000 to the American Academy of Arts and Letters to assist that group "in an effort to determine its duty regarding both the preservation of the English language in its beauty and integrity, and its cautious enrichment by such terms as grow out of modern conditions."[3] As a result, the academy sponsored and printed nine lectures on the English language and then discreetly withdrew from the language lists. In England, the Society for Pure English, a private group led primarily by the poet Robert Bridges, published a series of tracts between 1919 and 1948 whose modest aim was the tasteful improvement of our tongue. In his first tract, Bridges states,

> It is therefore proposed that a few men of letters supported by the scientific alliance of the best linguistic authorities, should form a group or free association, and agree upon a modest and practical

99

scheme for informing popular taste on sound principles, for guiding educational authorities, and for introducing into practice certain slight modifications and advantageous changes.[4]

The Blashfield Lectures and the Society Tracts make interesting reading, but neither group actually attempted to direct the course of the English language. The literary critic William Crary Brownell and the philologist and educator Brander Matthews advise the American Academy of Arts and Letters to avoid judgments on specific language questions. The correction of English, according to Brownell, is not the business of an academy but should be left to the schools and colleges. Matthews and Bliss Perry, editor of the *Atlantic Monthly*, advise the academy to show its support for language in America by encouraging literacy, giving prizes for well-written books, and reminding our citizens of the greatness of their linguistic heritage. Matthews doubts that any academy can do much more. Alluding to the French Academy he says, "The speech of forty millions of men and women cannot be confided to the exclusive control of forty elderly gentlemen however lofty their merits and however extended their learning" (*Academy Papers*, p. 86).

In the eighteenth and nineteenth centuries, attempts were also made to establish language academies, and the groups that did manage to form did not last long and had even less success than their twentieth-century counterparts.

Noah Webster's Philological Society was concerned with the arts and, to some extent, with the sciences, as well as with language. It was a short-lived organization that dissolved soon after Webster left New York, reforming as the Friendly Club and abandoning its philological pursuits for social and political ones. Legislative attempts to form an American academy also proved unproductive. In 1806 the poet Joel Barlow published a *Prospectus of a National Institution to Be Established in the United States*. Barlow envisioned an organization combining the functions of a Royal Society and a national university to counteract the centrifugal cultural forces at work on the vast American continent. Barlow wished to encourage the arts and sciences, particularly in the South and West, where the earth is easily worked "and leaves to the cultivator considerable vacancies of time and superfluities of wealth, which otherwise will, in all probability, be worse employed."[5] A Senate bill to establish Barlow's academy was defeated in 1806, and in 1811, despite the support of President James Madison, a House committee rejected a similar proposal to establish a national university.

The American Academy of Language and Belles Lettres

The most successful attempt to establish a language academy on our shores was that of William S. Cardell, a grammarian and author of children's stories, who, together with a few associates, founded the American Academy of Language and Belles Lettres in 1820. Cardell's academy survived for three years, publishing its language proposals and some of the public reaction generated by them. Cardell was more conservative in his view of the American language than was the young Webster: his idea was to make the American tongue not different, but better. To this end, he favored the introduction into the language of certain Americanisms, including French, German, and Native American place-names. At the time, such an attitude was still controversial, and, in a letter to Thomas Jefferson written in 1820 and containing the Academy's first circular, Cardell reassures the former president that the aim of the Academy is not, as some might fear, the reformation of the language: "To settle at once a point on which some difference might exist, [the Academy] is not designed independent of England, to form an American language, farther than as it relates to the numerous and increasing names and terms peculiarly American." Rather, its aim is to improve the common language of England and America. Specific tasks of the Academy will be to guard against local and foreign corruptions, to settle varying orthography, to determine the use of doubtful words and phrases, and "to form and maintain, as far as practicable, an English standard of writing and pronunciation, correct, fixed, and uniform, throughout our extensive territory." Cardell points to the example of the French Academy, noting its success in advancing the literature of that country and adding, "its literature has frequently saved the country when its arms have failed."[6]

Cardell feels that the Academy's job will not be difficult, because there are no great language corruptions in America to eradicate. Nonetheless, he reassures his readers that he is no radical: "Sound discretion will point out a middle course between a wild spirit of innovation and a tame acquiescence in obvious error" (p. 401). Once the Academy is established, it will invite cooperation from the British in a joint effort to regulate English, but Cardell makes it clear that he feels certain innovations labeled as Americanisms are necessary and proper expansions of the language.

Thomas Jefferson, a linguist in his own right who was an early advocate of the study of Anglo-Saxon in the universities, did not respond enthusiastically to Cardell's Academy. He feared that, like the French

Academy, it would attempt to fix rather than develop the language, and that it would favor the British standard at the expense of the American innovations he preferred. In a letter to the grammarian John Waldo some years earlier, Jefferson makes clear his stand on the question of the American language, rejecting the conservatism of British grammarians: "I am no friend, therefore, to what is called *Purism*, but a zealous one to the *Neology* which has introduced these two words without the authority of any dictionary. I consider the one as destroying the verve and beauty of language, while the other improves both, and adds to its copiousness." Jefferson deplores the attitude of English reviewers toward American literature: "They are particularly apprehensive that the writers of the United States will adulterate [the language]." Instead, he regards innovation in language as necessary, as virtually impossible to avoid: "The new circumstances under which we are placed, call for new words, new phrases, and for the transfer of old words to new objects. . . . Necessity obliges us to neologize." Such linguistic differentiation can have only one end: "An American dialect will therefore be formed; so will a West-Indian and Asiatic, as a Scotch and an Irish are already formed." While innovation and change characterize the English of America, in England "the dread of innovation . . . has, I fear, palsied the spirit of improvement." As a result, American and British English could become two different languages, with two different names, and Jefferson would place the blame for this as much on British sloth as on American energy: "Should the language of England continue stationary, we shall probably enlarge our employment of it, until its new character may separate it in name as well as in power, from the mother-tongue."[7]

James Madison, like Jefferson, declined Cardell's invitation to be associated with the Academy, although he was more sympathetic to its aims. While Madison sees America as soon to overtake England in the areas of population and literary output, and feels that all languages are capable of improvement, he favors the preservation of a common speech: "Instead of allowing this common tongue to be gradually fashioned into distinct ones, or even to diverge into different dialects, there should be at least a tacit co-operation in perpetuating its identity by a joint standard."[8] But George McDuffie, who was to become governor of South Carolina, and Thomas Bolling Robertson, governor of Louisiana, echoed Jefferson. They saw American English as diverging from the mother tongue, and both approved of the trend. Replying to Cardell, McDuffie says, "From the novelty of our situation, we *must* innovate upon our vernacular language. . . . would it not be an intolerable vassalage, which would restrain us from making a corresponding enlargement of our language?" He resents the "British tribunals of criticism" that more often than not had scorned Americanisms, and he sees the Academy as a native authority for sanctioning the newly developing language. Robertson, also replying to Cardell, feels "the American language will, in progress of time, necessarily differ from that of England." Arguing that languages change as the ideas of their speakers change, he concludes that, "unless the American and English people think alike, and change their opinions at the same time, and in the same manner, their language cannot be the same" (Read, "Projects," pp. 1160–61).

Despite his assurances to Jefferson that the Academy would seek to preserve the common language of England and America rather than encourage separation of the two tongues, Cardell, like the young Webster, is concerned with establishing "national uniformity in Language." Cardell feels that such an enterprise could succeed in America, where conditions are more favorable than in England, and although he does not consider the possibility that this might lead to linguistic divergence, he repeatedly stresses the connection between language and nation. In his own grammar writing, Cardell argues that if, for example, the system of teaching English is based on false principles, "it is of great importance, in a national point of view, that it should be set aside."[9] His aim, he tells us, is to promote "excellence of speech, as the means of personal and national intercourse" (p. 16).

Unlike the typical linguistic purists, Cardell has a high opinion of the state of language in America, and of the desire of the American people to achieve perfection in speaking and writing:

> Tho in a country as diversified as ours, there are, from various causes, many particular corruptions, there is hardly anything which can properly be called a provincial dialect. We have at present no very inveterate habits to correct, where gross barbarisms through large districts are to be encountered. The attempt therefore seasonably & judiciously made, presents a prospect, not only of success, but of comparative facility. Our scattered population seem only to want, from a competent tribunal, a declaration of what is proper, to guide them in their practice." [Read, "Projects," pp. 1152–53]

Clearly, Cardell's patriotism and idealism are reminiscent of Webster. In his *Essay on Language* (New York, 1825), Cardell is even more assertive about America and its right to lead the world in the preservation of the English language. He notes that English has now spread to the four corners of the globe, and he criticizes Americans for submissively following the false lead of British grammarians, who have, among other things, privileged the pronunciation and vocabulary of London, and misled us into thinking that English is a fixed language. He once again emphasizes that America is in a unique position to improve the language: "We have no account of any nation, a prime object of whose government was to diffuse instruction among the entire body of their people. The attempt has never been made, on a national plan, to produce uniformity, among all classes of people, in the speaking of a national language. Both these objects are of prime importance in the United States." In fact Cardell, like Webster, sees language as the very foundation upon which the United States rests: "Our public happiness, our union and peace, within ourselves; all which tends to develop our resources, improve and perpetuate our institutions; all which may give us wealth, strength, and glory, among nations" depends on "the goodness of our national language" (pp. 30–31).

Like Webster, Cardell takes a practical as well as a political stand on language planning, emphasizing the role of uniform, national education in the development of the American language, and stressing the need for native textbooks to replace the foreign books Americans had come to depend on. One of the prizes to be offered by the Academy was for the creation of a new reading text for the common schools. (Cardell himself wrote a reader, *The Story of Jack Halyard, the Sailor Boy*, published in 1853.) Although he had corresponded with the author of what was already a highly successful homegrown text, Cardell never mentions Webster in his printed works. This silence may be evidence of Cardell's reluctance to be associated with a man who had received a rough reception in many of the circles where Cardell himself hoped to exert some influence. Webster was considered a radical, and Cardell tried consistently to adopt a moderate position on language issues. In the circular issued by the Academy in 1821, he takes a tempered stand on the question of language change, admitting it as a natural process subject to control: "The changes of a living language can never be, nor ever ought to be, wholly arrested; but that some guiding influence may be exercised in their improvement and use, is beyond all doubt" (Read, "Projects," p. 1156).

Cardell's Academy will be the authority to exert this guiding influence. He mentions the existence of a philological committee engaged in the collection of "a list of the prevailing departures real or imaginary, from correct usage, in the written or spoken language of the country." In a burst of optimism, he assures his readers that the recommendations of this committee will be sufficient to discourage inappropriate forms of language. Cardell feels that there could be no "rational motive" for opposing the Academy's improvements and, although there will always be some who do not mind making fools of themselves, coercion will not be necessary: "Without any dogmatical exercise of authority, if such words as 'lengthy,' 'to tote,' and 'to approbate,' should be published as doubtful or bad, they would generally fall into disuse."[10]

Another task for the philological committee was to be the preparation of a list of words of doubtful accent or pronunciation, such as *academy* itself, *wound*, and *satire* (for this last, Cardell claims four distinct pronunciations, though unfortunately for us he does not attempt to describe them phonetically). Rounding off the Academy's concern with language will be the creation of a standard dictionary, incorporating all the decisions made on Americanisms, usage, and pronunciation. In the realm of belles lettres, the Academy was to encourage research, publish monographs by its members, and award prizes. One particular area Cardell singled out for research was the detailed study of native—and "savage"—American languages and customs, to be contrasted with those of the more civilized European settlers. Cardell also wanted the Academy to support American literature, and he argued forcefully for the nation's literary independence and vitality.

In the third and final circular issued by the Academy, Cardell prints letters he has received encouraging his project and defining the goals of the organization, adding several of his own replies, which are actually short essays describing his plans for the group. Cardell appeals to the patriotism of Americans, urging them to support the Academy, and American letters in general, so that the nation will become known throughout the world for its peaceful arts. He assures his readers that the Academy can succeed despite its apparent weaknesses: a far-flung membership, the lack of a national literary capital, and the newness of American literature. Cardell cuts America off from European tradition: "We are beginning in some degree, not only a separate nation, but another world, and opening a new destiny for the race of man. . . . We do not trace our origin to the offspring of a pretended God, nurtured by a wolf; but to men whose example and worth are the subject of authentic history" (p. 13).

Cardell feels that, as an independent nation, we must now purge ourselves of unnecessary British influence: "It was in the nature of things that, while colonies, they should look to the parent country as the chief seat of excellence in customs, opinions, talents, and laws, and this influence naturally continued after we became politically independent. The books which guided our thoughts and actions were not made for us" (p. 17). He feels that we have copied enough, perhaps too much, and that it is time for reason to replace imitation: "Is not our general system of legislation, as well as the fashion of our thoughts, too slavishly drawn from precedents in foreign countries, and with too little reference to a rational investigation of facts in our own?"

Cardell sees the American dilemma clearly. He is the first commentator on language to recognize our ambiguous feelings toward American English: "Our distinctive national character has been unsettled and fluctuating between an attachment to our own institutions, which we know to be good, and the desire of foreign applause which we have too blindly cherished." This ambiguity has produced in us, "in motley confusion, a debasing submissiveness and a spirit of rancorous and misguided hostility." To remedy the situation, to restore our sense of self-worth, we need a literary organization that will unite us in the same way our political organization has: "It is literature, in its connexion with national character, habits, laws, and religion, which, more than any thing else, must make us one people" (pp. 18–19).

Defending the value of an Academy, Cardell resorts to an economic analogy, comparing free enterprise to government regulation: "We hear the frequent repetition of the dogma, that business does best when left to itself. It is true that no public regulation can supply the want of personal enterprise; but . . . individuals of limited information do not always manage to the best advantage. . . . Individuals, sometimes those of ordinary talents, pursuing their separate interests, may do much in the examination of detached facts; but enlightened systems, or great plans of national unity, are not produced in this way." Cardell may have been thinking of the single-minded Webster, or he may simply be referring to the collective failure of individual language reformers. He concludes his defense of committees and organization with a military allusion: "The necessity of discipline, combined strength, and guiding talent, are well understood in the army; but the effect of national concert in great moral operations, has never been sufficiently tried" (p. 21).

Cardell alternates between eloquence and pragmatism, stressing not only the artistic but the commercial value of language as well. English, as a potential universal language, is the medium of trade, and naturally so: "The English language prevails chiefly among commercial and cal-

culating people." This being the case, Cardell argues that any econo-
mies resulting from language reform will be visible in terms of dollars
and cents: "How much time is unavoidably employed in [the] acquisition [of English], and admitting a gain of ten, five, or two per cent in
the facility of attaining it, what would be the aggregate amount?" (p.
30). As we have seen, this same money-saving argument was used by
several generations of spelling reformers, who point to the savings in
manpower and in paper that their new alphabets and orthographic prac-
tices would guarantee.

According to Cardell, America is in an excellent position to bring
about changes in language usage: "We undoubtedly have the advantage
of England, in promoting a comparative purity in language among the
entire mass of our population, and we may, if we will, enjoy in this
respect a proud pre-eminence over every other nation." One reason for
our superiority to the British is found in the sociolinguistic organization
of the parent country: "England has been subject to the double evil of
having its language directly and grossly vitiated by the vulgar, and of
being capriciously changed by the fashionable, to avoid the appearance
of being common." This destruction of the British language both from
above and below is in part permitted to exist by a too strong reverence
for the doctrine of usage. Cardell claims that "Horace has been frequently and gravely quoted as almost interdicting scholarship and taste,
from an interference in language" but adds disparagingly, that Horace
"was not suspected of being a deep philosopher." Cardell backs this
opinion up by citing Quintilian's statement that Latin was spoken well
by comparatively few. Cardell rejects the doctrine of usage as inappropriate in the New World: "'Jus et norma loquendi' . . . has no proper
reference to the United States of America," implying once again his
distrust of a free enterprise system. He returns to utilitarianism as he
urges the adoption of whatever reforms the Academy's philological
committee may recommend: "To facilitate the acquisition of what so
many millions must use, is a matter of as obvious utility as to smooth
and shorten a farmer's road to market"(pp. 30–31).

Letters to Mr. Cardell

The letters published by Cardell in his third circular, coming from
such notables as Thomas Jefferson, John Adams, and John Marshall,
are calculated to encourage membership in the Academy, although none
of the writers claims any special qualifications for the task of regulating

and encouraging language and letters. Some of the writers briefly express their ideas on language, and these opinions are interesting in that they reflect the general climate of language philosophy in America at the time.

John Adams, who for a long time had supported the idea of a language academy, writes to Cardell to express the hope that the American government will endow the Academy. He notes that this is an area where Americans can do something the British have neglected to do, and in his statement he reveals his own peculiar linguistic prejudice against women: "Men of letters throughout all Europe have long expressed their wonder, that the British Parliament have been so inattentive to the cultivation of their own language. . . . [they] have instituted nothing for the improvement of their language. Even the synonymous words of that language, which requires [*sic*] the profoundest knowledge in philosophy and metaphysics, as well as philology, to discriminate with precision, have been left to the talents and application of a lady" (p. 5). The lady referred to by Adams is Mrs. Hester Lynch Thrale Piozzi, an intimate of Samuel Johnson and a biographical competitor of Boswell, and the work in question is her two-volume *British Synonymy* (1794), one of the first collections of English synonyms. Adams may or may not have seen the work itself, but his phrasing leads one to believe that he had read the generally favorable notice that appeared in the *Monthly Review* of London. The reviewer, referring to Mrs. Piozzi as "this lively female Philologist" and "our ingenious female philologer," praises the work even though it is written by a woman: "We could not help being a little envious and ashamed that the honour of this enterprise should have been usurped in England by a female" (ser. 2, 15 [1794]: 242).

Levi Woodbury, a judge of the New Hampshire Supreme Court, feels that the Academy can play a role in the reformation of spelling and usage. He would have the language conform generally, though not categorically, to a rational design: "The evils of a doubtful and fluctuating orthography, pronunciation, and use of particular words, are not few. . . . It is of much importance that all questions on these subjects should be settled with accuracy; but it is of still more importance that they should be settled, though not in all cases, in strict conformity to philosophical principles" (p. 6).

John Trumbull, who made his living as a jurist but was widely regarded at the time as one of America's leading literary figures, asserts that the Academy's role must be a limited one. Revolutionary language schemes cannot work. Instead, the various committees must concentrate on the refinement of the existing language: "To attempt the formation of a national language, different from the English in its dialect, would indeed be absurd and impracticable. To fix the standard of a living language, and think to arrest the progress of innovations which many will adopt as improvements, though condemned by others as corruptions, is a task of equal difficulty. Yet much advantage may be derived from the united efforts of distinguished scholars. Their influence will assist us to banish cant phrases; to correct vulgar solecisms and improprieties; to check the affected pomp of pedantry, and prevent the introduction and increase of foreign phraseology, inconsistent with the idioms of the English language." Trumbull favors the use of certain necessary Americanisms, which England simply cannot supply: "To adopt them is not to change the language, but only to supply the deficiencies of its vocabulary" (p. 6).

Oliver Wolcott, governor of Connecticut and an associate of the poets Trumbull and Joel Barlow, sees no reason why Americans should hesitate to regulate the English language, for it belongs to them as much as to anybody else. The use of English as a vehicle for the advancement of knowledge is relatively recent, and its rapid spread places it in need of systematic regulation: "I perceive no sufficient reasons why [the proposed association] should be commenced with any indications of conscious inferiority. It is scarcely two hundred years, since the English language was first adopted as the language of science and philosophy in England itself. During the last century, some of the best specimens of British literature, are to be found in the writings of men who were neither Englishmen, nor educated in English universities. . . . The English language . . . is daily becoming more and more the language of commerce throughout the world. Nothing now tends to destroy its purity, symmetry and elegance, so much, as its rapid extension" (pp. 7–8).

In his letter to Cardell, Thomas Jefferson vigorously opposes measures that would inhibit the development of the language. An advocate of change, he believes that English has progressed from a more primitive initial stage. For continued progress, he favors the introduction of new words. Jefferson does not regret the formation of an American dialect separate from the British: "There are so many differences between us and England, of soil, climate, culture, productions, laws, religion, and government, that we must be left far behind the march of circumstances, were we to hold ourselves rigorously to their standard. If, like the French Academicians, it were proposed *to fix* our language, it would be fortunate, that the step was not taken in the days of our Saxon ancestors whose vocabulary would illy express the science of this day. Judicious neology can alone give strength and copiousness to language, and enable it to be the vehicle of new ideas" (p. 10).

The chief justice of the United States, John Marshall, also defends our right to the English language, but he feels that as a common property, it ought to be jointly administered by the United States and Britain. He concedes to the British a temporary superiority in the area of letters, but he defends the rights of Americans to act as critics whose aim is to preserve and improve, but not to change, the language: "Americans may co-operate in the joint work, and may exercise their own judgment on the performance of their fellow laborers, as well as on their own." The Academy may be useful in assuring linguistic uniformity in the United States. Marshall attributes the present uniformity to particular circumstances in the American environment, but sees these as only temporary. The Academy is therefore necessary for the perpetuation of some standard of English:

> Were its only good, the tendency it will have to preserve a sameness of language throughout our own wide spreading country, that alone would be an object worthy of the public attention.
>
> At present, the intermingling of classes; the intercommunication of well educated persons with those whose improvement is very limited; the removals from one neighbourhood and state, to another distant neighborhood [*sic*], and another state; the intimate intercourse thus kept up between all ranks, and the different parts of our extensive empire, all contribute to preserve an identity of language through the United States, which can find no example in other parts of the world.
>
> As our population becomes more dense, these causes will diminish in their operation; and, without some standard which all will respect, and to which all may appeal, it is not probable, that our language will escape those casualties and deteriorations, to which all seem to be exposed." [pp. 10–11]

George McDuffie of South Carolina, mentioned earlier as favoring American linguistic independence, sees the progress of nations "affected, more by the state of their language, than by any other single cause not even excepting their political condition." His example, one we have already seen to be popular, is that of the Chinese, an ancient people who have never been conquered, "yet how comparatively insignificant are their intellectual attainments!" McDuffie finds the Chinese language responsible for this. It is imperfect and cumbersome, and as a result, "it is impossible for any people to make much progress in science, when it is the labor of a life time to become a proficient in their language." In contrast, McDuffie sees a sudden and visible acceleration of progress in Europe accompanying the introduction of Latin there. McDuffie resents British criticism of American English and feels that the Academy as an institution will have the strength to withstand the transatlantic attacks that have been so devastating to individual writers and speakers in America. His main concern, as a language reformer, is in the preservation of what he calls the symmetry of English, neglected both in England and America. He sees French borrowings as a threat to this symmetry: "Such a word as '*eclaircissement*' ought never to deform the symmetry of our language, when '*explanation*' and '*elucidation*' are amply sufficient to convey the same idea." Returning to the classics, he adds, "I think the Latin and Greek languages furnish decidedly the best materials for improving our own: for . . . the words are so modified as to receive an English form; but in improvements derived from the French, the original termination and pronunciation are retained" (pp. 15–16).

Thomas Bolling Robertson, mentioned earlier as a proponent of the American language, warns Cardell that the Academy must be prepared to stand alone against the world: "I doubt whether in an attempt to 'harmonize and determine the English language,' we shall be aided or countenanced by foreigners." Yet Robertson urges Cardell to go forward: "As our plan is a good one, I would wish it to be exclusively American, and perhaps the propriety of this will be apparent, when we consider the Society in relation to its *national* character" (pp. 25–26).

The last full letter Cardell includes in the circular is from Gen. H. A. S. Dearborn of Roxbury, Massachusetts, who, besides having had a distinguished military career, was a politician and a prolific writer as well. Dearborn emphasizes the necessity for proper language instruction in order to ensure language stability: "How important is it then, that our seminaries of learning, of every grade, should be furnished with all the means, requisite for inculcating a perfect knowledge of the national language; that it may be spoken and written with correctness and uniformity, throughout the Union." Dearborn dismisses British critics of Americanisms, pointing out that "the English language has been a progressive one, and cannot even yet, be considered as perfectly established." He notes that Chaucer and Spenser, once considered the finest of writers, are now virtually unintelligible because of changes in language that have taken place (p. 37).

Circular III breaks off without explanation in the middle of a letter from Theodore Lyman, Jr., author, philanthropist, and, as one biography puts it, an "able but undistinguished mayor of Boston." The break comes, ironically, as Lyman is predicting that the Academy will facilitate communication and understanding between members scattered across the country. As for the work of the Academy, Cardell's optimistic plans were never realized. While the philological committee, or at least its head, the Rev. John M. Mason, formerly provost of Columbia University, did begin collecting Americanisms which Mason had slated for elimination, the Academy accomplished nothing material beyond the printing of its three circulars. This was due in part to the loose organization of the Academy: honorary members were selected and many of them, although they accepted the honor graciously and contributed funds for the support of the Academy, were decidedly inactive. The membership was scattered across the country, a factor which prohibited meetings and threw the burden of organization on Cardell. The deathblow was dealt the Academy in its third year by Edward Everett, the noted critic and orator.

Everett and the American Academy

Reviewing the Academy's published circulars in the *North American Review*, the journal which he edited, Everett, an avid supporter of American English, accused Cardell of being all talk and no action. Finding Cardell's proposals vague in the extreme—unlike Webster, Cardell gave almost no examples of language forms he wished either to preserve or stigmatize—Everett is blunt, and withering: "We have been unable . . . to obtain any idea of what the Academy is designed to be."[11] Everett argues that Cardell's group is not an Academy: it has no clear membership and no place to meet. Its duties are uncertain, and it seems to be the operation of a single man: "Does the secretary [i.e., Cardell] mean to say, with Louis XIV, *l'academie, c'est moi?*" Everett finds Cardell's prose unsatisfactory: his essays "are by no means free from grammatical errors, and are vague and wordy." And Everett concludes, "we are constrained to pronounce the whole enterprize one of the most signal displays of unprofitable fuss-making, we have ever witnessed" (pp. 356–59).

Edward Everett's own ideas about language had changed over the course of several years. In 1810, at the age of sixteen, Everett published an essay in the *Harvard Lyceum* on the topic "Whether the language of a country be more perfect for being in part derived from other languages," warning that the creation of new words in America invites certain censure from the British. After visiting England, he modified his views somewhat. Writing to John Pickering concerning the latter's *Glossary*, Everett reveals his new attitude, a resentment both of British idiom and reactions in the British literary reviews toward American usage: "I have ever been an enemy to every thing under the name of an Americanism, & disposed to deny, to the last, our right to make any alteration—improvement or not—in our language. . . . [but] we ought neither to be *reviewed* out of the right of coining any Words w'h the peculiarity of our situation requires, nor browbeaten into the belief, that in respect to New Words we speak and write the language more corruptly than we do. . . . [English] is no where in England spoken better, than by well educated people in America, and in many English provinces much worse, than in any part of America I have visited."[12] Everett finds the English guilty of all the faults they ascribe to Americans. They coin and borrow words freely—he cites as examples Johnson, Milton, and Shakespeare—but they complain when Americans do so. Everett finds the English too strict with their own language. He puts forth as a desirable alternative the example of classical Greek (Everett, at twenty-one, was appointed professor of Greek at Harvard), where no single dialect was privileged: "One dialect was as honorable of old as another, & the Poets took from each such peculiarities, as they thought would unite in the most harmonious whole" (p. 115).

Everett resents the British assumption that Americans speak an exotic form of the language. His own experience is representative of what happens to many Americans, even today: "An American, on arriving in England, is not unfrequently requested, by intelligent persons, to give a specimen of his native tongue, in the supposition that this is either a distinct dialect of English, or even an Indian language." While he feels that Americans in general do not pay enough attention to their pronunciation—he says, "The Negligence of Pronunciation, with us, is most criminal"—he argues that Americans ought to be permitted their own standards: the distance from England alone requires it. He complains that English standards are slippery, that words held to be corrupt Americanisms can be found in respected British authors: "They have denied the authority of Johnson and all other Individual Writers, & maintained that the only standard was a vague general usage—a thing not very definite in idea, or easy to be ascertained in Practice" (pp. 120–21).

Everett celebrates the lack of dialect in America, finding one general difference between the speech of Americans and Britons: "We are apt to drawl, to pronounce every syllable." He echoes the commonplace that Americans must get their language from books: "In this country, so long as England remains the centre of our civilization, we must have some book Standard, because the living Standard is not accessible to the Community" (p. 126). Yet on the question of standards he reveals a characteristic American ambivalence, longing for a British purity and defending American usage at the same time: "Whatever standard be taken, we engage to detect in English writers of respectable standing, and in respectable English society, more provincialisms, more good words in false acceptations, and more newly coined words, than can be found in an equal number of American writers, or in American society, of the same relative respectability" (p. 123).

When his resentment is unleashed it becomes easier to see why Everett was so critical of Cardell and the American Academy of Language and Belles Lettres. To Everett the Academy is a weak, confused organization incapable to taking the kind of strong linguistic stand necessary to turn the tables on the British and to legitimize the American language:

> We submit it fearlessly to any person, who has had the means of making the comparison, and is at all qualified to do it, whether one might not rather suppose that America were the native country of the language, and England a remote colony, exposed to all the chances of corruption, so villainously is the language spoken in all the provinces of the latter country, so wholly distorted in a score of rustic jargons, that do not deserve the name of dialects. [P. 122]

This sentiment was echoed by James Russell Lowell in *The Biglow Papers* (1848): "It might be questioned whether we could not establish a stronger title to the ownership of the English tongue than the mother-islanders themselves."

Everett's *North American Review* was as supportive of Noah Webster as it was critical of William S. Cardell. Reviewing Webster's *An American Dictionary of the English Language* in the number for April 1829, it devotes over forty pages to an analysis of the new dictionary. Webster's detractors are soundly dealt with, and attention is drawn to the intense climate of opposition that greeted Webster's original proposal for the dictionary and that followed his labors. Some critics went so far as to suggest "that in this dictionary some plot was contriving against the purity of the language" (28:434). In his review, Everett defends not only Webster but America itself against British attack: "Much more attention is paid to the authority of good writers, and to the decision of lexicographers, in the United States, than in England" (p. 462). Webster's etymologies are explained, his definitions found to be superior in many instances to those of Johnson, even some—though not all—of his spelling reforms are condoned. Everett states that he himself is not out to revolutionize the spelling system, but he feels that evils in that system exist, and Webster should not be castigated for trying to eliminate them.

Later Literary Views of English

Edward Everett expressed a patriotic view of the American language, but Walt Whitman added a poetic one. His "American Primer," composed in the 1850s but not printed until 1904 when it appeared in the *Atlantic Monthly*, was a high-spirited plea for national independence in language that touched on many ideas that were commonplaces, as well as some that were not. Whitman is noncommittal on spelling reform, expressing the rather weak opinion that phonetic spelling may prevail "if it is best it should." The fact that "for many hundred years there was nothing like settled spelling" makes this not a crucial issue for the poet. Although he objects to one aspect of American English, the nasal pronunciation of New Englanders, Whitman has nothing but exuberant praise for the rest. The American language will embody the ideals and character of its people as well as the new political facts of the nation: "The Americans are going to be the most fluent and melodious voiced people in the world—and the most perfect users of words. Words follow character,—nativity, independence, individuality." Whitman speaks of the "renovated English of America": "These States are rapidly supplying themselves with new words, called for by new occasions, new facts, new politics, new combinations." All of this calls for a new, democratic spirit of lexicography: "The Real Dictionary will give all the words that exist in use, the bad words as well as any. . . . Many of the slang words among fighting men, gamblers, thieves, prostitutes, are powerful words. These words ought to be collected,—the bad words as well as the good. Many of these bad words are fine." Whitman's sense of language is not bound by a restrictive purism, a guilt-ridden reverence of things English, or a disproportionate obedience to the written word. He recognizes the relationship between language and culture, and celebrates it: "What do you think words are? Do you think words are positive and original things in themselves? No. Words are not original and arbitrary in themselves. Words are a result—they are the progeny of what has been or is in vogue."[13]

A more cautionary mood is expressed by George Perkins Marsh, our Minister to Italy for twenty-one years and a specialist in Scandinavian languages and literature, who wrote such diverse books as the *Grammar of Old Icelandic* (1838) and *The Camel* (1860). In *Lectures on the English Language* (New York, 1860), a collection of his talks delivered at Columbia University, Marsh comments on the state of the English language in America, summing up the linguistic situation in this country in a way that reflects much of the discussion of the previous eighty years. Still concerned with the question of one language or two, Marsh counsels us to avoid "Americanizing, and consequently denaturalizing, the language in which our forefathers have spoken, and prayed, and sung, for a thousand years." He is opposed to the spelling reform movement in general, but particularly to the type of reform advocated in Webster's earlier works, a reform designed to establish the American language as distinct and independent from the English. Marsh phrases his comment in politically tinged rhetoric to indicate the political nature of the issue: "Let us not, with malice prepense, go about to republicanize our orthography and our syntax, our grammars and our dictionaries, our nursery rhymes and our Bibles, until, by the force of irresistible influences, our language shall have revolutionized itself."

The only kind of language change Marsh recognizes as legitimate is natural change. Nonetheless, he is not reluctant to intervene in another area of the American language. Unlike most of those who voiced their opinions on language matters, Marsh was abreast of developments in linguistic science (although Webster claimed such knowledge, he worked in a self-imposed intellectual vacuum, and was woefully ignorant of the significant linguistic thought of his day). Marsh is not an armchair purist, like his contemporary, Richard Grant White, nor is he a crusader like Webster. But on the subject of language standardization his opinions are those of any self-respecting proponent of Federal English. Marsh rejects dialects as politically and culturally counterproductive: "The inconveniences resulting from the existence of local dialects are very serious obstacles to national progress, to the growth of a comprehensive and enlightened patriotism, to the creation of a popular literature, and to the diffusion of general culture" (p. 676). Marsh finds dialects to be more divisive than religious differences, and more offensive than foreign languages. We must do everything in our power to retard the decay of our tongue, and to prevent its dissipation into a multitude of independent dialects. Despite these warnings, Marsh is optimistic. He finds that there are no dialects threatening to shatter English in America, attributing their absence in part to our political organization and our geography: "The physical character of our own territory is such as to encourage the hope that our speech, which, if not absolutely homogeneous, is now employed by 25,000,000 of men, in one unbroken mass, with a uniformity of which there is perhaps no other example, will escape [division into dialects]." Marsh then goes on to list the social and economic forces in America that will be conducive to the maintenance of linguistic homogeneity, for example, the newspapers, journals, and presses; the insurance companies, businesses, and industries whose operations and stockholders are spread across the country; the federal monetary system; universal education; charitable and religious organizations; and the absence of social rank (pp. 679–80).

In contrast to Whitman's effusive but perceptive essay and Marsh's more scientific account, "The Real American Language," by the poet Vachel Lindsay, which appeared in the *American Mercury* in 1928, is simply and unabashedly sentimental. For Lindsay, what he calls United States language, Virginia with the *r* put back in it, is spoken along the back roads of the nation, by "the hermits, and their wives and shirt-tail kids." It is antique, retaining its "colonial purity." And it is mellow. Its speakers "come forward during completely national upheavals—as Andrew Jackson in the war of 1812—or Sergeant York in the late war. . . . Sometimes they speak a dialect, but not often the aristocracy among them. . . . They believed in grammar just as they believed in paying their debts" (13:257–58).

A century and a half after independence, despite the continued language controversies and the failure of language reforms, one idea about the English language in the New World had not materially changed. Whether they spoke of one English or two, it was clear to observers that, just as language influenced the organization of society, society made its mark on language. No one could deny the fundamental differences between British and American society. No matter how similar the languages of the two peoples, their national differences were felt, for better and worse, to be reflected in their speech. Although individuals tried to assert their influence, no Academy was ever created, in either country, to regulate language matters, and while standards, both national and international, were agreed upon in general, the specifics of these standards have always been the subject of hot debate. What began in the minds of the federal philologers as Federal English, that form of English which bore the influence of democracy and revolution, has become, in the present century, Standard English, an equally vague but expressive notion for the actual as well as the ideal state of the American language whose fine points were never definitely fixed. The more political term for the language did not survive the beginning of the nineteenth century, perhaps because it smacked too much of a governmental control of language that speakers of English have always avoided, but the term that has replaced it has not altered to any great extent the popular or official notions of what the American language is.

6 Schoolmastering the Language: The Seventeenth and Eighteenth Centuries

American schools have been a major force in language planning from their inception. In the schools, children were exposed to specific examples of language which they were told either to imitate or to avoid. The notion that language was either good or bad, appropriate or inappropriate, welcome or forbidden was drilled into them, often without explanation. Grammar and spelling texts from the late eighteenth and early nineteenth centuries do not attempt to elucidate their own linguistic claims. Students were expected to learn—that is, to memorize—and not to question. Although the more comprehensive grammatical treatises did go into lengthy discussions of the pros and cons of particular constructions, most teachers were either too unfamiliar with their subject to understand the complex arguments, or they simply did not wish to devote classroom time to the explanation of points made in the elementary textbook grammars. Some educators and writers looked back with dismay at the inadequacy of their early training and were not surprised to find that they had retained little or nothing of their monolithic language instruction apart from a vague sense of their own linguistic incompetence.

At another level, language reformers went to work on the educated, adult population of the country. Emphasizing a continuation of the process begun in the common, or elementary, schools, experts who as often as not lacked specific linguistic expertise advised America's readers on points of usage and language etiquette. As in the case of the grammar texts, the usage commentaries, which will be discussed in the final chapters of this work, dealt with extremely specific points. And, although explanations often accompanied the judgments that were rendered, it is unlikely that a reader of either the "Hints on Language" that appeared in *Godey's Lady's Book* or of the columns by Richard Grant White that appeared in *The Galaxy* and the *New York Times* would be left much more satisfied than a student struggling with Lindley Murray's *Grammar*. The concern with monitoring the language of young and old alike is reflected in William Dwight Whitney's phrase, *schoolmastering the language*, from which the title of this chapter derives.

The Idea of English as a School Subject

In the twentieth century we have come to equate the English language with the school subject of the same name in which we studied reading and writing, grammar and spelling, speech and literature. It is surprising to many to discover that the study of the English language is a relatively recent addition to the liberal arts curriculum, and that it first flourished not in England, the ancestral home of the language, but in the United States, aided no doubt by the colonial mentality that accorded New World English a second-class status that it still possesses in the eyes of many, both at home and abroad.

Grammar and language had long been respected parts of the school curriculum in England as well as in the United States, but they consisted of the grammar and language of classical Greece and Rome. In *Some Thoughts Concerning Education* (1693), the philosopher John Locke called for the introduction of English language study in the schools. Locke is concerned in his essay with language education in general. He feels that grammatical instruction is an ineffective way to teach language and prefers that Latin be taught by the conversational method, as English and French are: "*Latin* is no more unknown to a Child, when he comes into the World, than *English*: And yet he learns *English* without Master, Rule, or Grammar; and so might he *Latin* too, as *Tully* did, if he had some Body always to talk to him in this Language." In this way, "a Child might without Pains or Chiding, get a Language, which others are wont to be whip'd for at School six or seven Years together."[1]

Locke rejects the notion that learning grammar precedes learning language: "I have never yet known any one who learnt his Mother Tongue by Rules." Yet he does see the need for certain people to study the grammar of their native language. Of those who live by their tongues and pens Locke says, "it is convenient if not necessary that they should speak properly and correctly, whereby they may let their Thoughts into other Mens minds, the more easily and with the greater impression." A professional speaker or writer cannot allow his or her words merely to be understood. The effect of the words on an audience must be considered as well: such a person "ought to Study Grammar amongst the other helps of Speaking well, but it must be the Grammar of his own Tongue, of the Language he uses, that he may understand his own Country speech nicely, and speak it properly without shocking the ears of those it is addressed to with solicisms [*sic*] and offensive irregularities." According to Locke, good grammar is the sign of the gentleman or woman. Without grammatical propriety, one gets "the censure of having had a Lower Breeding and worse Company, than suits with his quality" (pp. 305–06).

Locke advocates the study of the grammar of one's native language rather than of the dead ones. He feels that foreigners will not understand why the English spend so much of their school time on Latin grammar, which can be of no practical use to them when they enter the business world: "Would not a *Chinese*, who took notice of this way of Breeding, be apt to imagine that all our young Gentlemen were design'd to be Teachers and Professors of the Dead Languages of Foreign Countries, and not to be Men of Business in their own?" (p. 307). Returning to the question of grammar education, Locke presses the point that grammar is a tool for polishing language. The ancients studied their own grammar, not that of other languages. Locke points out that while we revere dead languages, the ancients regarded foreign tongues with suspicion, if not disdain. They saw grammar as an introduction to rhetoric, and Locke feels the English ought to do the same: "If Grammar ought to be taught at any time, it must be to one that can speak the Language already, how else can he be taught the Grammar of it. . . . Grammar being to teach Men not to speak, but to speak correctly and according to the exact Rules of the Tongue" (pp. 308–09).

In *British Education: or, the Source of the Disorders of Great Britain* (London, 1761), the lexicographer Thomas Sheridan asserts his desire to ascertain and fix the English language, and he calls for the schools to play a role in this process. Like Locke, Sheridan decries the general neglect of English education in Great Britain, where pupils are committed "to the care of the most ignorant and lowest of mankind." He says of the language that "there are hardly any who speak or write it correctly" (p. 196). Sheridan cites Locke on the need for learning English in schools: "Boys are often able to write exercises in pure and correct Latin, who at the same time can not express their thoughts with the best grace or propriety in their own language" (p. 205). He concedes that before the Reformation there was no need to study English because very little of any use was written in it, but he argues that the situation has now changed, that Latin and Greek are no longer repositories of learning and therefore no longer deserve the attention they once merited. Sheridan's plea had little effect on the British system of education. In the New World, however, interest in English language study was considerably stronger.

Franklin's English School

Benjamin Franklin, seeing the need for English in the schools, borrowed Locke's ideas on native language instruction and tried to implement them. In 1748 he published George Fisher's *American Instructor*, a book which stressed the need for good English and handwriting in the business world, and in 1749 Franklin began to organize an academy in Philadelphia in which students could either study the traditional curriculum, which included the classics, or attend an "English School," where they would be given instruction in the structure of their own language by an English Master. The English School was designed to provide the student with a practical education. Franklin recognized that not all students were interested in or able to benefit from the study of Latin. He felt strongly that such students should not be denied an adequate education and that, in fact, the study of the classical languages was necessary for only a very few callings. In his "Sketch of an English School," Franklin showed how his academy could provide a proper education for the mass of students: "Thus instructed, youth will come out of this school fitted for learning any business, calling, or profession, except such wherein languages are required; and, though unacquainted with any ancient or foreign tongue, they will be masters of their own, which is of more immediate and general use . . . the time usually spent in acquiring those languages, often without success, being here employed in laying such a foundation of knowledge and ability as, properly improved, may qualify them to pass through and execute the several offices of civil life, with advantage and reputation to themselves and country."[2]

According to Franklin's outline of the proposed course of study, pupils entering the English School would already know how to read and write. In their first year they would cover English grammar and orthography (Franklin favored spelling competitions to encourage learning) as well as reading. In the second year they would learn how to modulate their voices when reading aloud, and how to use the dictionary. Franklin was concerned with what we now call reading comprehension: "When our boys read English to us, we are apt to imagine they understand what they read, because we do, and because it is their mother tongue. But they often read, as parrots speak, knowing little or nothing of the meaning." In later classes the students would begin the study of rhetoric and composition, first by writing short letters involving imaginary business transactions, and essays summarizing or commenting on their reading. The English Master would correct their speech and their written work: "Let all their bad habits of speaking, all offences against good grammar, all corrupt or foreign accents, and all improper phrases, be pointed out to them. . . . All their letters to pass through the master's hand, who is to point out the faults, advise the corrections, and commend what he finds right" (pp. 126–30).

Franklin repeats his emphasis on the practical value of an English education for school pupils in "Proposals Relating to the Education of Youth in Pennsylvania" (1750): "Art is long, and their Time is short. It is therefore propos'd that they learn those Things that are likely to be *most useful* and *most ornamental*, Regard being had to the several Professions for which they are intended."[3] He cites Locke and other authorities on the importance of studying one's native language. But ultimately Franklin's utilitarian approach to education was too revolutionary for the school's founders, and the prestige of the classics was too strong. When the school was actually formed, the Latin Master was hired at twice the salary of the English Master to teach half the number of students. The English School prospered for a while, despite the obvious bias of the trustees toward the Latin School, but a succession of English masters found they could make more money by forming their own schools. In 1789 in "Observations Relative to the Intentions of the Original Founders of the Academy in Philadelphia," Franklin all but acknowledged that the English School was defunct.

The Rise of Vernacular Instruction

Franklin may have jumped the gun in trying to establish an English school, but his advocacy of vernacular education proved to be prophetic. After the American Revolution, English schools became the rule rather than the exception. According to Rollo Laverne Lyman, who has written the only history of early grammatical education in America, the rise of vernacular instruction in the United States after the Revolution was as striking as the rise of vernacular literature in England two centuries earlier: "Just as the new national life of England in the sixteenth century, with the accompanying pride in its self-sufficiency, brought forth a vigorous demand for the vernacular, so the national independence of America cooperated powerfully with other causes in transferring generally to the public schools the higher branches of the vernacular."[4]

William Cobbett shared Franklin's views. Cobbett was an Englishman who lived in America for a number of years as a political refugee. He wrote satirical essays under the name Peter Porcupine, and he published his *Grammar of the English Language* in New York in 1818 as a book designed "especially for the use of soldiers, sailors, apprentices, and plough-boys." Although he was a loyalist, Cobbett's book reflects the American patriotic boom that lasted until well after the War of 1812. Stressing the importance of the vernacular, Cobbett sees grammar as the gate of entrance to all the paths of knowledge and of the means of communicating that knowledge to others. And he identifies grammar with the aims of the Revolution. It will help every young man, he writes, "to assert with effect the rights and liberties of his country . . . for tyranny has no enemy so formidable as the pen" (p. 9). Holding up Great Britain as a model of decayed usage, Cobbett disparages the language both of the king and the prince regent. A political journalist and inveterate satirist, Cobbett was convicted of libeling Dr. Benjamin Rush, the popular American physician, having accused him of excessively bleeding and purging patients during the yellow fever epidemic of 1797. It was said that John Adams thought seriously of deporting Cobbett. In 1819 his house was burned, and Cobbett returned to England for good, though his views on the American language were apparently not modified by his later experiences in this country.

Along with the rise in interest in the vernacular, Lyman notes a marked increase in the teaching of English after the Revolution. English teachers began to be paid as much as or more than Latin teachers. States changed their educational requirements, reflecting a new attitude toward vernacular instruction. In 1789, for example, Massachusetts relieved 120 of its 270 towns of the necessity of keeping a Latin school, substituting a requirement for English schools instead. And the study of English grammar began to be prescribed for elementary as well as higher schools (*Grammar in American Schools*, p. 72).

Lyman sees two forces at work to place English on a par with Latin in America: the desire to standardize and preserve English by the cultivation of a style of pure speech, and the need to keep English free from the influence of other languages and to establish it as the standard language of the New World (p. 61). Eighteenth-century language theory assumed that the classical languages had been standardized and saw no reason why the same should not be done for English. The fear of language decay, strongly felt at home in England, was even more ominous in the wilds of North America, and the failure to study the grammar of the vernacular was seen as a direct cause of incorrect speech as well as a contributor to cultural decay.

Language was an important concern from early on in the New World. In New England, an area with an unusually high proportion of educated inhabitants, the Puritan emphasis on reading the Bible in the vernacular assured a literate population aware of the benefits of schooling. Compulsory education was established in the Massachusetts Bay Colony in 1647. The study of English was seen as a preparation for the study of the classics, which in turn was considered a necessary part of leadership training up to the time of the Revolution. Speech was as important as literacy, and there was a tendency in Puritan New England to equate speech with morality. Physical punishments were meted out to those considered guilty of various linguistic infractions, including swearing, anger, scolding, and gossiping.[5] Verbal behavior was subject to correction by the rod—appropriateness of speech is still of great concern to American teachers—but there was also a very positive emphasis on oratory, not only in New England but in all the colonies, giving rise to the stereotype that America was a nation of public speakers. Vernacular education in America did indeed center around the book. Lyman says, disapprovingly, "Book learning in the eighteenth century had an even more literal significance than it has to-day in many an ill-conducted classroom" (*Grammar*, p. 7). Primary texts were geared to the teaching of reading, and all subsequent learning involved the memorization and repetition of book material. Oratory was not extemporaneous; it was instead the reading aloud, and with proper emphasis, of speeches, essays, and, sometimes, poems. Even composition, or rhetoric, involved the rewording or amplification of reading matter, or the imitation of a model.

Early Grammar Books

The *New England Primer*, first published between 1680 and 1690, and many of the textbooks that followed it, adapted methods of classical education to the vernacular. Basically a speller and reader, the *Primer* begins with a description of the alphabet, first vowels, then consonants. The construction of simple syllables is then demonstrated, followed by lists of words of one, two, three, four, and five syllables (one hundred ninety-one words in all are listed in the edition of 1777, and their treatment affords us some insight into the state of the language at the time; for example, the combinations *tion*, *ious*, and *ial* are treated as disyllabic). The balance of the book is religious and moralistic. A series of behavioral imperatives, among them *Pray to God; Love God; Fear God; Strive to learn; Mind your Book; Be not a Dunce; Play not with bad Boys*, is followed by a series of woodcuts illustrating the alphabet with Biblical and moral scenes accompanied by explanatory verses: *In Adam's fall / We sinned all; Elijah hid / By Ravens fed*. The *Primer* concludes with a Bible quiz, a series of moral lessons, a collection of religious verse for children, a list of male and female names whose purpose was "to teach Children to spell their own," a catechism, and a dialogue between Christ, youth, and the Devil. Although later texts were not as obviously intended to double as devotional works, many of them preserved the stamp of Christian morality in their syntax examples and reading passages, and the connection between good speech and good character persists to this day in American schools and culture.

English education in America was hampered during the eighteenth century by a lack of adequate textbooks. *The New England Primer* was popular, and was reprinted many times, but its linguistic content was minimal. Spelling, according to Lyman, began as an incidental school subject in the first quarter of the eighteenth century, and eventually came to occupy an undue portion of attention in the schools until the middle of the following century, when grammar began to dominate English instruction (*Grammar*, p. 8). The earliest grammar written in the New World was by Hugh Jones, professor of mathematics at William and Mary College and the author of *The Present State of Virginia*. His *Short English Grammar* was published in England in 1724, but it was apparently never imported to America. Benjamin Franklin brought out an edition of Thomas Dilworth's *New Guide to the English Tongue* in 1747. Although it contained a grammar and a reader, Dilworth's was primarily a spelling text, and with it spelling became a universal subject in American schools. Abraham Lincoln is thought to have used this text, which proved to be one of the most popular schoolbooks in America before 1800, going through nearly forty editions in its first hundred years. Noah Webster sought to replace Dilworth with his own series of books, and a pseudonymous correspondent known as Dilworth's Ghost (actually a New York City schoolteacher named Hughes) exchanged a heated series of letters with Webster in several newspapers during 1784 and 1785 over the relative merits of the two spellers.

It was not only a lack of textbooks that caused problems before the Revolution. Before 1775, grammar was offered more in the private than the public schools. Lyman says, "The newness of the subject, the abject ignorance of the village schoolmasters, and the general absence of textbooks make it appear likely that English grammar did not generally make its way into the public schools until some time after it was taught in the more prosperous private schools of the cities" (p. 23). And there has always been some feeling that the teaching of grammar was unnecessary and should be minimized. For example, in *The Pennsylvania Spelling Book* (2d ed., 1779), Anthony Benezet, a Quaker schoolteacher and vegetarian who was an early advocate of the rights of women, blacks, and Indians (he opened a female seminary and a school for blacks in the 1750s), recommends "That such parts of Grammar as are applicable to the English tongue, be taught those boys who are fit for it, in order to make them write properly, but that they be as little as possible, perplexed with such nice distinctions, as have no foundation in the nature of our language" (p. 165).

The preparation—or rather lack of preparation—of schoolteachers has been a constant problem in the area of grammar in particular, and of the English language in general, in American schools. Texts through the mid-nineteenth century were generally designed to be self-teaching, partly to attract an adult readership and to serve in frontier areas where schools were not yet established, but partly, no doubt, to make up for the ignorance of the subject matter prevalent among the instructors. Lyman notes complaints in Massachusetts and Vermont about the poor preparation of teachers and the confusing multiplicity of texts in use. New York, for example, did not require English language study of its prospective teachers until 1834. In 1838, Ohio complains of "the almost utter incompetency of teachers" of grammar. And some school districts refused to let grammar be taught altogether because of the lack of competent staff. In 1854 the Pennsylvania legislature required grammar instruction in the schools, but many districts complained that the subject was unpopular and that many teachers could not teach it. Indeed, grammar was generally regarded as a difficult upper-level subject, and when it was taught, few pupils took it (*Grammar*, pp. 88–94). Noah Webster regrets that grammar was not offered when he went to school, but those who did take the subject may have been equally unfortunate.

Early Grammar Failures

In 1841, a correspondent identifying himself only as "Thrifty" reports in the *Common School Journal* (edited by Horace Mann, and later by W. B. Fowle) that his son learns proper grammar from his textbook and improper grammar from his teacher. Eight years later Fowle, who in addition to being an educator and active critic of American schools (he encouraged such innovative teaching methods as the use of the blackboard and was an early opponent of corporal punishment) was the author of several grammar texts, dismisses the teaching of grammar as humbug: "All our people study grammar, but not one in ten thousand can write or speak the English language correctly, and with facility." Fowle criticizes teachers and the teachers of teachers for their poor writing, and indicts his grammatical colleagues as well: "Strange as it may seem, the grammarians who pretend to be the arbiters of the language, have generally been unable to write or speak pure English." Fowle also questions the role of grammar books in the process of language decay: "It is an interesting inquiry, whether the publication of grammars has not prevented improvement, for its tendency is evidently to fix a language." He blames grammarians and their doctrine of usage for the perpetuation of error. They "took the language as it was, and declared that imperfect thing to be the rule and model for future generations; and the whole tribe of grammarians, from that day to this, have done little else than to confirm abuses, and perpetuate deformity." Like Webster, Fowle looks to the democratic organization of society to defeat these negative influences: "In spite of this attempt of grammarians to fix error, the common people, the uneducated, following the analogy of the language, have rectified a large number of [its irregularities]."[6] Speaking of his own inefficient language training, Fowle emphasizes its lack of practical significance:

> We were two or three years in the grammar; . . . we were never required to write a sentence of English, and we never did write one as a school exercise. [*Common School Journal* 12 (1850):5] We were *educated* at one of the best schools . . . but, although we studied English Grammar seven years and received a silver medal for our proficiency, we never wrote a sentence of English at school and never did anything which implied a suspicion on our part that grammar had anything to do with writing or conversation. [*Common School Journal* 11 (1849):258]

Even with competent teachers, methods of grammar education justi-fied comments like the ones above. There was a considerable emphasis on the memorization of grammatical rules, definitions, and paradigms. As with the study of Latin, English grammar was taught incrementally: students could not go on to the next step until they had mastered its predecessor. Reliance on the textbook was virtually absolute, and, ac-cording to Lyman, the general feeling was that the textbook alone was sufficient to make one a grammarian (*Grammar in American Schools*, p. 111). There was no clear application of the rules to be memorized, hence many pupils felt grammar to be totally abstract and mysterious.

Generally speaking, improvements in nineteenth-century grammar textbooks consisted of the development of new memory aids: repetition, rhyme, large type for emphasis, a catechetical question-and-answer for-mat, a foldout chart summarizing the rules. The writers of these books had little or no knowledge of linguistics, and they chose not to confuse their readers by discussing theory or asking open-ended questions that might stimulate thought. One of the boldest and most controversial in-novations was the introduction of examples of false syntax for the stu-dent to identify and correct—although in most cases the identification and correction were provided, lessening even further the amount of involvement between reader and text. The use of false syntax was con-sidered by a number of grammarians to be inappropriate as it might lead students into the inadvertent imitation of errors.

Grammars and Grammarians

Lyman divides grammar education in America into two large periods. The first, which extends to 1848, in which grammar was generally con-sidered an art, consists of an initial stage (1750–84) during which ver-nacular education was considered simply as a preparation for the study of Latin. During the rote period (1784–1823), English had established itself as an alternative to, not a preparation for, the classics, and gram-mar education was largely a process of rote memorization. In the pars-ing period (1823–47), greater attention is paid to the students' active participation in their education, and grammar becomes training in the parsing of sentences and paragraphs. In the second large period (1848–1920), grammar is considered more as a science than an art. This period is also subdivided into smaller ones where the emphasis is on analysis (1848–73) and rhetoric (1873–91), and a final one (1891–1920) in which grammar becomes once again an incidental study in the schools (p. 103).

Lyman's broad categorical distinctions are useful, but they are also misleading, for many influential writers spoke of grammar as both science and art well before 1850. Bringing Lyman's account up to date, we observe that grammar has continued to show cyclical popularity in American schools, being alternately revived and abandoned in response to continued complaints about the writing of school pupils. Complaints about teachers' ability to handle the subject, and of the difficulty of interesting students in it and giving it practical application to their lives, also continue. Even the progression Lyman noted from grammar as art to grammar as science has proven cyclical. Despite the increasing intensity of linguistic research, the popularity of school grammars incorporating linguistic theory has declined in recent years and the "science" of grammar seems to have fallen once again into educational disfavor.

Grammar, as defined by grammarians from Ben Jonson through Noah Webster, Lindley Murray, and Goold Brown, is the art of speaking and writing correctly. Webster of course was concerned with language as a science, and Dilworth mentions the science of letters, though he seems basically to be concerned with the art, not the science, of language. Peter Bullions, clergyman, classicist, and author of a number of popular textbooks, wrote much later in *The Principles of English Grammar* (Albany, New York, 1841) to explain the dual position of grammar as science and art, trying to reconcile factual description and classification with linguistic prescription and the doctrine of usage: "Grammar is both a Science and an Art. As a Science, it investigates the principles of language in general: as an Art, it teaches the right method of applying those principles to a particular language, so as thereby to express our thoughts in a correct and proper manner, according to established usage" (p. 1).

Dilworth: A Typical Grammar

Thomas Dilworth wrote textbooks on bookkeeping and arithmetic as well as English. His grammar is only one section of his *New Guide to the English Tongue*, the most popular American language text before 1800. The title page of the Bradford edition (Philadelphia, 1793) advertises the book as "being recommended by several *Clergymen* and eminent *Schoolmasters*, as the most useful *Performance* for the Instruction of *Youth* . . . designed for the Use of SCHOOLS in *Great Britain*, *Ireland*, and *America*." Besides a major section on spelling, the book contains a number of prayers and devotional readings which reveal its original purpose as a text for the religiously supported charity schools of England. Like most grammars of its time, Part III of the *New Guide*, the "Practical English Grammar," begins with a definition of its subject. Here Dilworth speaks both of science and art interchangeably, though his definition, couched in catechetical, or question-and-answer form, is otherwise quite traditional:

Q. *What* is Grammar?
A. Grammar is the Science of Letters, or the Art of Writing and Speaking properly and syntactically.[7]

Although they had already been treated in the first section of the book, on orthography, the grammar proceeds to list the letters of the alphabet and discuss their pronunciation. One interesting point made in this section concerns mute consonants. Although Dilworth recognizes the existence of a final silent *e*, he seems unwilling to allow for the possibility of silent consonants. In his list of examples of letters that do not always keep their sound, he notes that "*L* is sounded like *m* in Salmon" and that "*T* is sounded like *s* in Whistle, Thistle" (p. 89).

Dilworth's grammar is outside one tradition of American grammar texts: it is not reformatory in tone. Dilworth describes, fairly neutrally, some aspects of the English language, but his book contains more a setting forth of grammatical terminology than an attempt to make any of his readers alter their usage. This is not to say that Dilworth was no prescriptivist. Like most of the authors of language texts of his or any time, he surely felt there was a right and a wrong way to speak and write. It is just that his work contains no comments on correct usage. Ben Jonson's grammar (1634), which is specifically designed to rid the language of barbarisms, is similarly silent on usage questions. Dilworth's attempts at description are also traditional. His rules would not do much to help a non-native speaker learn English, nor would they correct and improve the language of those born and bred in English-speaking households. His definition of a sentence, for example, is simple and inconclusive: "Words duly joined together in Construction, make a *Sentence*; as, *Pride is a very remarkable Sin*" (p. 94). Just what *duly* joined constructions are is not made explicit. His definition of syntax is not quite as vague, and with it he gives an illustrative example, which, though circular, is also more pertinent:

Q. *What is* Syntax?
A. It is the disposing of Words in their right Case, Gender, Number, Person, Mood, Tense and Place, in a Sentence.

Q. *Give an Example.*

A. *Good Boys are not beaten*; here the Words are placed according to *Syntax*: Whereas should I say, *Beaten not are Boys good*, it would be unintelligible; because here is no *Syntax* in this Sentence. [P. 123]

Noah Webster complains that Dilworth's grammar is just an English translation of a Latin grammar, since Dilworth conjugates English verbs according to Latin tenses and declines English nouns with a full paradigm of Latin cases, including the vocative: *O Book, O Church, O Man*; and the ablative: *From a Book, From Men, From Churches*. What may concern Webster even more, although he leaves it unsaid, is the fact that Dilworth's grammar is not a usage guide, but simply a brief account of English grammar. As we have seen, although he considered himself a descriptivist, Webster's was a normative temperament, and he could be as dogmatic in his ideas of language structure and usage as he was on spelling. In his *American Selection of Lessons on Reading and Speaking* (Boston, 1793), the third part of his *Grammatical Institute*, Webster's purpose is, as always, "to refine and establish our language, to facilitate the acquisition of grammatical knowledge, and diffuse the principles of virtue and patriotism." His rules for speaking are unequivocal. He will permit no "whining, drawling, lisping, stammering, mumbling in the throat, or speaking through the nose" (pp. 5–7). But it is in his several grammars that he evokes the linguistic purism that had permeated eighteenth-century linguistic thought.

Webster on Grammar

In the second part of the *Grammatical Institute, A Plain and Comprehensive Grammar* (Hartford, 1784), Webster rejects the traditional dependency of English grammars on their classical predecessors: "The English nation at large have till very lately, entertained the idea that our language was incapable of being reduced to a system of rules; . . . even now many men of much classical learning warmly contend that the only way of acquiring, a grammatical knowledge of the *English Tongue*, is first to learn a *Latin Grammar*." Webster calls this a "stupid opinion" that shows the influence of habit. Finding that it has "now arrived to a great degree of purity," he would have English freed from its subservience to the classical languages. Webster particularly praises the elegant and sublime style of writers of the last and present age, and he takes as his task the perpetuation of this state of purity: "To frame such a Grammar as to instruct our own youth, as well as foreigners, in this purity of style, is the business of a Grammarian—a business that appears to be not yet accomplished" (pp. 3–4). For Webster, there is no adequate grammar text available: Dilworth is too Latin; Lowth is not suitable because of its difficulty; Buchanan and Ash are not bad books, but like Lowth, they contain errors.

Webster's approach to grammar, like his approach to spelling, is revisionistic. While much of his description is traditional, borrowed freely from his predecessors, Webster seems most content when he is making the rules and setting the styles. In his grammar he comments on some questions of usage, and he revises some of the traditional grammatical categories. For example, Webster rejects the group genitive (a phrase inflected in the possessive as if it were a single noun), "the King of Great-Britain's soldiers" as ungrammatical, although he mentions that Lowth approves such constructions. For Webster, it is ungrammatical because there is no grammatical rule that will account for it: "Every phrase that cannot be resolved or analyzed by the rules of Grammar and the established idioms of the language, ought to be rejected as a corruption" (p. 13). In discussing the subjunctive, however, Webster concedes that popular usage has a powerful effect on linguistic change, and that it is difficult to regulate such usage even when it goes against grammatical principles. He regrets the apparent decay of the English subjunctive "mode," and its replacement by the indicative: "This is . . . an error and a real misfortune to the language, because it destroys a distinction that is essential and ought to be preserved" (p. 41n). Webster also recognizes that popular usage will not be swayed by arguments from grammarians: "Custom is sovereign in the use of language; and when universal invariable custom has introduced and established any form of expression, we may possibly doubt its analogy to the rules of other languages, but ought not to scruple its propriety in our own" (p. 42).

Webster finds fault with some traditional grammatical analyses. He prefers classifying verbs as transitive and intransitive, rather than active, passive, and neuter, supporting his claim with references to Lowth, who argues for the existence of a passive in English but fails to identify it when parsing a sentence, and to Ash, who finds no true passive in English. Webster's treatment of the auxiliary (known informally nowadays as the helping verb) under the rubrics of mode and tense is an expansive dissertation on the subject, going beyond what is usually found in grammar texts. He attempts to fix with precision the various meanings of the modal auxiliaries (*shall, will, can, may,* and so forth) in a great number of their tenses and moods, arguing, among other things, for the preservation of the shall / will distinction that seems to have been more a product of prescriptive grammars than popular usage. Of *will*, Webster says:

> This is also a sign of the future tense; but for the most part, is directly the reverse of *shall*; that is, it has the same force or meaning as *shall*, but in different persons. In the first person, it promises; as, "I will write:" In the second and third, it simply foretells; as, "you will or he will go to Philadelphia." [P. 28]

Webster's definition of a sentence goes beyond Dilworth's to include a semantic notion: a sentence is "a number of words, ranged in *proper* order and making complete sense" (p. 66). He distinguishes a solemn and a familiar style of sentence construction, the solemn corresponding more or less to a religious register in which are preserved the second person singular pronoun and verb forms, for example, *thou art*, and the third person singular verb in *-th*, *he readeth*. Webster then gives examples of false constructions in both styles, providing the correct forms at the bottom of the page. When he presents the rules of syntax, Webster gives examples and explains them, commenting on difficult or unusual cases that are likely to occur, and giving his opinion of current trends in speech.

As an example, Rule XI of Webster's syntax states simply, "Prepositions govern an objective case or word." In a remark on the rule, Webster adds that prepositions should not be separated from words which they govern, as in "*Whom* did you give it *to?*" Webster is reluctant to allow such a form even for informal situations: "Grammarians seem to allow of this mode of expression in conversation and familiar writings; but it is generally inelegant, and in the grave and sublime styles, is certainly inadmissible. But this is much more pardonable than another error that has crept into general use; which is to make prepositions govern a nominative case; thus, *Who* did you give it *to?*" One has the sense that Webster already sees the battle lost on this one, but there is no mistaking his reluctance to concede a point to fashionable speech. Nominative pronouns separated from their governing prepositions are "in every person's mouth and yet they will be shocked to hear the preposition pronounced where it ought to stand; thus, *To who* did you give it? . . . Yet these last are as proper as the first, though not so familiar to the ear" (pp. 78–79).

The grammar concludes with a sample passage that is parsed and a series of examples of false syntax found in approved authorities such as the Bible, Shakespeare, Dryden, and Swift. These examples are corrected and the reader is referred to the appropriate syntax rule as explanation. There are also discussions of ellipsis, prosody (that is, accent and emphasis), morphology, and punctuation. Although Webster's grammar presents a much more complete course than Dilworth's does, neither the second part of the *Grammatical Institute* nor any of its subsequent revisions was to achieve much popularity as a text.

Six years later Webster published the *Rudiments of English Grammar* (Hartford, 1790), in which he acknowledged that his original *Plain and Comprehensive Grammar* was both too comprehensive and not plain enough to be a suitable schoolbook. Webster clarifies the significance of grammatical rules: "It is a mistake that children ever learn their nativ tongue by rules; they learn it by the ear and by practice. Rules are drawn from the most general and approved practice, and serve to teach young students how far their *own practice* in speaking agrees with the *general practice* of the nation, and thus enable them to correct their errors." Webster also seems to admit the possibility that grammatical instruction may be an ineffective device for language reformation in school children, although he is optimistic that such instruction may have some future influence on students' lives: "Altho the young pupil may not fully comprehend [the grammatical rules], when at school, yet if he commits them to memory, he will afterwards recollect them with ease and apply them with advantage" (p. 4).

A third grammar, *A Philosophical and Practical Grammar of the English Language*, was published by Webster in New Haven in 1807. In this work Webster makes his most radical suggestions for the reformation of grammatical terminology. He emphasizes the importance of etymology, a study which preoccupied him while he undertook the preparation of his great dictionary, and he makes a clear case for language study as a science that cannot be thwarted by the individual prejudice of particular grammarians: "In the sciences prescription cannot legalize error" (p. 5).

Webster is concerned with what has since come to be called the explanatory power of a grammar: "A Grammar, to deserve the title, must contain a true explanation of the several species of words, a correct classification of them, and a developement of the real principles of combination in the structure of sentences" (p. 3). He rejects the classification of the article as a part of speech, and he proposes to simplify the terminology of grammar by renaming the other parts of speech:

"Nothing facilitates the study of the sciences more effectually than the use of plain intelligible terms." Thus Webster suggests *name* as a replacement for *noun* or *substantive*, although he himself continues to use the term *noun* in his book. For *pronoun* Webster recommends *substitute*, arguing that pronouns "are often used in the place of sentences and adjectives, as well as of nouns" (pp. 6–7). For *adjective* Webster prefers *attribute*, for *adverb*, *modifier*, and for *conjunction*, *connective*. Although Webster does not like the term *verb*, he can find no other word to replace it, and he reluctantly decides to keep it. John Sherman, a Unitarian minister, teacher, hotelkeeper, and the author of *The Philosophy of Language Illustrated* (1826), also rejects traditional categories for the parts of speech, though unlike Webster he is not interested in reducing their number. Sherman creates nine new terms whose use is not always entirely clear: names, attributes, possessives, assertors, relatives, connectives, appendants, indexes, and ejaculations.

Webster is firmly committed to the concept of language as a science, not an art, although like others he defines grammar as "the art of speaking and writing our thoughts with propriety" (*Plain and Comprehensive Grammar*, p. 7), but Webster realizes that most people do not yet share this outlook, that linguistics is not yet well established in the public eye: "The science of Grammar is nearly in the condition in which chemistry stood, about thirty years ago. . . . For the honor of our native tongue, the key to every science, it is presumed this subject will hereafter receive more attention." Webster's fascination with etymology and the study of language families led him to propose some outlandish connections and bizarre derivations, but where grammar was concerned he argued forcefully for a description of English independent of the grammar of any other language: "The better way is, to explain every language just as it is, and frame a grammar of each language upon its own idioms" (pp. 9–10), although this reverses his earlier stand that idiom must follow, not precede, grammatical rules.

According to Webster, the grammar of each language is a combination of linguistic universals and idiosyncratic particulars. Natural distinctions such as sex, number, and time give rise to linguistic ones, and it is the job of a grammar to connect the realm of ideas with that of expression: "Grammar, as a science, treats of the natural connection between ideas, and words which are the signs of ideas, and develops the principles which are common to all languages. . . . The grammar of a particular language is a system of *general principles* derived from natural distinctions of words, and of *particular rules* deduced from the customary forms of speech in the nation using that language. These usages are mostly arbitrary, or of accidental origin; but when they become common to a nation, they are to be considered as established, and received as rules of the highest authority" (pp. 12–13).

Usage is thus elevated to a position of the highest authority in the determination of grammatical propriety, but this is a doctrine that, as we have seen earlier, Webster has some trouble accepting in practice. Usage here is said to determine the principles, or genius of a language, yet usage is also occasionally seen as the violation of these principles. This position is of course not unique to Webster. It is the stance taken by many eighteenth- and nineteenth-century grammarians, as well as by influential writers on language in the present century, and it is a stance that ultimately allows the grammarian the freedom to contradict him or herself. Opinions can then be justified either on the basis of usage or of reason, and the privileged or stigmatized grammatical form can be accounted for with ease. In the *Plain and Comprehensive Grammar* Webster discusses a change in the English pronoun system: the introduction of the plural *you* as a replacement for the singular *thou*, now only to be found in what Webster calls the sacred or solemn style. He observes that the new form, *you*, retains its notion of plurality and should never be conjugated with the singular form of the verb: "Thus, *you was*, is as improper as, *you art*, *you hast*. We ought to say, *you were*" (p. 15).

This particular usage question was often considered in the eighteenth century. According to the grammar historian Sterling A. Leonard, Lowth, Priestley, and Withers rejected *you was*, while it was approved by Blair and found in many of the standard authors of the time.[8] In the *Philosophical Grammar*, Webster reverses his earlier position. He condemns the rejection of singular *you* by other grammarians as arbitrary (he fails to mention his own earlier stand on the subject), and he turns the controversy into a question of patriotism: "National usage rejects the arbitrary principle. The true principle [that is, national usage], on which all language is built, rejects it." Webster now favors *you was* because national usage determines correctness in grammar, and because, in the United States, *you was* is "not merely popular usage, tho this, when general, is respectable authority; but the practice of men of letters" (*Philosophical Grammar*, pp. 33–34n).

Webster only occasionally relies on men of letters as style setters. In the case of singular *you* their opinion is simply extra ammunition for him. Later on in the grammar he discusses the opposition between popular and literary usage, regretting it as a stumbling block in the

creation of a uniform national language. Webster does not scoff at literature. In fact he often proclaims his warm support for the development
of a national literary canon and relies heavily on American writings in
his reading and oratory textbooks. But he makes a strong case for the
folk language as the proper idiom, because the usage of the common
people retains more of the genius of the original language.

Webster on the Double Negative

The problem of multiple negation, particularly the double negative, was
often mentioned by eighteenth-century grammarians. Lowth, Johnson,
and most others who deal with the question argue that two negatives
make a positive, and this is the school grammar rule that has survived
to the present day. The conflict between the requirements of logic and
the realities of usage is in fact noted as early as the sixteenth century in
sonnet 63 of Sir Philip Sidney's *Astrophel and Stella* (London, 1591)
which deals directly with the problematic double negative:

> Oh Grammer rules, oh now your vertues showe,
>   So Children still read you with awfull eyes,
> As my young Doue may in your precepts wise,
> Her graunt to me by her owne vertue knowe.
> For late with hart most hie, with eyes most lowe;
>   I crau'd the thing which euer she denies.
> Shee lightning Loue, displaying *Venus* skyes,
> Least one should not be heard twise, said no no.
> Sing then my Muse, now I do Paean sing.
> Heauens Enuy not at my high triumphing:
> But Grammers force with sweete successe confirme,
>   For Grammer sayes ah (this deere *Stella* way)
>   For Grammer sayes (to Grammer who sayes nay)
> That in one speech, two negatiues affirme.

Of the eighteenth-century grammarians, Joseph Priestley (now better
known for his discovery of oxygen than for his work on grammar) and
a few others accept the double negative, citing its use in older forms of
English, its popularity in common speech, and its occurrence in such
standard authors as Addison. Webster too approves of this construction,
regarding the single negative as an innovation. In his comment he reiterates his belief that the genius of the language is democratic, not auto-
cratic, and he celebrates the language of the average American:

The learned, with a view to philosophical correctness, have rejected the use of *two* negatives for *one* negation; but the expedience of the innovation may be questioned, for the change has not reached the great mass of the people, and probably never will reach them; it being nearly impossible, in my opinion, ever to change a usage which enters into the language of every cottage, every hour and almost every moment. Such usages are always regulated by tradition. The consequence is, we have two modes of speaking directly opposite to each other, but expressing the same thing. . . . It makes no difference that men of letters denounce vulgar language as incorrect—Language in a nation should be uniform; the same words should, among all classes of people, express the same ideas—and rash indeed is the innovator who attempts to change an idiom which has the stamp of the authority of thousands of years . . . and which is so incorporated into the language of common affairs, as to render hopeless every effort towards a reformation. To create essential differences between the language of polite and common life, is a serious evil. In this instance, the people have the primitive idiom. . . . It is not expected that any change can now be effected in the practice of one class of people or the other: but these remarks are intended to suggest a salutary caution against indulging a spirit of innovation, under the pretext of reforming what is supposed to be wrong. [*Philosophical and Practical Grammar*, p. 192]

It would seem that Webster kept his ideas about spelling and grammar in separate compartments. Although he became pessimistic about enforcing orthographical changes, he never really felt his spelling reforms were out of place. But in matters of grammar, perhaps because so many reformers in the eighteenth century had already staked out their ground, or because of his need to defy the established British linguistic tradition, Webster was much less prescriptive. This may in part account for the lack of popularity of his grammars, although Webster's tendency to overwrite may also be a contributing factor. Of all his textbooks, the grammars are the most difficult to read.

7 Schoolmastering the Language: The Nineteenth Century

The American school grammar that proved most popular in the early 1800s was that of Lindley Murray, an American-born merchant who had studied at Franklin's English Academy in Philadelphia and moved to England, ostensibly for reasons of health, after amassing a large fortune by trading with the Royalists during the Revolution. Murray's grammar, written at the request of friends for use in an English girls' school, is based largely on the grammar of Robert Lowth, bishop of London. Lowth's work, often considered today as the archetypal eighteenth-century prescriptive grammar, achieved less success in the United States than that of Murray, although Lowth's *Short Introduction to English Grammar*, first published in England in 1762 (the first American edition was printed in Philadelphia in 1775), was used in American colleges, including Harvard and Yale, while Murray's work was a standard common school text until 1850.

Robert Lowth's *Grammar*

Robert Lowth was a clergyman, Murray a businessman. But Lowth's grammar is much more secular in tone than Murray's. Lowth's position is openly that of a corrector of improper usage. He begins by praising the development of the English language over the previous two hundred years: "It has been considerably polished and refined; its bounds have been greatly enlarged; its energy, variety, richness, and elegance, have been abundantly proved, by numberless trials, in verse and prose, upon all subjects, and in every kind of style." But there is one area where the language has proved disappointing: "It hath made no advances in grammatical accuracy."[1] Lowth does not believe that English is irregular and incapable of being reduced to a system of rules—his grammar clearly demonstrates this. But he does feel that "the English language, as it is spoken by the politest part of the nation, and as it stands in the writings of the most approved authors, often offends against every part of grammar" (p. iv).

Lowth praises the simplicity of the English language (he is referring primarily to its inflectional system), but he feels that this very simplicity contributes to the current usage crisis: "The construction of this language is so easy and obvious, that our grammarians have thought it hardly worth while to give us any thing like a regular and systematical syntax" (p. v). Native speakers of English take for granted their ability to speak and write the language well, and this, according to Lowth, produces a false sense of security as well as some serious grammatical improprieties. Grammar is not part of the school curriculum (Lowth is here addressing a British audience; the situation in American schools was somewhat different), and it cannot be learned simply by an imitation of prominent authors, for, as Lowth makes every effort to show, "our best authors have committed gross mistakes, for want of a due knowledge of English grammar, or at least of a proper attention to the rules of it" (p. viii).

Lowth's method, in his grammar, is twofold. He shows by the use of rules and examples what he feels the structure of the English language ought to be. And he also introduces what he regards as a new method of education which "teaches us what is right, by shewing what is wrong," a method he hopes may be even more effective (p. ix). Lowth feels, in addition, that the study of English grammar should be undertaken before the study of any foreign languages, so that a student will not have to learn both the principles of grammar and the principles of a new and unfamiliar language at the same time.

Grammar, for Lowth, is prescriptive. It "is the Art of rightly expressing our thoughts by Words"[2] and it should be designed to enable us to "judge of every phrase and form of construction, whether it be right or not" (1775 ed., p. x). The way Lowth has arranged things, judgments of correctness cannot be made without recourse to his grammar, whose rules serve as a touchstone. Lowth does not derive these rules from the genius of the language, from the application of reason, or from a doctrine of usage. His opinions frequently go against usage, and he often cites the language of some of the most respected works and authors— the Bible, Swift, Donne, Milton, Addison—in illustrating what ought not to be written. Lowth criticizes Shakespeare's choice of pronouns; past participles used by Swift and Milton; Pope's employment of a neuter verb as an active one; improper tense constructions on the part of Dryden; and a present participle "vulgarly" used as a passive by Locke and Sidney, to name only a scant few of the illustrations of false syntax. Translations of the Old and New Testaments provide Lowth with numerous examples of incorrect usage and, unlike the American grammarians, Lowth does not cite these examples to evoke pious sentiment, but to show that the best writers are occasionally incompetent.

Authority in usage rests solely with the grammar book, and although Lowth admits that his own work is fallible and subject to correction, he sees the grammar book as the highest of linguistic authorities and he dispenses his judgments on the structure of English ex cathedra, without recourse to any justification based on reason, analogy, the historical development of the language, or even other grammarians.

Lowth is aware of language change, and he does not oppose it. He often cites earlier forms, but he objects to their retention when they have become obsolete. Discussing the past participle of the verb *sit* Lowth says, "Frequent mistakes are made in the formation of the participle of this verb. The analogy plainly requires *sitten*; which was formerly in use: 'The army having sitten there so long'. . . . But it is now almost wholly disused, the form of the past time *sat*, having taken its place. 'The court *was sat*, before Sir Roger came'" (p. 53). Lowth regards the forms of the reflexive *himself, themselves* as corruptions of *his self* and *their selves*, citing Sidney's use of the latter, and reversing his original opposition to these forms. However, despite Lowth's support, *his self* and *their selves* have never lost their stigma.

Murray's *Grammar*

Lindley Murray's *English Grammar, Adapted to the Different Classes of Learners*, first published in 1795, sold over a million copies, in its various editions, by 1850. Using Lowth's grammar as a base, Murray makes some changes in presentation so the book will be more suitable as a text. Rules to be memorized are set in larger type. To make them more easily memorized, the author "has been solicitous to select terms that are smooth and voluble; to proportion the members of the sentences to one another; to avoid protracted periods; and to give the whole definition or rule, as much harmony of expression as he could devise." Murray continues Lowth's use of false syntax as "more instructive to the young grammarian, than any rules and examples of propriety that can be given."[3] But Murray adds a characteristically American pietistic flavor to the schoolbook. While he sees grammar primarily as an aid to communication, education for Murray involves more than subject matter. In the preface he says that the author "wishes to promote, in some degree, the cause of virtue, as well as of learning; and, with this view, he has been studious, through the whole of the work, not only to avoid every example and illustration, which might have an improper effect on the minds of youth; but also to introduce, on many occasions, such as have a moral and religious tendency"(1:ix).

It has been suggested by Christopher Niebuhr that the general pietism of American schoolbooks may result from the fact that many eighteenth-century schools were staffed by teachers who had trained for the Presbyterian ministry but could not secure ministerial posts. After the Revolution, education in America became more religiously conservative, while religion became more liberal, swinging away from Puritanism toward Methodism.[4]

Murray's work was so successful that he published an expanded, two-volume edition, the second volume consisting largely of exercises. In the introduction to this volume Murray reiterates his belief in the value of moral education:

> Even sentiments of a pious and religious nature, have not been thought improper to be occasionally inserted in these Exercises. . . . The importance of exhibiting to the youthful mind, the deformities of vice; and of giving it just and animating views of piety and virtue, makes it not only warrantable, but our duty also, to embrace every proper occasion to promote, in any degree, these valuable ends. [*English Grammar*, 2:vii]

Murray is aware of the potential aridity of schoolbook grammars, but he is convinced that his own perambulations among the finer points of his subject will be regarded as pleasant, if not invigorating, by the right kind of student:

> The author conceives that the occasional strictures, dispersed through the book, and intended to illustrate and support a number of important grammatical points, will not, to young persons of ingenuity, appear to be dry and useless discussions. He is persuaded that, by such persons, they will be read with much attention. And he presumes that these strictures will gratify their curiosity, stimulate application, and give solidity and permanence to their grammatical knowledge. [1:xn]

Correctness of style is a major concern to Murray, and many of the strictures mentioned above concern appropriate style. Murray's Rule XVI, on the double negative, contains such a discussion:

Two negatives, in English, destroy one another, or are equivalent to an affirmative: as, *"Nor* did they *not* perceive him;" that is, "they did perceive him." "His language, though inelegant, is *not ungrammatical;*" that is, "it is grammatical."

It is better to express an affirmation, by a regular affirmative, than by two separate negatives, as in the former sentence: but when one of the negatives is joined to another word, as in the latter sentence, the two negatives form a pleasing and delicate variety of expression.

Some writers have improperly employed two negatives instead of one: as in the following instances: "I never did repent of doing good, nor shall not now;" *"nor shall I now."* [1:187]

Murray does not recognize multiple negation as characteristically English, and he argues against it on logical grounds. In his next rule, XVII, which states that prepositions govern the objective case, Murray is more inclined to evoke the genius of the language. He rejects such statements as "Who do you ask for?" but he is less strict about separable prepositions in examples like "Whom will you give it to?" Webster found this construction intolerable, but while Murray feels such prepositional movement is inappropriate for solemn and elevated discourse, he recognizes that "this is an idiom to which our language is strongly inclined; it prevails in common conversation, and suits very well with the familiar style in writing" (1:188). Murray goes even further, rejecting certain constructions as being too foreign. He favors *averse* (or *aversion) to* over *averse from* because it is "more truly English." Citing George Campbell's *Philosophy of Rhetoric* on the subject, he goes on: "The argument from etymology is here of no value, being taken from the use of another language. If, by the same rule, we were to regulate all nouns and verbs of Latin original, our present syntax would be overturned. It is more conformable to English analogy with *to*: the words *dislike* and *hatred,* nearly synonymous, are thus construed" (1:189).

Analogies with French are similarly to be avoided, and even English analogies are to be rejected in the face of approved usage. Murray feels that our best and most correct writers now use *means* and *amends* as singular forms, and he would not have them return to *mean* and *amend*:

It can scarcely be doubted, that this word *amends* (like the word *means*) had formerly its correspondent form in the singular number, as it is derived from the French *amende,* though now it is exclusively established in the plural form. If, therefore, it be alleged that *mean* should be applied in the singular, because it is derived from the French *moyen*, the same kind of argument may be advanced in favour of the singular *amende*: and the general analogy of the language may also be pleaded in support of it. . . . An attempt therefore to recover an old word, so long since disused by the most correct writers, seems not likely to be successful; especially as the rejection of it is not attended with any inconvenience. [1:151–52]

Standard language, according to Murray, may violate the constraints of etymology and analogy, but only when it is the language of established authors and when it has been carefully considered: "The practice of the best and most correct writers, or a great majority of them, corroborated by general usage, forms, during its continuance, the standard of language; especially, if, in particular instances, this practice continue, after objection and due consideration." But this standard, while it may go against tradition and may itself be subject to alteration in the future, may not go against the bounds of good taste: "Every connexion and application of words and phrases, thus supported, must therefore be proper, and entitled to respect, if not exceptionable in a moral point of view" (1:152).

Murray's discussion of linguistic anomalies reveals a strong conservative tendency: he often accepts popular usage, instead of trying to reform it. He approves *none* with a plural verb: *"None* of them *are"* and allows an objective *himself* to become a nominative: "He *himself* shall do the work." He also allows a formerly objective *you* to replace *ye* in the nominative, commenting that these forms, though anomalous, "are to be considered as strictly proper and justifiable." This leads him to a consideration of the role of the grammarian in language controversies:

> With respect to anomalies and variations of language, thus established, it is the grammarian's business to submit, not to remonstrate. In pertinaciously opposing the decision of proper authority, and contending for obsolete modes of expression, he may, indeed, display learning and critical sagacity; and, in some degree, obscure points that are sufficiently clear and decided: but he cannot reasonably hope, either to succeed in his aims, or to assist the learner, in discovering and respecting the true standard and principles of language. [1:152]

According to Murray, meddling with the established language should be avoided at all costs. In one of his exercises, on ambiguity, we find the following example of false syntax, a commentary on some of the author's colleagues: "The pretenders to polish and refine the English language, have chiefly multiplied abuses and absurdities" (2:112). The grammarian's role is not to reform what has already become established as correct, no matter how much it violates the dictates of reason or how much it deviates from past usage. Only in the case of what is doubtful may the grammarian "reason and remonstrate on the ground of derivation, analogy, and propriety and his reasonings may refine and improve the language: but when authority speaks out and decides the point, it were perpetually to unsettle the language, to admit of cavil and debate. Anomalies, then, under the limitation mentioned, become the law, as clearly as the plainest analogies" (1:152–53).

The genius of English is again defended in Murray's discussion of style. Here authority is to be found at home, not abroad: "Purity requires that those words only shall be employed, which are of classical authority. . . . Classical authority consists of speakers and writers, who are deservedly in high estimation: speakers, distinguished for their elocution, and persuasive eloquence; writers, eminent for correct taste, solid matter, and refined manner. . . . Foreign and learned words, unless where necessity requires them, should never be admitted into our composition. Barren languages may need such assistance, but ours is not one of these" (1:282–83). Despite his frequent appeals to English idiom, Murray feels free to reject usage whenever it disagrees with a higher, though often unspecified, authority. Thus Murray tells us, "In some dialects, the word *what* is improperly used for that, and sometimes we find it in this sense in writing: 'They will never believe but *what* I have been entirely to blame'. . . . instead of 'but that'" (1:145). This stigmatizing of dialect forms is not surprising, and Murray is actually fairly restrained here.

Murray does not hesitate to extend his authority to matters that are apparently not in dispute. For example, in an elaborate treatise on the genitive, he is concerned with matters of language etiquette rather than grammaticality as he dictates appropriate usage in a broad range of cases including compound noun phrases, group genitives, poetic genitives, explanatory phrases interrupting the genitive, and double genitives. At one point he advocates the use of the periphrastic genitive (that is, the expression of the genitive using a prepositional phrase introduced by *of*), appealing to popular usage in his dismissal of the native English inflected form: "The English genitive has often an unpleasant sound; so that we daily make more use of the particle *of* to express the same relation"(1:166). Murray finds inappropriate such expressions as "in the army's name" and "the kingdom's condition," classing them in the same category as "the Lords' house" (for the idiomatically established "house of lords"). On another point of etiquette, Murray feels that the subject of a sentence should be repeated when different moods or tenses are found in its different clauses. He would improve *Anger glances into the breast of a wise man, but will rest only in the bosom of fools* either by making the tenses agree (*but rests only*) or by repeating the subject (*but it will rest only*). Similarly, he rewrites *Virtue is praised by many, and would be desired also, if her worth were really known* by changing *and would* to *and she would* (1:193).

The proper sequence of tenses was a subject of intense and often confusing debate among grammarians in the eighteenth century and Murray enters the lists with a rejection of usage—even respectable usage—when it violates grammatical and logical propriety. It is the grammarian, more specifically Murray himself, who determines grammatical propriety: "With regard to verbs in the infinitive mood, the practice of many writers, and some even of our most respectable writers, appears to be erroneous. They seem not to advert to the true principles, which influence the different tenses of this mood. We shall produce some rules on the subject, which, we presume, will be found perspicuous and accurate" (1:175).

When a construction violates Murray's strictures, it is harshly censured. For example, *I intend to have written*, permitted by some grammarians, is condemned by Murray for containing a verb, *intend*, which implies futurity, and the construction *to have written*, which he regards as the past tense of the infinitive and equates with Latin *scripsisse*, producing the paradoxical "I intend to produce hereafter an action or event, which has been already completed." Although elsewhere Murray rejects analogies with Latin and French and supports the notion that anomalies in language can arise and become sanctioned, in this case there can be no exceptions to the rule: "By admitting such violations of estabished grammatical distinctions, confusion would be introduced, the language would be disorganized, and the most eccentric systems of grammar might be advanced and plausibly supported." Murray's rejection of the perfect of the infinitive with any verb implying futurity is, he tells us, based on the grammatical authority of Harris, Lowth, Campbell, and Pickbourn, as well as "on the authority of reason and common sense" (1:176). Murray admits that some of his examples may be fallible, although the principles they illustrate are not. Some examples may be subject to question, or to alternate interpretation, but we are cautioned to remember, "a rule is not to be invalidated, because all the examples given under it, are not equally obvious, or even equally tenable" (1:180).

Sometimes the grammarian's judgments are equivocal. Murray is flexible regarding the placement of adverbs, permitting them before adjectives, after verbs, and between auxiliary and verb. But he does not permit them elsewhere. Thus he rejects *We always find them ready when we want them* in favor of *we find them always ready* (1:184). In some cases he merely states a mild preference for one of two competing forms: "It is a matter of indifference with respect to the pronoun *one another*, whether the preposition *of* be placed between the two parts of it, or before them both. We may say, 'They were jealous of one another;' or, 'They were jealous one of another;' but perhaps the former is better" (1:192). But even if a rule can be contradicted, it cannot be weakened. Murray says of exceptions to Rule XVIII, which states that conjunctions connect the same moods and tenses of verbs, and cases of nouns and pronouns, "If criticism should be able to produce some exceptions to this rule, we presume it will, nevertheless, be found a useful and proper general direction. Rules are not to be subverted because they admit of exceptions: *exceptio probat regulam*" (1:193–94).

In Rule XIX, Murray outlines a number of conditions for determining when the subjunctive should be used, and when the indicative. He attributes certain deviant constructions to ellipsis. For example, *We shall overtake him though he run* is to be regarded as a shortened form of *We shall overtake him though he should run*. Although he earlier rejected arguments based on historical analogy, here Murray appeals to the history of the language—or what he feels is the history of the language—to support his position. He generalizes on the nature of grammatical variation: "Almost all the irregularities, in the construction of any language, have arisen from the ellipsis of some words, which were originally inserted in the sentence, and made it regular." By restoring the original, lost forms, we "enable the student to examine the propriety of using them, by tracing the words in question to their proper origin and ancient connexions" (1:195). Later, in Rule XXI, Murray forbids any ellipsis that "would obscure the sentence, weaken its force, or be attended with an impropriety" (1:206). He concludes his discussion of the subjunctive by noting that popular usage does not yet follow the proposed distinctions between subjunctive and indicative (there is an implication here that speakers of English have strayed from rules set down for the original language), and by expressing some hope that the situation will change: "If these rules, which seem to form the true distinction between the subjunctive and the indicative moods in this tense, were adopted and established in practice, we should have, on this point, a principle of decision simple and precise, and readily applicable to every case that might occur." Murray recognizes that blindly following the rules he has set down may result in awkward constructions, and he advises his readers to rephrase rather than violate the grammatical rules for any reason: "It will, doubtless, sometimes happen, that, on this occasion, as well as on many other occasions, a strict adherence to grammatical rules, would render the language stiff and formal: but when cases of this sort occur, it is better to give the expression a different turn, than to violate grammar for the sake of ease, or even of elegance" (1:197). We are told elsewhere that the most correct form is not necessarily the form of choice: some forms, "though they are contended for as strictly correct, are not always the most eligible, on account of their unpleasant sound" (1:182).

Murray's syntax concludes with a series of parsing exercises, almost all of them based on moral sentences, literally *sententiae*, such as *Vice produces misery*; *Peace and joy are virtue's crown*; and *We are not unemployed*. Reason, analogy, the history of the language, and the opinions of other writers and grammarians all bow to the authority of piety in Murray's work, and it is this moral grounding of grammar that excuses, or perhaps accounts for, some of Murray's slipperiness in establishing grammatical certainty. Authorities are set up in one part of the grammar, only to be undercut elsewhere. The only argument of any import is the argument of the moment. If the examples do not satisfactorily illustrate the rule, then the examples, not the rule, are defective. No discernible standard of choice emerges from the conglomeration of rules, and it is no wonder students complained that the study of grammar bore no obvious connection with the workings of the language.

In a final "Address to Young Students," Murray returns to the connection between learning and virtue. The study of grammar is meant to provide the student with "an employment calculated to exclude those frivolous pursuits, and that love of ease and sensual pleasure, which enfeeble and corrupt the minds of many inconsiderate youth, and render them useless to society." According to Murray, education fails if it does not focus the mind of the student on God and the next world. He warns students not to "grow vain of your real or imaginary distinctions, and regard with contempt, the virtuous, unlettered mind." He also admonishes them not to let "your heart and principles be debased and poisoned, by the influence of corrupting and pernicious books, for which no elegance of composition can make amends. . . . [nor to] spend so much of your time in literary engagements, as to make them interfere with higher occupations, and lead you to forget, that pious and benevolent action is the great end of your being" (1:343–45).

Samuel Kirkham's *Grammar*

Lindley Murray's grammars had enormous success, being widely read and widely imitated. Many subsequent school texts openly credit Murray as their source. Samuel Kirkham's *English Grammar in Familiar Lectures* (1825) adapts Murray's rules to his own format, a self-teaching, "progressive" method requiring little or no questioning of the student by the teacher. Students will learn the principles of grammar by applying them in systematic parsing exercises, abolishing "the absurd practice . . . of causing learners to commit and recite definitions and rules without any simultaneous application of them to practical examples." Memorization will be facilitated by the application of the rules, and Kirkham states that it will now take only two months to learn what formerly required a year. Reacting to the absence of explanation in earlier grammars, and to the somber strain of piety and morality that had come to be associated with grammar more than any other school subject, Kirkham claims that the simplicity of his system will accelerate "the march of the juvenile mind in its advances in the path of science," while at the same time endeavoring "to render interesting and delightful a study which has hitherto been considered tedious, dry, and irksome." In a daring contrast to the tone of Murray's work, Kirkham characterizes his own as a method "in which pleasure is blended with the labors of the learner."[5]

Kirkham calls grammar the science of language. As the foundation of human communication, grammar is the sine qua non for all our knowledge: "Grammar is a leading branch of that learning which alone is capable of unfolding and maturing the mental powers" (p. 13). Kirkham is not referring to a mentalistic concept of human grammar, an innate and universal linguistic mechanism. Rather, he means the explicit, prescriptive rules of correct usage imposed by means of external authority. To Kirkham, the notion that a language can be spoken or written with propriety without the knowledge of such grammatical rules is absurd: "You have undoubtedly heard some persons assert, that they could speak and write correctly, or, at least, so as to be *understood*, without a knowledge of grammar. But . . . probably you have many hundred times witnessed the reverse of this assertion, for it is not universally true. From a want of grammatical knowledge, many often express their ideas in a manner so improper and obscure, as to render it impossible for any one to *understand* them."[6] He adds, in a later edition of his book, "Without the knowledge and application of grammar rules, it is impossible for any one to think, speak, read, or write with accuracy" (11th ed., p. 14).

Kirkham is not as heavy-handed as Murray in the areas of piety and religion, but these motifs are not absent from his work. He reminds us that the study of grammar is secular, and therefore subordinate, although he repeatedly stresses the importance of his subject: "Nothing of a secular nature can be more worthy of your attention . . . than the acquisition of grammatical knowledge" (p. 14). Unlike Murray, who wrote initially for a British audience, Kirkham is able to evoke American patriotism in recommending his grammar. Reminding his readers of the sacrifices of their forefathers, of the blood shed in the Revolution in order to achieve independence and freedom, Kirkham forbids "that you should ever be so unmindful of your duty to your country, to your Creator, to yourself, and to succeeding generations, as to be content to grovel in ignorance." Murray's puritanical tone is gone, but the message is similar: "Become learned and virtuous, and you will be great. Love God and serve him, and you will be happy" (p. 15).

The format of Kirkham's work is innovative. He presents a series of lectures, short essays on the parts of speech and the rules of syntax, giving examples and explaining them, providing exercises in parsing and noting the pertinent rules to be applied. As a pedagogic tool, there is a large foldout sheet containing a summary of these rules which the student is to use while parsing the exercises. Accompanying the text is a series of notes on philosophical grammar, in which Kirkham presents some shaky historical derivations for present-day parts of speech. He has an ambivalent attitude toward linguistic history. He stoutly rejects a historical approach to English grammar, regarding our ancestors as barbarians. Kirkham will have nothing to do with "the dubious and wildering track struck out by those innovators and visionaries who absurdly endeavor to teach modern English, by rejecting the authority and sanction of custom, and by conducting the learner back to the original combinations, and the detached, disjointed, and barbarous constructions of our progenitors" (pp. 30–31n). Yet he himself resorts to historical argument to demonstrate what he considers to be the growth of English adverbs from nouns and verbs, a process which, by making the language more concise, saved "an immense amount of time and breath" (p. 84n). He also states that students have no time for such historical treatment, and that it should be reserved for philosophical grammars, not school texts.

Kirkham sets as his highest authority "the established practice of the best speakers and writers." He defines established practice as "reputable, national, and present usage" (a trilogy of terms borrowed by many grammarians from George Campbell's *Philosophy of Rhetoric* [1776]), and the best speakers as "those who are deservedly in high estimation; speakers, distinguished for their elocution and other literary attainments, and writers, eminent for correct taste, solid matter, and refined manner." He reconciles the desirability for rationality in grammatical structure with the imperfect realities of usage: "In the grammar of a *perfect* language, no rules should be admitted, but such as are founded on fixed principles, arising out of the genius of that language and the nature of things; but our language being *im*-perfect, it becomes necessary, in a *practical* treatise, like this, to adopt some rules to direct us in the use of speech as regulated by *custom*." Kirkham regards language as both variable and progressive, subject to improvement and innovation. It is conventional, having been invented by human beings, and "it assumes any and every form which those who make use of it choose to give it." In an apparent acceptance of the status quo of language, he states that we must "take language as it *is*, and not as it *should be*, and bow to custom" (pp. 17–18).

Kirkham sees himself as neither innovator nor restorer. He does not claim to reform language into a rational mode better suited to its genius, nor does he long for a return to a golden age when usage was at a peak of refinement. But he does see his role as that of a corrector. Present custom is—paradoxically—not universally observed, and it is not only with examples of correct and false syntax that Kirkham hopes to get his students to emulate the best writers and speakers of the time. Appended to the grammar is a list of provincialisms and vulgarisms, labeled by area (New York and New England; Pennsylvania; Maryland, Virginia, Kentucky, Mississippi; and so on) and, in one case, by ethnic group (the Irish), and Kirkham prefaces his list by saying, "It is hoped these corrections will be found useful in the districts to which the various phrases respectively belong" (p. 205).

There are a few general errors that Kirkham proscribes, particularly a number of contractions that have since become perfectly standard. Along with such forms as *aint*, *haint* 'have not', and *baint* 'are not', Kirkham rejects *wont*, *wer'nt*, *woodent*, *mussent*, *izzent*, *hezzent*, and *whool* (the spelling, loosely phonetic, is basically eye dialect). Kirkham also censures the New York and New England forms *akst* 'asked', *hizzn* 'his', *natur* 'nature', *fortin* 'fortune', *heft* 'weight', *muss* 'disorder', *dump* 'unload', *foxy* 'reddish', and *stoop* 'porch'. His correction of *When ju git hum from Hafford?* to *When did you return from Hartford?* reveals a dislike of r-lessness, as well as disapproval of the running together of *did* and *you* and of the idiom *get home*. Kirkham proscribes a number of Pennsylvania usages, including *ornary* 'ordinary', *we bit* 'small piece', *ort* 'ought', *wisht* 'wish', *wunst* 'once', *spook* 'ghost', *wanity* 'vanity', and *disremember* 'do not remember'. He also rejects "southern" *bar* 'bear', *war* 'were', *mout* 'might', *shet* or *shut* 'rid', *gwine* 'going', *tote* 'carry', *carry* 'lead', *hopd* 'helped', and *cahoot* 'partnership'. Kirkham censures southern l-lessness, correcting *Who hoped you to sell it?* to *Who helped you to sell it?* And one of several faults he finds with the language of the Irish is a rather interesting advertisement for grammar education. Kirkham corrects *Let us be after pairsing a wee bit* to *Let us parse a little*.

Despite the evocation of science, reason, and description, and despite the differences in tone from Murray, his model, Kirkham manages to cast the study of language into the same basic categories of right and wrong that form the backbone of American grammar education. Piety is redirected toward the student's duty to God and country to learn, and the material to be learned is still, despite some changes in terminology and presentation, the same four basics of English grammar texts: orthography, etymology, syntax, and prosody.

Some Innovative Grammars

Operating from a more theoretical standpoint than most grammarians of the time, Joseph Neef, a follower of the progressive Swiss educator Pestalozzi, presented the work of his mentor to America. His *Sketch of a Plan and Method of Education* (Philadelphia, 1808) was one of the first strictly pedagogical works published in America. In it, Neef—who describes his own talents modestly: "The education of children and rearing of vegetables, are the only occupations for which I feel any aptitude" (p. 2)—outlines an inductive method for learning all the old things in a new way. Proceeding in the minutest gradation from point to point, the pupil will leave nothing behind without having mastered it. Neef recommends to the teacher Pestalozzi's practice: "Not to introduce any thing into his pupil; but to develope what he finds in him" (p. 6). For example, in learning reading and writing, the pupil will, after suitable exercises in drawing, discover how to write. After all, Neef tells us, "the inventor of the writing art, *wrote* before he *read*; *and so shall we*" (p. 48). It is anybody's guess what the pupils engaged in this activity will devise: "Perhaps Cadmus's genius inhabits the head of some future pupil of mine; perhaps the Chinese system will be re-contrived; perhaps we shall hit upon the syllabical method." But Neef will not allow his pupils to continue uncorrected in their vagaries, for he believes in an absolute truth independent of the accidents of induc-tion. Implying a lack of judgment on the part of the Chinese and Cher-okee as well as in his own students, Neef adds, "These two latter schemes, however, if they should be resorted to, would be soon aban-doned, because we should soon be convinced of their inconveniency and impracticability" (pp. 49–50). Induction, it seems, is useful only to a point.

Rejecting the past as uncivilized, Neef, a native of Alsace, advises America to seize the chance to reform its alphabet and orthography. He recognizes that such a task must be the work of a nation, not an indi-vidual, and he appeals to the spirit of the Revolution in his plea: "People of America, sole and only sovereigns of a free nation on this globe . . . for you it is to discard those nonsensical remains of an ignorant and barbarous antiquity; to assimilate instruction to the mild spirit of your laws . . . abolish the scourge and rack, and torture of harmless child-hood. . . . let the instruction of infancy be conducted with the same wisdom that directs your government" (pp. 55–56). Neef advises the selection of a committee to determine the necessary number of sounds, and to commission geometricians to design a totally new alphabet. Fu-ture generations will be grateful for this revision: "By comparing the plain and apt characters which you have created, with the Gothic, bar-barous, and inexplicable hieroglyphics, that they will find in your actual books, they will be fully convinced that you are their greatest benefac-tors" (p. 58).

Neef also recommends a reform in grammatical instruction. He would begin by rejecting the traditional terminology, replacing it with his own. Grammar is to consist of three parts: ideology (roughly, seman-tics), lexigraphy (morphology, or, as it was called then, etymology), and syntax. Neef requires only four parts of speech, to be named for their functions: substances (nouns), adjectives, conjunctives (verbs), and super-adjectives (adverbs). His syntax is to be based on reason, for "in speech, as well as in nature, nothing exists without reason." Syntax consists of two parts, a universal general syntax, which "is absolutely independent of all human convention, since it consists in expressing our ideas in the same succession as they are necessarily conceived by our thinking power. Thus, when I say, for instance, God is just, my speech is conformable to general syntax; because I express my ideas in the same successive order, in which my mind necessarily conceives them." Particular syntax is to cover "all the cases, in which our usual language deviates from the rules of general syntax" (pp. 73–74).

Neef's suggestions met with mixed reactions in America. He himself established a number of schools, including one in Robert Owen's experimental community in New Harmony, Indiana, and perhaps his most famous pupil was Admiral David Farragut, the Civil War hero. Goold Brown, himself a prolific grammarian, treated Neef's ideas with derision and scorn, but others, like the textbook writer Roswell C. Smith, were more open to them. In *Smith's New Grammar: English Grammar on the Productive System* (Hartford, 1842), a popular textbook in the mid-nineteenth century, the author credits the Swiss and German Productive School with embodying the best of all previous educational systems, including that of Pestalozzi. Claiming to offer more pedagogical innovations than Kirkham, but in fact following Kirkham closely in terms of actual content, Smith favors Neef's inductive method, regarding the child "as an agent capable of collecting, and originating, and producing most of the ideas which are necessary for its education, when presented with the objects or the facts from which they may be derived" (p. 5), an idea that comes directly from Neef. For Smith, the inductive method involves a painstakingly programmed approach to grammatical rules, with terms being defined at every stage of the process. But the notions of grammar in this work are no different from those of previous grammars, no mention being made of Neef's curious ideas of self-discovery and reform. Smith, like his predecessors, copies entire passages from the books of others without any attribution. His examples contain references to the rules they illustrate, but they are otherwise unremarkable reflections of grammar book sentences, displaying the piety, morality, emphasis on hard work and education that had become standard.

As early as 1841 Robert Gordon Latham, physician, philologist, and professor of English language and literature at University College, London, warned against the assumption made by the common schools that the study of prescriptive grammar correlated with improvement in student writing. In *The English Language* he asserts that usage is learned not from rules but from habit, not in school but in conversation. Echoing Alexander Pope, Latham makes the even more daring claim that "in Language, *whatever is, is right*" (2d ed., London, 1848, p. xvii). For him, language is not bound by logic; usage can change prescriptive rules. Grammar must be studied as grammar, not as something else. We must examine how words and phrases have been used and study the amount of latitude language can accommodate and still remain language. According to Latham, grammar as an art is only required in the acquisition of a foreign language.

In his *Elementary English Grammar* (3d ed., Cambridge, Massachusetts, 1854), Latham criticizes the work of his predecessors, whose grammars "either contain that which is incorrect, and better not known at all, or something that was known before, and would have been known independent of any grammatical lesson whatsoever." Adopting a more scientific and philological approach, Latham attempts to replace rules with principles, authority with demonstration. His work is specifically intended for those "desirous of either knowing the history, or of reasoning on the principles of the English language." Students requiring simply to master the English language have no need of his, or any, grammatical text: if they "merely mean to speak and write with average correctness, they can get what they want without any grammar at all; viz. by attending to the language of the best sort of their acquaintance, and by applying to some good authority in doubtful cases" (p. vii). This book, addressed to the understanding, not the memory, is descriptive in principle, providing paradigms, examples, and discussions of the basic parts of speech, although syntax is presented in the form of rules. Latham stresses the history of the English language, giving examples of its older forms and relating them to present ones, and tries to provide a more scientific account of phonetics than the average school text had done. But Latham's work is addressed more to the specialist than the common school pupil, and his influence on school grammar is minimal.

A more popular text, *A Grammar of the English Language* (Philadelphia, 1863), one of a series of schoolbooks written by Samuel S. Greene, who was professor of didactics at Brown University, does reflect some of the newer thinking in educational methodology that began to appear in the second half of the nineteenth century. Greene's earlier *Elements of English Grammar* (1853) was "constructed upon the obvious principle that what is *seen* by a child reaches the understanding at once." Greene disapproves of memorization, preferring to demonstrate his rules. Grammar, for him, must be verifiable "by direct appeals to the usage of standard authors." They, and not the grammarian, are the source of authority: "It is not the province of the grammarian to legislate in matters of language. . . . He does not *make* the rules and definitions which express these analogies; they had already existed, and were obeyed,—unconsciously, it is true—long before he formed them into words and published them." Like many who wrote before him, Greene speaks of the grammarian as a discoverer, not an inventor or dictator. The grammarian's statements on language are not "authoritative *because* he has uttered them, but simply because they are just and faithful interpretations of the already existing laws which underlie and pervade the language itself" (pp. iii–v).

In making explicit the unconscious rules obeyed by native speakers, Greene attempts to characterize the structure of the sentence in terms he calls elements and ranks. Preferring to deal with ideas rather than simply forms, he begins with the notion of the sentence as the basic unit of communication, consisting of the expression of a single thought. The sentence is composed of elements which in turn are made up of words. Elements of the sentence are classified according to rank, an indication of dependency; thus the subject and verb are elements of the first rank, prepositional phrases elements of the second rank, and so on. Despite these modern-sounding structuralist touches, Greene's grammar begins like all the rest: "English Grammar treats of the principles and usages of the English language; it teaches us to speak and write it correctly," and it contains the four basic elements of grammar: orthography, etymology, syntax, and versification (p. 13). Some of the examples Greene uses are moralistic; many are classical or pseudoclassical; still others are descriptions of nature. Religious and aphoristic examples are minimized, and many examples are taken from the standard literary canon as illustrations of proper, not improper, usage. But Greene's innovations, like those of Kirkham, Neef, and Smith, do little to alter the basic content of grammars established by Lowth and Murray.

Goold Brown: Grammarian's Grammarian

In the *Institutes of English Grammar* (1825), Goold Brown, an autodidact who read Greek at the age of five and left a career as a merchant to become a teacher, portrayed his role as one of language educator, not legislator: "It is not the business of the grammarian *to give law* to language, but to *teach it*, agreeably to the best usage." Brown's stance is moderate. He claims to provide no new ideas about the English language, although he does intend to correct misconceptions about it. He is quick to challenge those who would mold the language to suit their theories. Declaring himself opposed to "fantastic innovation, and to a pertinacious adherence to the quaint peculiarities of ancient usage," Brown criticizes the prose as well as the thinking of his colleagues: "Correctness of language and neatness of style are as rarely to be found in grammars as in other books" (pp. iii–v).

In his encyclopedic *Grammar of English Grammars* (1851), the product of twenty-three years of labor, and itself an example of inexcusable wordiness, Brown tried to provide the most comprehensive treatment of the subject yet attempted. In doing so, he managed to find fault with almost every one of his contemporaries. Commenting, "I have turned the eyes of Grammar, in an especial manner, upon the conduct of her own household" (10th ed., New York, 1878, p. 143), Brown dismisses Roswell Smith's Productive System as "'*productive*' of no good to any body but the author and his publishers." While Brown admits that a student can memorize all the rules of grammar, and still know very little about the art, he does not see this as a valid argument against the study of the subject. Memorization, for Brown, is the only adequate way to master the principles of language. He rejects Smith's inductive method: "The chief argument of these inductive grammarians is founded on the principle, that children cannot be instructed by means of any words which they do not perfectly understand. If this principle were strictly true, children could never be instructed by words at all" (pp. 102–08).

Brown's argument with Samuel Kirkham was more personal. In an exchange of reviews in various periodicals, Kirkham responded to Brown's attacks by calling him a knave, a liar, and a pedant. The last of these charges was certainly a true one, for in the eleven hundred pages of his magnum opus Brown refers in one way or another to almost every extant treatise on English grammar, well known or obscure, establishing himself as the unchallenged grammarian of English grammars, if nothing else. Brown criticizes everyone. While he is respectful of Webster's lexicographical accomplishments, he does not hesitate to point out that Webster's grammars were unpopular and that Webster changed his mind on major grammatical points with each new grammar he published. Brown says of him, "It is impossible to place any firm reliance upon the authority of a man who contradicts himself so much" (p. 133). Brown acknowledges Lindley Murray's influence on his own work but reminds his readers that Murray was a compiler and imitator who had no special knowledge of his subject and who managed to perpetuate many serious misconceptions about the language.

Believing that the principles of grammar must be so mastered that they become intuitive, "so as to regulate . . . language before it proceeds from the lips or the pen," Brown feels that only the parsing of what is right and the correcting of what is wrong are suitable textbook methods. Brown subscribes wholeheartedly to the doctrine of usage, and, paradoxically, like many who do, he finds much in the language of his day that is in need of correction: "With respect to our present English, I know not whether any other improvement ought to be attempted, than the avoiding and correcting of those improprieties and unwarrantable anomalies by which carelessness, ignorance, and affectation, are ever tending to debase it, and the careful teaching of its true grammar, according to its real importance in education." And he finds much of the grammar of his day to be equally unsatisfactory: "Of the quackery which is now so prevalent, what can be a more natural effect, than a very general contempt for the study of grammar?" (p. v).

Brown is a philological conservative. Rollo Lyman describes him as the last major grammarian in the nineteenth century to insist on the treatment of grammar as an art rather than a science. Although Brown does speak of the science of letters, and he does give a brief account of the historical development of the English language, he ignores all of the major developments in philology of his day. He maintains an aristocratic view of language, arguing that grammar does not precede, but only follows, literacy. Speech, for Brown, is always subordinate to writing, and he takes a dim view of language varieties that have no written codes: "Over any fugitive colloquial dialect, which has never been fixed by visible signs, grammar has no control; . . . the speaking which the art or science of grammar teaches, is exclusively that which has reference to a knowledge of letters" (p. 22).

For Brown, letters provide the opportunity for stabilizing a language: "A language, indeed, after its proper form is well fixed by letters, must resist all introduction of foreign idioms, or become corrupted" (p. 129). However, fixing the form of the language is not as simple as it might seem. Of the usage doctrine, Brown says, "The ultimate principle, then, to which we appeal, as the only true standard of grammatical propriety, is that species of custom which critics denominate GOOD USE; that is, present, reputable, general use." Unfortunately, Brown admits, this is easier to say than do, for the definition of good use has proved elastic in the hands of grammarians: "Good use is that which is neither ancient nor recent, neither local nor foreign, neither vulgar nor pedantic; and it will be found that no few have in some way or other departed from it, even while they were pretending to record its dictates." Brown is again critical of his colleagues: grammars are continually being written, and while new ideas are added to our linguistic store, old errors are left standing, and "positions that were never true, and sentences that were never good English, have been published and republished under different names, till in our language grammar has become the most ungrammatical of all studies" (p. 31).

Brown cites Noah Webster's comment on the effectiveness of his fellow grammarians:

> From all the observations I have been able to make, I am convinced the dictionaries and grammars which have been used in our seminaries of learning, for the last forty or fifty years, are so incorrect and imperfect, that they have introduced or sanctioned more errors than they have amended; in other words, had the people of England and of these States been left to learn the pronunciation and construction of their vernacular language solely by tradition, and the reading of good authors, the language would have been spoken and written with more purity than it has been and now is, by those who have learned to adjust their language by the rules which dictionaries and grammars prescribe.[7]

If the usage of the grammarians, and of the best and the brightest writers and speakers, is suspect, so is that of the least and the dullest, for that is how Brown views the language of the common people. He violently disagrees with Webster's theory that the language of the common folk preserves the true and original genius of English: "The great mass of uneducated people are lamentably careless of what they utter, both as to the matter and the manner; and no few seem naturally prone to the constant imitation of low example, and some, to the practice of every abuse of which language is susceptible" (Brown, p. 33).

Brown rejects William S. Cardell's praise of the unlettered: "That people who make no pretensions to learning, can furnish better models or instructions than 'the most enlightened scholars,' is an opinion which ought not to be disturbed by argument," and he accuses Webster of "supposing the true principles of every language to be best observed and kept by the illiterate." He cites Webster's comments in the *Philosophical Grammar*: "Having suggested that the learned must follow the practice of the populace, because they cannot control it [Webster] says:

It is commonly supposed that the tendency of this practice of unlettered men is to *corrupt the language*. But the fact is directly the reverse. . . . nineteen twentieths of all the corruptions of our language, for five hundred years past, have been introduced by authors—men who have made alterations in particular idioms which they did not understand. . . . The tendency of unlettered men is to *uniformity*—to *analogy*; and so strong is this disposition, that the common people have actually converted some of our irregular verbs into regular ones. . . . It is a fortunate thing for language that these *natural* principles generally prevail over arbitrary and artificial rules. [*Philosophical Grammar*, p. 119]

Brown apparently feels that these words are sufficiently damning to undermine Webster's democratic position and to demonstrate the correctness of Brown's own aristocratic stance, for he turns from his assault on the uneducated to an attack on those with pretensions to learning. If the authority of the learned is to be the standard of usage, how are we to determine the legitimacy of a given authority? For this, we are told, "there is no tribunal but the mass of readers, of whom few perhaps are very competent judges." While an author's reputation may be influential, "every man is at liberty to form his own opinion, and to alter it whenever better knowledge leads him to think differently" (p. 34). This doctrine of the marketplace is later rejected when Brown attacks the successful grammars of Kirkham and Smith, and it is tempered here with the caution that those who are most in need of correction are least able to judge the worth of the available authorities: "To two thirds of the community, one grammar is just as good as an other; because they neither know, nor wish to know, more than may be learned from the very worst" (p. 51).

According to Brown, the acquisition of taste and refinement in language is a perpetual struggle for many of those he regards as potential clients. Catering to those who wish to acquire the trappings of the leisure class as well as those wishing to preserve their language from the threat of decay, Brown recommends the study of grammar as the foundation for "a graceful and easy conversation in the private circle, a fluent and agreeable delivery in public speaking, a ready and natural utterance in reading, a pure and elegant style in composition." The mastery of grammar will not guarantee accomplishment in these areas, but ignorance of the subject will assure failure. Appealing to middle-class aspirations, he exclaims, "How can he be a man of refined literary taste, who cannot speak and write his native language grammatically?" (p. 96).

Brown cites the Quaker moralist Jonathan Dymond's argument, in *Essays on Morality* (1829), that the study of grammatical rules has little to do with the production of language: "Men learn their own language by heart, and not by rules. . . . A compiler of grammar first observes these habits, and then makes his rules: but if a person is himself familiar with the habits, why study the rules?" Dymond does not object to philosophical grammar as a science, but he does question its usefulness in the curriculum of the common schools: "The objection is, to the system of attempting to teach children formally that which they will learn practically without teaching." Brown admits the validity of Dymond's argument, but only to a point. Ideally, explicit grammatical rules should reflect a person's innate linguistic knowledge, but unfortunately the forces of corruption are such in our society that students must be armed with grammatical knowledge to prevent linguistic decay: "As they cannot always be preserved from hearing vulgar and improper phraseology, or from seeing it in books, they cannot otherwise be guarded from improprieties of diction, than by a knowledge of the rules of grammar" (pp. 97–98).

Fowler's College Grammar

In his monumental history *The American Language*, H. L. Mencken calls William Chauncey Fowler's *English Grammar: The English Language in Its Elements and Forms* (New York, 1868) the first college English language text. Lowth's *Short Introduction* had been in use in American universities, but Fowler's book, written a century later, was the first designed specifically for that purpose. Fowler was a Congregationalist pastor who taught chemistry at Middlebury College and rhetoric and oratory at Amherst. Married to a daughter of Noah Webster, he edited the University edition of Webster's Dictionary. In the preface to his *English Grammar*, Fowler notes the absence of competing texts, recommending that the study of English should not be confined to the lower schools: "Besides what it has in common with other languages, is there not in it enough of inherent interest, enough of difficulty, enough of fruit in disciplinal influence and practical knowledge to entitle it to a place in colleges by the side of the Classical languages as a part of a liberal education? 'The grammar of a language,' says Locke, 'is sometimes to be studied by a grown man'" (pp. xi–xii). It is clear from Fowler's remarks that the place of English language study is not yet firmly established in any curriculum, upper or lower. Fowler sees his book serving as an aid to teachers as well as students, to "help to give breadth and exactness to their views, and thus qualify them to impart oral instruction to their pupils who study some smaller work." The study of grammar is also suitable for those in professional life: "Unless men, at least occasionally, bestow their attention upon the science and the laws of the language, they are in some danger, amid the excitements of professional life, of losing the delicacy of their taste and giving sanction to vulgarisms, or to what is worse" (pp. xii–xiii).

Fowler regards grammar as both science and art, citing John Stuart Mill on the difference between the two: "Science is a collection of truths; art is a body of rules or directions for the conduct." As a science, grammar is "a system of principles and a collection of facts peculiar to the English language, together with those which are common, also, to other languages." As an art, it is "a system of rules for the practical application of these principles to the English language." The student who applies these principles in writing and speaking makes "science the minister of art" and uses the language correctly (p. 232).

Fowler sees a need for controlling the growth of language as well as for the cultivation and preservation of a correct taste in usage. The American language is irrepressible: "As our countrymen are spreading westward across the continent, and are brought into contact with other races, and adopt new modes of thought, there is some danger that, in the use of their liberty, they may break loose from the laws of the English language, and become marked not only by one, but by a thousand Shibboleths. Now, in order to keep the language of a nation one, the leading men in the greater or smaller communities, the editors of periodicals, and authors generally, should exercise the same guardian care over it which they do over the opinions which it is used to express; and, for this purpose, they should be familiar with works which treat of its analogies and idioms, that they may understand what are the laws of normal and of abnormal growth, and by their own example and influence encourage only that which is strictly legitimate" (pp. xiii–xiv).

Keeping with this line of reasoning, Fowler uses a sort of germ theory of language decay to warn against the dangers of including examples of false syntax in grammar books (ironically his own grammar also contains such examples): "By becoming familiar with incorrect forms of speech, one is in danger of falling into the use of them" (p. xvi). Language, for Fowler, is necessarily imperfect because of its basic subjectivity: "The term in a proposition, if it has any meaning in the mind of the speaker, has a different one from what it has in the mind of the hearer" (p. 41). Furthermore, language is constantly growing and decaying. Old words die and new ones are born. The mere changing of a government assures a change in the language. Fowler appreciates the value of variation in language and argues for the need to study dialects to understand linguistic history. He does not see dialectal differences between the better English and American writers and feels that the speech differences that do exist are minimal. He sees the fear that Americans will speak not "English but an American language" as diminishing, and he feels that the influence of schools, common textbooks, and the press "will help to keep the people of the United States one in language as one in government" (pp. 127–28). Fowler cites the optimistic view of the philologist Thomas Watts, Keeper of the Printed Books at the British Museum: "Our solid and increasing establishments in America, where we less dread the innovations of barbarisms, promise a superior stability and duration to the English language," and he predicts that English will become the universal language of the future (p. 135).

Fowler voices his suspicion of the doctrine of usage, preferring the more informed opinion of language experts: "Usage is not uniform. There is ancient usage and present usage, general usage and local usage. Custom or usage, therefore, in given cases . . . must be an uncertain guide, because it is divided; and even if it were undivided, it might be contrary to other important considerations" (p. 228). In the matter of spelling reform, he favors phonetic respelling, the dropping of unnecessary silent letters, the retention of such letters when they are etymologically significant, and a general preservation of analogy, recognizing that these principles often conflict.

In addition to extensive treatment of the sounds of English, its history (here Fowler includes material on Indo-European), and the parts of speech, syntax, and prosodic forms of the language, Fowler discusses logic and rhetoric and provides both a subject index and a detailed index of words discussed. But given the completeness of the treatment of the subject matter, and the occasional intrusion of relatively up-to-date ideas about language, Fowler's book remains a traditional school grammar. His syntax rules are couched in categorical terms: they *are*, *should*, or *must* be obeyed. He hints at spelling reform, but refuses to decide cases of doubtful spelling one way or another. Concluding his discussion of spelling concerns, he says, "These instances are brought forward, not for the purpose of deciding any doubtful questions in orthography, but only to exhibit the considerations which the orthographist must take into view in order to come to a correct decision" (p. 231).

The Schoolmasters' Failure

In the century that passed between the work of Bishop Lowth and that of Goold Brown and William Chauncey Fowler, the scope of school grammars had increased considerably. New topics were added, and old ones were treated in what, in Brown's case, amounted to encyclopedic detail. Attention was paid to new methods of education and new discoveries in linguistics, and increasing concern was voiced over the effectiveness of the presentation of the material. But the basic content of the texts remained the same. This is not to say that they presented a monolithic uniformity. Differences were often quite significant. Terms and categories were discarded or invented, positions on spelling and syntax varied, doctrines of usage, analogy, and reason were asserted, rejected, or ignored. But the rules of language behavior, as a body of doctrine, survived unscathed, and the position of the grammarian as lawgiver went unchallenged. In 1927 the American linguist Charles C. Fries noted, "Even a hundred years of the historical method in linguistic scholarship has failed to affect in any marked degree the common grammatical ideas and ideals of the general public," and Robert C. Pooley agreed in 1934 that "Eighteenth-century theories of language resulted in attitudes and specific rules concerning usage which became fixed and arbitrary in nineteenth-century schoolbooks, and which still persist in the textbooks of today in total disregard for the objective facts of English usage."[8]

Even when grammarians claimed to be cataloguing the behavior of the best speakers and writers, or serving as transmitters and preservers of the language of the average American, their authority, and that of their predecessors, lent to grammar an air of the mystical. Students and teachers tended to approach the subject carefully and timidly, and their expectations of finding in the study of grammar a difficult and obscure doctrine that could not easily be connected to actual human discourse were often confirmed.

The appeal to religion, morality, or patriotism that underlay almost all the school grammars published in the era we have surveyed showed little sign of weakening. Even in Fowler, the most scientific of the school grammars, we find buried among the more mundane examples of syntax, such as *I shall be in Boston next month* and *Passengers are forbidden standing on the platform of the cars*, others which preserve a tone of reverence and piety for church, state, the ethical life, and pseudoclassical culture: *In Federal money a dime is ten cents*; *Virtue rewards her followers*; *Christ, and him crucified, is the head, and the only head of the Church*; *Brutus killed Caesar*; and *He eats temperately*. This pietistic tone reinforced the authority of the rules of grammar as they were presented and contributed to the aura of reverence and fear that surrounds grammatical study in the schools to this day.

The effect of the schoolmasters on the American language is difficult if not impossible to measure. Certainly they influenced some students to make their own language use conform to that advocated by the textbook and the teacher. But if observations of the teaching of grammar in the twentieth century are any indication, such instruction did less to reform the language of the mass of students than it did to instill in them a conviction that their own usage could never really match up to a linguistic ideal which in many cases they could not even understand. Infinitives continue to be split, prepositions end sentences, subjects and verbs fail to agree, tense sequences go unobserved, *shall* and *will* remain interchangeable, new words continue to be invented, and, to borrow a phrase from our motion picture ratings code, the idiom and grammar of our best writers and speakers are often not suitable for pre-teenagers.

In the early twentieth century the failure of grammar courses to improve the usage of schoolchildren led to their abandonment by the educational system. They were replaced by an emphasis on speech and composition, but this did little to calm the well-established public sense that the English language was not being used as well as it should be, or as well as it used to be. After a while, grammar was reinstated in the curriculum. It has since been abandoned and reinstated several times, and at the present time, in response to what is called a back-to-basics movement, prescriptive grammar is once again felt to be a necessary and proper tool of language engineering.

The cyclical popularity of school grammar in our educational system may partly be a result of the misconception of grammar as a body of etiquette rules to be learned and applied rather than as a body of knowledge to be studied for its own sake. We do not teach biology in the schools so that students can be better able to use their bodies. We teach it so they can understand how bodies work. But we do not feel the same way about English language instruction. While linguistics has made tremendous strides in the nineteenth and twentieth centuries as a theoretical and descriptive science, school grammar continues to treat language as normative. For educators, linguistics as a science is useful only insofar as it can be applied to the standardization of language. Schools seek to regulate the language of students in the same way they regulate the length of their hair or the kind of clothing they will be permitted to wear in the school building.

The attempts of nineteenth-century language teaching in the schools created, or rather, perpetuated, an attitude toward correctness in language that students, teachers, and writers have had a difficult time living with and living up to. The result for some must be a sense of linguistic insecurity which results in the creation of new linguistic variants as speakers and writers attempt to imitate prescribed forms or avoid proscribed ones. These new "errors" unwittingly add to the reformational zeal of the schoolmasters. Other students no doubt shy away from a public demonstration of their language use, refusing, in the classroom, to read, write, or talk, lest they subject themselves to continued censure.

Like those patriots who advocated a Federal Language, the schoolmasters and grammarians did more to affect attitudes about language than they did to change the actual course of American language behavior. The proliferation of literally hundreds of school grammar texts in the nineteenth century virtually assured that no one system would become the Federal grammar to be used in every schoolroom in the country. But despite the absence of a uniform text and the evident inadequacy of the methods of instruction used by teachers, the common schools managed to establish in the minds of Americans the inherent connection between language and morality. Many students learned to hate or fear their grammar lessons. And many of the nineteenth-century commentators on usage rejected formal grammar instruction, partly in reaction to their own classroom experiences and partly because it had proved unable to schoolmaster the language, to assure the kind of language standardization they deemed necessary for American cultural and political supremacy. But what most people did learn in school was that there was right and wrong in matters of usage, and that language was subject to a higher law. One of the clearest statements of this grass-roots attitude is the following excerpt from an examination paper received ten years ago in an undergraduate grammar course at Eastern Illinois University. The question called for an evaluation of descriptive and prescriptive grammar:

> I think I support prescriptivism. I believe that some words are absolutely unacceptable in any situation. I think there should be an accepted way of speaking and deviation would not be tolerated. I believe in a set of absolute values. I believe there is one right and wrong for everyone. Perhaps what I think is right is not what you think is right but in the final analysis that isn't going to matter. What God thinks is right is what really matters and He doesn't have one right for you and one right for me.

8 Grammar and Good Taste: Part I

A number of years ago a certain brand of cigarettes was advertised as tasting good, "like a cigarette should." Many people felt the use of the preposition *like* in place of the conjunctive *as* was a serious violation of the grammatical integrity of the language, and strong complaints were lodged against the slogan. The cigarette manufacturers capitalized on the publicity generated by these complaints with a television commercial campaign in which they asked the musical question, "What do you want, good grammar or good taste?" The choice for viewers was a clear one. They could identify with the actor representing good grammar, a stereotypically pedantic, puritanical, and ineffectual language purist, or with the young, attractive, happy, and energetic singers and dancers who personified good taste. This dichotomy between grammar and taste was created primarily to sell tobacco. But the glorious defeat of artificial grammatical prescriptions by the democratic representatives of realistic language use had additional significance. It was a rare public display of strong negative reaction to the high-handed purism of the commentaries on English usage that we will look at in these last chapters. These commentaries played a major role in the nineteenth- and twentieth-century attempts to shape the American language into a vehicle suitable for the transmission of the refined thoughts to which the writers of such guides felt we should all aspire. And they produced in the democratic-minded, socially ambitious American people a sense of linguistic insecurity manifested at once by a desire to improve the quality of their linguistic production and a resentment of the purists' assumption that their language was not good enough for admission to polite society.

Usage guides have existed for some time. One of the most influential, for a modern language, was that of Claude Favre de Vaugelas, one of the first members of the French Academy, *Remarqves sur la langve françoise* (1659). This work, more known about than known by writers on English, establishes the genre with an appeal to usage and a case-by-case discussion of linguistic problems that includes points of spelling, syntax, diction, and language etiquette. Vaugelas insists that the usage of a group, not that of an individual, makes linguistic law, but for him usage is a severely limited term. There is good usage and bad usage; the former is the language of the elite and the latter, unfortunately, is the language of the majority. Usage, or more narrowly, good usage, is established in France by the royal court and the best writers of the age: "It is the manner of speech of the best of the Court, together with the manner of writing of the best of our contemporary authors."[1] In no way does Vaugelas perceive usage to be democratically based:

> From this great Principle, that *good Usage* is the Master of our Language, it follows that they are mistaken who give all authority to the people, misled by the incorrectly understood example of the Latin tongue, which, as they see it, recognized the people as its Sovereign. [Biv recto]

In fact the undemocratic foundations of the French language were so clearly felt that during the French Revolution attempts were made to revise the sociolinguistic structure of the new republic. A report by the Comité de Salut Public in 1794 called for the destruction of "the 'distinctions of nobility,' that is to say the reservations and privileges in the linguistic interactions of the citizenry." This was to be accomplished by a massive campaign to educate the people in the use of the French language. The report continues, "It is necessary to popularize the language, to destroy this aristocracy of speech which threatens to establish a polite nation in the midst of a barbarous one. . . . Let us therefore also revolutionize our language."[2] The linguistic revolution which was to spread standard French to the provinces and among the middle and lower classes called for the publishing of all laws in French. Official teachers of French were to be appointed by the newly created centralized national educational system, and an official national grammar text was to be selected for the schools. (Ironically, an inquiry made after the Revolution revealed that three-quarters of the nation's thirty-eight million citizens already possessed an adequate knowledge of the standard language, and the official grammar chosen by the State was one that had served the schools of the old regime as well.) Language uniformity was imposed in France both by law and through the continued efforts of the French Academy, which had been founded about 1630. Because of these language planning efforts the French have come to think of themselves as a nation of grammarians concerned with the purity of their national tongue. Although standard French spread as an administrative and literary language at the expense of local dialects and provincial languages, it has recently been argued that the French language never became as fixed and conservative as the French would like to believe. The linguistic centralism imposed by the Revolutionary language reform is even now being shaken by renewed interest in regional culture and language in Brittany and Provence, and French linguists have begun to study dialectal variation in present-day French.[3]

We have already seen that the idea of the legal or quasi-legal imposition of linguistic uniformity was distasteful to the British and Americans. Their reaction to the teaching of grammar in the schools has also shown a suspicion of constituted authority or at least a reluctance to grasp the connection between the material being taught and the English language as they know and use it. But the more informal guides to usage, no matter how cranky or censorious, have proved popular since their inception. They seem both to feed on and calm our sense of linguistic insecurity. English speakers have traditionally reached for these books as they have for the other trappings of politeness and culture sought after by a largely middle-class society. And those who found even books on usage to be too threatening could send for the home study English improvement courses that were advertised in the back sections of newspapers alongside ads for resorts and patent remedies. The language historian Sterling Leonard calls the publicity for such courses "no better than . . . those medical advertisements which all decent papers rigidly exclude, that inquire: 'Do you ever have a burning sensation in the left ear?' . . . and thus proceed to terrify healthy young people into swallowing whatever pill or drug the advertiser has to sell."[4] In a description in the *Christian Science Monitor* (1926) of such a home study English course devised and marketed by Grace Miller, of Boston, the discontent that people may feel about their own language use is reinforced. Using an analogy with another cultural acquisition activity of the upwardly mobile in society, music lessons, Miller implies that good speech cannot be acquired without proper instruction: "Learning to speak by ear is like learning to play by ear. It is both superficial and dependent."[5] Writing almost three hundred years earlier, Vaugelas succinctly states the fear that fuels our linguistic insecurity: "One incorrect word is all that is needed for a person to be scorned by a group" (*Remarqves*, Ci recto).

A concern with the purification of the English language led to proposals for its reform on both sides of the Atlantic. Although our purpose in this study is to deal mainly with attempts to alter the course of American English, it is important to realize that questions of usage in the nineteenth century often involved British as well as American writers. In order to explain such twentieth-century American phenomena as the *Harper Dictionary of Contemporary Usage* or the writings of self-styled language guardians, which continue to be produced in great number, it will be necessary to deal with a tradition developed both in England and America. There are three types of usage regulation that we will consider. In the first, reformers call for a few narrowly defined changes. For example, the British novelist and inveterate letter writer Horace Walpole, influenced by a classical model, suggests in 1785 adding -*a* or -*i* to our nouns as plural markers.[6] And Theodore Roosevelt, in 1906, orders the adoption of spellings recommended by the Simplified Spelling Board. In the second type of usage reform, such writers as Dean Henry Alford and Richard Grant White comment in the tradition of Vaugelas on a broad variety of language questions, often engaging in debates or controversies in the press and then distilling their arguments in the form of more complete books on usage. Related to these are the advice columns or letters to the editor appearing in popular journals. Here writers usually deal with discrete problems: the determination of what is proper (is *different from* preferable to *different than* or *different to*?) or the recommendation of a specific change (should we adopt a common gender pronoun for the third person singular?). These questions are often dealt with in the larger commentaries as well. A third type of usage regulation is found in the lists of common errors promulgated without comment or explanation, for example the collection of words to be avoided that was developed by William Cullen Bryant when he was editor of the *New York Evening Post*, or the little book of proscribed words and phrases published by Ambrose Bierce, *Write It Right*. While the usage commentaries often contained elaborate arguments and were aimed at an educated class of readers presumed already to be familiar with questions of correctness and concerned with the perfection of an already accomplished style, the lists of common errors presented no rationale to explain their judgments and only a bare minimum of commentary, and they catered to an audience of lower socioeconomic status. Such works played on the fears of this group that their language would give away their lower social origins or, what was felt to be an even worse linguistic fate, reveal them to be no more skilled in English than newly arrived immigrants.

Some Calls for Specific Modification of English

In addition to changes in spelling and in the alphabet, some of which were discussed earlier, we often find calls for the grammatical reorganization of the language. Thomas Cooke, known for his translations of Hesiod, suggests, in 1729, that strong verbs—that is, those verbs in English which form their principal parts by means of an internal vowel change, for example, *sink, sank, sunk*—be made weak. Thus *strove* and *striven* would become *strived*; *shone* would become *shined*. Cooke finds the strong verbs anomalous: "These barbarous Changes in the Formation, which are in many more Words, are made by no Rule, but from the Tyranny of Custom." However, he is willing to bow to custom when "Propriety and Sound" must be preserved: in Cooke's system *sit* and *see* will form their preterites as *sat* and *saw*. Just as *-ed* will form the principal ending for what Cooke calls the "passed Tenses," *-s* and *-es* will become the markers of the plural in nouns. With the exception of *man* and other "words of authority," we find Cooke recommending such plurals as *Libertys, Discoverys, Difficultys,* and *Irregularitys*. Similarly he does not respell *y* to *i* in the comparison of adjectives, writing *happy, happyer, happyest,* or in the formation of the preterite, as in *layed*. Cooke would reform spelling to omit superfluous letters, except in the case of Latin and Greek derivations, and he recommends changing final *re* and *le* to *er* and *el*, because in speech the consonant follows the vowel. Thus he writes *participel, reasonabel, agreeabel, exampel,* and *capabel*, but keeps the spelling *particle* to avoid the pronunciation of *cel* as *sel*. A proponent of cultural as well as linguistic change that is properly motivated by concerns of reason and faith, Cooke urges the adoption of his suggestions unless better ones come along. Alluding to the Reformation, he reminds his readers that change can be beneficial: "We might still have been cursed with the Religion and Style of Chaucer had we feared to reform in either."[7]

Jonathan Swift concerned himself with both the light and serious sides of language study. In his *Discourse to Prove the Antiquity of the English Tongue* (1765), a delightfully scatological attempt to prove that Hebrew, Greek, and Latin were originally derived from English, Swift claims that English is 2,634 years old, and he shows that Biblical and classical names are actually disguised forms of English. For example, *Ajax*, often incorrectly assumed to come from *a jakes*, is actually from *age-aches*, one of the Greek hero's frequent complaints. Swift argues that Andromache's father was Scot, and that his name is really *Andrew Mackay* pronounced with a "Grecian accent." The name of *Mars*, the war god, comes from *Kiss my a——se*, which he would say when he was angry, and *Leda* derives from *laid a*, because she *laid a* couple of eggs.[8]

In his more serious *Proposal for Correcting, Improving and Ascer-*

taining the English Tongue (1712), Swift calls for the creation of an Academy to oversee the conservation of the language. Citing the examples of Greek, Chinese, German, Spanish, and Italian as languages that have altered very little over time, Swift says, "I see no absolute Necessity why any Language should be perpetually changing."[9] Ignoring any possible connection between variation and change, Swift rejects the notion of phonetic spelling because pronunciation varies from place to place and because such spelling would destroy the etymology of words. Swift sees a climatological factor at work in languages: "The same Defect of Heat which gives a Fierceness to our Natures, may contribute to that Roughness of our Language, which bears some Analogy to the harsh Fruit of colder Countries," but this does not prevent him from taking linguistic swipes at the Scots or the French. Charging that, since the Restoration, playwrights and poets have been contributing to the decay of the English language, Swift accuses them of forming "such harsh unharmonious Sounds, that none but a *Northern* Ear could endure" (p. 11). And although the French have worked hard to refine their language, their efforts seem doomed to failure: "The *French*, for these last Fifty Years, hath been polishing as much as it will bear; and appears to be declining by the natural Inconstancy of that People" (p. 8; here Swift uses the progressive passive in *hath been polishing*, the equivalent of today's *has been polished*).

The historian and pamphleteer John Oldmixon, replying to Swift's proposal for an Academy, objects to Swift's suggestion that women be consulted in the reformation of the language. Swift had not actually called for women to be members of the Academy, although he did feel that the absence of women from meetings of such groups had caused conversation to degenerate. Oldmixon, however, seems to resent any hint that women be allowed to participate in the process of language fixing. To him, Swift's notions of women and language smack of popery:

> Imagine, that the Two Universities would give up so Essential a Branch of their Privileges to the Ladies, and take from them the Standard of *English*. This puts me in mind of *Fontenelle's* way of Learning a Language, which he recommends to be by having an Intrigue with some Fair Foreigner; and beginning with the Verb *I Love*, *You Love*, &c. It is well enough from Him, a *Papist*, or *Layman*, but for a Protestant Divine to erect an Academy of Women to improve our Stile, is very extraordinary and gallant.[10]

This is just the start of Oldmixon's attack. Oldmixon feels that Swift is far from gallant. He accuses the Dean of being bawdy and lewd in his own style, and suggests that, in the area of philology, Swift is a quack. He takes exception to Swift's claim that certain languages failed to deteriorate: "Did not the *Roman* Tongue even by [Horace's] own confession, change as much as ours has done" (p. 24). Rather, Oldmixon claims that change is natural to language: "I should rejoyce with [Swift], if a way could be found out to *fix our Language for ever*, that like the *Spanish* Cloak, it might always be in Fashion, but I hope he will come into Temper with the Inconstancy of Peoples Minds, of which he complains, and that we are in no Fear of the Invasion and Conquest he talks of" (pp. 13–14). Taking the example of French, Oldmixon declares that English has changed less in a hundred years than has French, and without the benefit of an academy, and he adds that the French Academy has failed to save the language of France from decay.

According to Oldmixon, all the efforts of an academy of language will be doomed to failure:

> It will be in vain to pretend to *ascertain* Language, unless they had the Secret of setting Rules for Thinking, and could bring Thought to a Standard too. For every Age, as well as every Nation, has its different manner of Thinking, of which the Expression and Words will always have a Relish, and be Barbarous or Polite, according as the Times take their Turn. [Pp. 26–27]

Oldmixon suspects Swift of sympathy for the French: he "has already impos'd on us the Court Style of *France*, and their Politicks wou'd soon come after it" (p. 30), and Oldmixon's comment on the destructive effects of reformers is frequently repeated by later critics of language planning: "I believe the Reformation of our Language would have just as much success as the Reformation of our Manners, which, 'tis said, none have more corrupted than the very Reformers" (p. 21).

English Pure and Undefiled by French

In his *Reason, the True Arbiter of Language* (London, 1814), the clergyman and grammarian James Gilchrist issues a sweeping condemnation of grammars and grammarians. English, according to Gilchrist, was once a simple primitive language like Hebrew or Gothic. It has been spoiled and corrupted by the influence of Greek, Latin, and French. Gilchrist suggests that Greek actually derives from Gothic. He argues that Greek *eis* 'one' comes from Gothic *ein* by means of a regular sound change which causes the dental consonant *n* (Gilchrist says that *n* is a dental) to change to *s*. Gilchrist denounces the *-est* and *-eth* endings of English present tense singular verbs. He feels that the original Gothic verbs had no endings, for verbal endings are redundant, providing information already made plain by nouns and pronouns. Gilchrist derives *-eth* and *-est* from Latin verb endings rather than from native English morphology. He adds that such endings are not natural to English: "Children speak the verb right before they are taught it wrong; and it is with much difficulty that these younglings of nature and simplicity are brought to say *est* and *eth* properly, I mean improperly, or to hiss like a serpent at the end of third person singular" (p. 16).

The simple primitive tongues, according to Gilchrist, preserve the order of nature in their syntax, attaching adjectives to their nouns. Languages such as Latin violate natural order unnecessarily. Gilchrist objects to synonyms: one thought should be expressed by one word. Redundancy for him is sinful: "Mere variety in language, without utility, is luxury; and luxury in language is as hurtful to the understanding as the luxuries of life are to health and morality. Once covet vain show and useless sound, and the eye is never satisfied with seeing, nor the ear with hearing" (p. 42; the word *luxury* referred at the time both to 'lustfulness' and 'excess in general'). Gilchrist even finds fault with the *m* in *whom*, *him*, and *them* on the grounds of luxury.

Gilchrist argues against the validity of most of the traditional syntactical rules of grammarians like Lindley Murray. He does not feel that verbs must agree in person and number with their nominatives, or that pronouns must agree in number and gender with their antecedents. Of concord he says, "The divine concord between adjective and noun is nothing but the absurdity of putting the article in twice or thrice oftener than it is really wanted; as a senseless baby or drivelling idiot chimes over the same word without meaning or reason." He adds, derisively, using pseudo-Latin rather than Anglo-Saxon concord to underscore his point, "Would *oneus manus* and *onea womana* and *oneum thingum* be an improvement?" (pp. 98–99). Rejecting rules and tyrannical custom, Gilchrist trusts only in reason and necessity. He argues from a utilitarian point of view: "Whatever is necessary to bring out the meaning of the speaker, or writer, is proper and good grammar, and nothing else whatever" (p. 90).

Although many of Gilchrist's arguments make little sense, his observations on morphological redundancy are interesting. His defense of native English against foreign influence, while philologically inaccurate, is sincere. His hatred of the influence of French prompts him to forget about linguistic argument altogether and launch into pure diatribe:

> The article *he* is said to be often elegantly put after the manner of the French. Yes; we have learned to do many things elegantly after the manner of the French. We have learned to bow and crouch elegantly after the manner of the French; we have learned to fawn and feign after the manner of the French; we have learned to despise *morality* after the manner of the French—who can go through the sickening catalogue of abject meanness and mawkish affectation? . . . The lesser antics of this drunken apishness I can make sport of; but when it is presented in all its length and breadth of vulgar grossness, it sickens the soul into silence; for one feels too much to be able to speak. Hardly a master and miss in all the land but must be puling and snivelling out French, and capering like a French goat. Go, goatish and apish as you are, and dangle at the heels of goats and apes! [Pp. 101–02]

Anti-French sentiment of this type has pervaded discussions of English usage since the eighteenth century, masquerading under the name of linguistic purism. The satirist Archibald Campbell combines it with a rejection of latinate diction in his *Lexiphanes, A Dialogue. . . . Being an Attempt to Restore the English Tongue to Its Ancient Purity* (1767). Directing his attack at Samuel Johnson's *Dictionary* (1755), Campbell warns against what he calls *lexiphanism* and affectation in English: the question is whether we shall preserve our own language "or whether we shall adopt, I will not say a new language, but a barbarous jargon, attempted to be imposed upon us, by a few School-masters and Pedants, who owe all their credit to their petulance and impudence, who are equally ignorant of books and men, and who think they have done a fine thing when they have tack'd an English termination to a Latin word."[11] Campbell is aware that even corruption has its fashions: "The corrupters of our tongue in the days of Swift and Steele, were pert lively fops; they were great curtailers of words, and took a pleasure in lopping off their first and last syllables, as owls bite off the feet of mice, in order to confine and fatten them" (p. xxxvii). According to Campbell, his own age shows an opposite taste for long and imported words.

Returning to his criticism of Dr. Johnson, Campbell cites a letter detailing the purported experience of a French hairdresser who ran afoul of the natives on coming to England because of his overzealous reliance on Johnson's definitions. The Frenchman's letter is valuable both as a criticism of definitions that Johnson did not intend as purely literal and as an illustration of an eighteenth-century British satirical stereotype of the visiting Frenchman:

> Me ave at de grand depense made one purchase of de Dictionaire of de Docteur S——l J——n, vor apprendre more facilement, and parlé more justement and proprement de English Tongué. But dat vilain Dictionaire ave ledé me into ver grand mistaké, and ave goté me kické, cuffé, beaté, and my teet drivé down my troaté.

The Frenchman, one M. Dugard de Belletête, gets into trouble for quoting from Johnson's dictionary. He tells a British soldier who has lost an arm and a leg in his country's service and is receiving a pension, "Jan Foutre, I be my own Maitré, but you be one slave hiré to obey your Maitré'; Docteur J——n tella me so, and that you be one Traitre to your country Begar." With his stump, the enraged soldier knocks the visitor down and drives three of his teeth down his throat. All this hinges on Johnson's definition of *pension*: "An allowance made to any one without an equivalent. In England it is generally understood to mean pay given to a state hireling for treason to his country." A *pensioner* according to Johnson, is "a slave of state hired by a stipend to obey his master."

Monsieur de Belletête then sees a notice for Consumers of Oats to meet at a tavern. He says, "I consult de grand Dictionaire of dis Docteur J——n, and I see dat Oats be de food of de horsé in Englandé, but of de peuple in Scotlandé. Le Diable, say I to myself, do de English horse and de Scottishmans meet and drinké togeder, in dis country! Begar I will go see dis Mervielle." Waiting in vain for horses to arrive, the Frenchman finally asks some of the tavern's patrons, "Vat Jentlemens be all your Horse sické, or take physické, dat you come here in deir place, and be de representative of de Horsé?" The affronted patrons promptly beat him up. Johnson defines *oats* as "A grain, which, in England, is generally given to horses, but in Scotland supports the people." De Belletête closes his letter with a demand for a public apology from Dr. Johnson and a declaration that he intends to seek legal redress (pp. 179–84).

Attacks against the French influence on English become common. Advocating the establishment of a society for the improvement of language, one T. Search writes in the *Gentleman's Magazine* (1787) to protest against the looseness of English usage: "Many will contend, that, as we are a free people, our language of course ought to bear some resemblance to the principles of the political constitution; and that a liberty of form in expression is nearly allied to freedom itself." His principal concern is with unwarranted coining and borrowing from French: "Under the present circumstances, a common writer may fabricate new words which in themselves are frequently dissonant to the real idiom and genius of our native speech." Search notes that although the French emulate British fashions, they borrow very little from the English language. He lists the borrowings *Boulingrin, Ridingotte, Rôt de bife, le Spline, Ponch,* and complains that such words ought at least to be pronounced with the proper French accent. He would much prefer, however, that new English words have a classical ancestry: "We often forget the superior *euphonia* of Greek or Latin primitives, inadvertently recurring to the disagreeable sounds of those French words which in their language are called *nasals*" (57:119–20).

Another anonymous complaint in the *Gentleman's Magazine* (1802) against French lexical imports objects to their prevalence in the register of advertising (for example, *fauteuil, armoire*), where they are used "to give a dignity to tables and chairs, to exalt cupboards and brackets, and to preserve the purity of our diction as well as morals, by obviating that indelicacy which frequently attended the mention of certain necessary articles" (72:803).

Robert Baker, whose *Reflections on the English Language* (1770) is modeled on Vaugelas's *Remarqves*, expresses the commonly felt sentiment that English would be better off unmixed with other languages:

> It would indeed be well if foreign Words could be intirely banished: The Use of them has something in it unnatural, and gives the Language, into which they are dragg'd, an Air of Poverty. Where we want a Word in our own Tongue to express any particular Idea, we ought either to take a foreign Word, and give it an English Form and an English Pronunciation, (as we have already done in many Instances) or to invent a Word ourselves.[12]

William Mitford, perhaps best known for his *History of Greece* (1784–1818), wrote in 1804 to object to a number of trends in the language of his day. He complains of spelling pronunciations, particularly of the tendency to pronounce *merchant* as *murchant* rather than *marchant,* and he urges his readers to resist "the Scottish confusion of *shall* and *will*" which if adopted would make English an inferior and defective language. Like many commentators in the eighteenth and nineteenth centuries, Mitford feels the *shall/will* distinction is practically genetic: "Every English child feels the difference of *shall* and *will*, and uses each in its proper place," but the constant reiteration of the naturalness of the distinction and the confused vagueness by which it is often explained (Mitford's own account of *shall* and *will* is virtually unreadable) are indirect indications that their use was beyond regulation. Mitford objects to Scotticisms in general (for example, *I'd be obliged to you*), and his low opinion of French comes through when he praises English over the Romance languages for its tense distinctions. Mitford finds English deficient in analogy because too many other languages, Norman French in particular, have been mixed with it. He does not approve of the mismanaged attempts to ape French pronunciation in words borrowed from that language into English, but he finds French to be poor in vocabulary and plagued with too many homonyms. To make up for its deficiencies, Mitford finds that French resorts to ingenious phrasing that is elegant or odd, and that the language is too quick to change fashion.[13]

The Saxonist Movement

The principal objection to the importation of foreign words into English concerns not so much the words themselves as their pronunciation and morphology. Most critics would have been appeased if needed words had been thoroughly Englished and if faddish expressions and needless borrowings had been avoided. In the sixteenth and seventeenth centuries, and again in the later part of the nineteenth century, however, a movement to purify English of immigrant words does arise. This "Saxonist" revival, led in Victorian England by the philologist William Barnes and supported to some extent by the poet and printer William Morris, had as its goal the replacement of the latinate vocabulary of English with terms felt to be more suited to the genius of the language. In *An Outline of English Speechcraft* (London, 1878), Barnes proposes revivals from Old English, provincial dialect forms, and new words created on an Old English model, in short, *Saxonisms* that he hopes will eventually uproot non-native lexical items. Morris did a translation of the *Odyssey* in which he employed Saxonisms to provide epic flavor, and as late as 1917 the translator Charles Louis Dessoulavy published his *Word-Book of the English Tongue*, a word list giving what he called Teutonic equivalents of French and latinate words in English (many of these equivalents were taken from Barnes).

The movement which, for want of a better name can be called Saxonism, was inspired partly by the continued complaints against foreign assaults on the English language (including the latinate diction of the rapidly growing languages of technology and science) and partly by the renewed interest in the study of Old and Middle English language and literature in the seventeenth and again at the end of the nineteenth century. The publication of texts by groups such as the Early English Text Society, and the work of the London Philological Society—particularly its support of the historical dictionary project that has come to be known as the *Oxford English Dictionary*—spurred interest in both the older and the nonliterary varieties of English. Barnes wrote treatises on his native Dorset dialect and even published poetry that he had written in it. But Saxonism had little influence on the language. Whether for personal or academic reasons, Barnes was not asked to read for the *Oxford Dictionary*, nor did the *Dictionary* cite much of his research. Morris's *Odyssey* did not prove popular. The British literary public preferred the more conservative approach of nativizing borrowed forms that was espoused by Robert Bridges and his Society for Pure English. The sorts of words proposed by Barnes and Dessoulavy, though analogically English, possessed more of an air of foreignness than the borrowings they were meant to replace. For example, for *criticism* Barnes proposes *deemster-hood*, for *botany*, *wortlore*, and for *active*, *sprack*. *Omnibus* is to become *folkwain*, a *butler* will be a *cellar-thane*, a *telegram*, itself a word that provoked criticism from purists who pointed out it could never have existed in Greek, would be a *wire-spell*. *Speechcraft* was Barnes's term for *grammar*, *rede-craft* for *logic*, and *manqualm* for *epidemic*. He began to write using the terms he created, and the following sample, about the Saxon's penchant for vandalism, prompted one reviewer to accuse Barnes of "a want of literary sanity":

> The mindstrength and body worksomeness of the Saxon, which are of great might for good when well spent, need a training in wisdom to keep them from mischief. The Saxon's mind . . . is destructive, and his sprackness wants the guidance of refined thought. . . . Thence it is that seats put out at towns are often wantonly wrenched asunder, that bars and stiles are notched by bearers of an axe.[14]

One Saxonism that has prospered partly as a result of this movement is the use of *foreword* in place of *preface* in printed books (another is *handbook* for *manual*, though when it was first revived in the nineteenth century it was poorly received). Dessoulavy in his *foreword* discusses the relationship of the English and French languages that sparked his own efforts at reform:

> English folk . . . have been seeking to shake off the Norman yoke that lies so heavy on their speech . . . [but] English is no English at all but sheer French. . . . There are many who feel not a little ashamed of the needless loan-words in which their speech is clothed. . . . For liveliness and strength, manliness and fulness of meaning, the olden English Tongue were hard to beat. The thought-world, too, of those who think in the olden Saxon Tongue is utterly other from that of those who think in Norman French. It is, maybe, to their love of the Tongue of their Fathers that our singers owe much of their witchery.[15]

Elias Molee: American Saxonist and More

There were some advocates of the Saxonist movement in America, although on the whole they had little influence. Webster's praise of pure, native English earlier in the nineteenth century may have helped to set the stage for later complaints against the excessive use of fashionable French terms and ornate latinisms, but it seems that most Americans were too preoccupied with defining their own linguistic relationship to Great Britain and with assimilating non-English-speaking immigrants to worry overly about the effects of the Norman conquest. One American who did worry about them was Elias Molee, the Wisconsin-born son of Norwegian immigrants, who studied at both Norwegian and English schools and settled on a farm in Dakota "to divert his attention as little as possible from linguistics." Molee felt that English spelling was "a cruelty to the native-born child and more than that to the foreign-born," and his own idiosyncratic usage is excused by an admiring biographer: "As he has spent so much time in meditating on what the English language ought to be and might have been, he may be pardoned for not always remembering what it is" (*Plea*, p. 16). In his *Plea for an American Language, or Germanic-English* (Chicago, 1888) Molee proposes a three-part reform of English to introduce phonetic spelling, revise the grammar, and replace Latin and French terminology wherever possible with Anglo-Saxon, German, or Scandinavian elements to make the vocabulary "transparent," or self-explaining. Molee's reform—which involves a revision of the alphabet and the use of alphabetic symbols in place of arabic numbers in order to "drill every person in the correct and separate pronunciation of the vowels and consonants" (p. 217)—is visionary in its overall design. He would create a "union language" to replace the individual Germanic languages (he advises a similar effort for the Romance languages) and to serve as a bulwark against Pan-Slavism. According to Molee, English is destined to be a world language, but first it must rid itself of its bondage to the Norman French conquerors.

Molee criticizes French for its double nominatives, double negatives, clumsy comparison of adjectives, bad spelling, lack of a neuter gender, and nasal twang, as well as for being "very full of idiotic expressions where words mean something entirely different from what they appear to mean" (p. 20). Claiming that "the English speak . . . as a conquered people" (p. 27), and that the British educational system has failed miserably in the task of spreading literacy, Molee argues that it is up to America to take the initiative. A union language would be the natural product of the American melting pot: "Americanism is to select what is best from other countries and adopt it here. This is a composite nation, a daughter of the whole western and central Europe. This nation is not a daughter of England" (p. 39). Because America has a composite population, "respect for English is less strong, and if we were wise enough here to take advantage of that fact, we have an opportunity now to put the world into the possession of the best language in existence, because it will have the light, experience and achievements of other languages to build upon. A language in which words and rules will be arranged in rows and beds, as plants in a garden, instead of growing up without order, as flowers on the wild prairie" (p. 112).

Molee repeatedly stresses the point that the "Old Natives," as he calls the Yankees, are only one of many immigrant groups in this country, and that English is a slave language: "English is not produced naturally by a free people, and it is hardly good enough for our free America, because it is too wasteful of mental energy and cannot be readily understood" (p. 50). Our present spelling system represents a waste of ten dollars per person, or $100 million each year. The latinate vocabulary with which we are burdened is undemocratic, for it excludes the common people, the poor and uneducated, from learning and science. Molee cites James Hadley, professor of Greek at Yale and author of a "Brief History of the English Language" that prefaced the 1864 edition of Webster's *Dictionary*: "It is a . . . *serious* disadvantage that in order to express our ideas we are obliged to translate them into dead languages" (p. 58).

While Molee finds our spelling too complex, he criticizes English grammar for being too simple. We make no distinctions between possessive and plural, between present participle and verbal noun, between preterite and past participle. English is poor in diminutive particles; it lacks augmentative particles and reflexive pronouns; and its feminine endings are most often proscribed. There are of course some advantages to the English grammatical system. We have done away with grammatical gender, verbal endings, and the dative case. But our prefixes and suffixes are wastefully redundant; we use too few vowels and too many little words; we place the accent too near the beginning of words; and we "hack" or contract our words excessively, a fault which greatly troubles Molee: "If this hacking of words is to continue we shall be reduced to Chinese monosyllables, to short *consonantal grunts*. . . . Alexandre becomes Al.; Albertina, Ali; Thomas, Tom. . . . The Greeks would not have tolerated such uneuphonious hacking of consonants and negligence of vowels" (pp. 131–32).

Molee sees his reform as the most conservative yet proposed. Whenever possible, English will be remodeled along the lines of its ancestor Anglo-Saxon or, if this is impracticable, along the lines of its modern Germanic cognate languages. Molee points to the case of Hebrew as an example of a well-conserved language that has had a beneficial effect on the character of its native speakers: "The Jews have clung to their Hebrew language. They say their prayers and chant their joys and sorrows in their ancient tongue, and yet they are the world's greatest business men, as well as the most famous in literature. They are also the least criminal part of our population. They have the greatest regard for old parents and young children, and have the least divorces. Fidelity in one respect produces fidelity in another" (p. 41). Molee's own *Amerikan* or *Teutonic-English* would have a similarly benign effect. It would open the mysteries of science and philosophy to the masses. It would reduce the amount of time spent in school on spelling. And it would lessen linguistic insecurity: "A homogeneous language allows a freer flow of vivacity and cheerfulness. . . . The spirit moves easier in a self-developed tongue, as there is less fear, at least with many of the guests [that is, immigrants], to misplace accent and to misapply some foreign word" (p. 157).

Molee admits that some Romance words must remain in English because they have become thoroughly ingrained: for example, *fine*, *person*, *butter*, *church*, and *anchor*. This does not represent a problem, for him, but an advantage, for it will satisfy the demands of the Romanic peoples who have settled in America. But most words of French origin must be replaced. *Prayer* must go, but since German *gebet* sounds too much like *betting*, Molee advises that we adopt the Scandinavian *bön*. Molee's *wördalist* is difficult to reproduce because of his use of a new phonetic alaphabet, or *stablist*. His *Amerikan* is more German than Anglo-Saxon: *animal* is *dir*; *away* is *weg*, *shön* is *beautiful*. Other examples include *winkl* 'angle', *hart-hind* 'pericardium', *sukdira* 'mammalia', *fadi* 'father' and *fada* 'mother', *broi* 'brother' and *broa* 'sister', *ar* 'honor', *adl* 'noble', *erin* 'remember', *umspikl* 'topic', and *ingehav* 'viscera'.

Molee proposes a number of morphological changes to make English more systematic and to introduce more vowels into our words. Words that end in vowels will add *s* to indicate plurality; words ending in consonants will add *a*: thus *da* 'day', *das* 'days', *hors* 'horse', *horsa* 'horses'. The possessive will be indicated not by *s* but by a final ↻ ,/o/ (the vowel sound in *boat*), or *n* ↻ , from ↻ *n* 'own'. Adjectives will end in -*i*; feminines in -*a*, and masculines in ʊ, /i/. Verbs will form their preterites by adding -*d* when they end in vowels and -*o* when they end in consonants: *I sow, I sowd*; *I drink, I drinko* (in Molee's scheme there will be no more strong verbs).

Molee also suggests some changes in the pronoun system. *Thee* will become *thoum* to avoid confusion with the article *the*. *She* will become *ha*. *Them*, when masculine, will be *hem* (*he* plus *them*); when feminine, it will be *lem* (*lady* plus *them*); and when neuter, *tem* (*it* plus *them*). In addition, Molee proposes to add a common gender pronoun to replace singular *he* and *she* and to replace the plural *tem* when gender is mixed rather than neuter: "There is a new pronoun that we actually need, and which has been pointed out many years ago by several grammarians. That is a pronoun to stand for hi or ha (he or she). Ex.: 'Let every person think of *his* and *her* duty.' If we had a pronoun of the third person, common gender, we would not need to repeat as above. The pronoun ʊ*r* (*eer*) has been taken, as it is short, of old standing, and as it will establish suggestive harmony between pronoun and the personal endings of many nouns, as *er* changed to ʊ*r* (old form), which will be explained under Comparison. Sendʊr (eer), writʊr, workʊr, payʊm (payee), etc." The complete paradigm proposed by Molee, rendered in conventional English spelling is, for the singular, ʊ*r*, ʊ*ro* (possessive), ʊ*m* (accusative), and for the plural, *tha, thar, them* (pp. 200–01).

Molee is careful to call himself a compiler, not an innovator. He repeatedly asserts that his proposals are not original but borrowed, although he never credits his sources and some of his suggestions do seem to be his own. For example, although over forty different forms have been suggested for the common gender pronoun since 1850, Molee is the only person to propose a plural as well as a singular form.[16] Molee is also flexible in his approach to language reform, recognizing that many of his suggestions will be difficult if not impossible to implement. He is willing to give up his insistence on lowercase letters and his revised number system, and in his later work he gives up many of his morphological suggestions as well. In none of his own prose writing does he replace the Romance roots of English in favor of the artificial Saxon vocabulary that Barnes used in his compositions. Molee's autobiography, published by the author in 1919, shows him to have abandoned most of the ideas suggested in the *Plea for an American Language*. In the autobiography, *molee's wanderings*, we find no capital letters. Molee employs abbreviations for the twenty most frequently occurring words (*e* for *the*, *hd* for *had*, *t* for *to* and *too*); alphabetic letters replace numbers; and an occasional lexical innovation appears: *wonderthing, crisifixion, animal lore* 'zoology', and *thru*. In an appendix, however, Molee prints two samples of *alteutonik*, his universal Germanic language (this time without alphabetic eccentricities), of which the following is a brief example: "di sprakeregla is ja schon angivn in mio buk," which translates as 'the grammar rule is already given in my book' (p. 120). Molee's quest for the perfect replacement for English seems never to have ended.

Reacting to Saxonism: In Praise of Status Quo

Not everyone who recognized English as a mixed language adopted the purist solution of the Saxonists. William Mathews, professor of rhetoric and English at the University of Chicago, echoes, in *Words; Their Use and Abuse* (Chicago, 1876), the anti-French sentiment that the Gallic language reveals the decadent national character, but he does take a stand defending Romance words as well as Saxon in the English language: "Of late it has been the fashion to cry up the native element at the expense of the foreign. . . . The English language has a special dowry of power in its double-headed origin; the Saxon part of the language fulfills one set of functions; the Latin, another" (pp. 168–70). Mathews recognizes that languages break with their own past, and that usage must concern itself with the present, asking "not what ought to be, or formerly was, the meaning of a word, but, what is it *now*?" (p.

203). Mathews sees the American temperament and social situation as responsible for innovation, both good and bad, in English: "Not only does political freedom make every man in America an inventor, alike of labor-saving machines and of labor-saving words, but the mixture of nationalities is constantly coining and exchanging new forms of speech." Mathews sees an English wildness and an American passion for freedom as the two major causes of barbarisms, solecisms, and improprieties:

> The chief cause must be found in the character of the English-speaking race. There is in our very blood a certain lawlessness, which makes us intolerant of syntactical rules, and restless under pedagogical restraints. . . . In America this scorn of obedience, whether to political authority or philological, is fostered and intensified by the very genius of our institutions. We seem to doubt whether we are entirely free, unless we apply the Declaration of Independence to our language, and carry the Monroe doctrine even into our grammar. [Pp. 327–28]

Mathews plays down Saxonism, and other commentators treat it as only one aspect of their discussion of language and purity. Writing in the *Encyclopaedia Britannica* (1842), philosopher Dugald Stewart is one of the few students of English after 1700 to regard his own era as a linguistic golden age. In a note to his article on Philosophy he quotes the novelist William Godwin as saying, "The English language is now written with more grammatical propriety than by the best of our ancestors." The reason for Stewart's optimism is the change he sees in the style of English composition: "The number of idiomatical phrases has been abridged; and the language has assumed a form more systematic, precise, and luminous. The transitions, too, in our best authors, have become more logical, and less dependent on fanciful or verbal associations." English for Stewart improves as it becomes more systematic and rationalistic, as it exchanges a dependence on arbitrary usage for a dependence on principle. He finds English to have gained as an instrument of thought and a vehicle of knowledge, and to have become easier for foreigners to learn as, "in proportion to its rejection of colloquial anomalies, more durable materials are supplied to the present generation for transmitting their intellectual acquisitions to posterity."

Stewart does not propose changes himself, but he does encourage the trend he observes toward simplification and nativization of the language. In this he echoes the Saxonists, although his major concerns are with comprehensibility in syntax and diction and with the competition between French and English as languages of scientific communication, not with a purgation of loan words that would have created numerous comprehension problems for native and foreigner alike. Stewart challenges Diderot's classification of French as a purely rational language more fit than any other for the transmission of learning, and of English, Latin, and Greek as languages better suited by their structures for literary purposes. Stewart is not without kind words for Samuel Johnson, but he feels Johnson, despite his successes, did much to hinder the proper development of English: "Johnson boasts, and with truth . . . that he had 'added some thing to our language in the elegance of its construction, and some thing in the harmony of its cadence;' but what a sacrifice did he make to these objects, of conciseness, of simplicity, and of (what he has himself called) *Genuine Anglicism*. To accomplish the same ends, without any sacrifice of these higher merits, has been one of the chief aims of the most eminent among his successors."[17]

Commentaries on Usage

Writers of more historically oriented works on the English language occasionally comment on questions of usage and style. The clergyman Matthew Harrison, in his *Rise, Progress, and Present Structure of the English Language* (Philadelphia, 1848), complains of the lack of formal English language study in British schools: "It is notorious, that, at our public schools, every boy has been left to pick up his English where and how he could" (p. v). In a brief section on the sources of corruption in English, Harrison blames Geoffrey Chaucer for helping to introduce French terms into the language (it was a widely held misconception that Chaucer's literary reputation did more for the position of French in England than the Norman invasion), and he is none too sympathetic with what he regards as the perversions of language taking place in America or in many of the British colonies. Harrison objects to inflated style, "embodying terms altogether disproportionate to the subject, and which is often so unfortunate as to combine in one sentence, or one paragraph, the pompous, the offensive, and the ridiculous" (p. 110). He criticizes incongruous terminology, which he defines only by example—particularly American example, although British novelist Fanny Burney is also cited as an offender for writing such phrases as "the *sudden-at-the-moment-though-from-lingering-illness-often-previously-expected* death of Mr. Burney's second wife." Harrison seems to feel that the following examples are characteristic of American usage, stereotyped as full of tall talk and fancified phrasing: *the advent of fun and fashion-dom; a foot like a jolly fat clam; pocketually speaking; unletupable nature, plumptitude, wide-awakeity, betweenity,* and *go-awayness* (pp. 112–14).

Harrison is one of the first writers to speak of the *facts* of language usage, arguing that facts are more significant than opinions: "We shall find that high authorities are no guarantee against the commission of flagrant error. There are facts in grammar, as well as facts in other matters; and against these no authority, however great, can contend. . . . it may not be a useless task to show that grammar has no aristocratic favorites—that there is no true standard except an impartial grammatical standard" (p. 167). Facts, for Harrison, are not what they are to such twentieth-century writers on language as Sterling Leonard, Albert Marckwardt, or Charles C. Fries, that is, the record of actual language use by speakers and writers. Rather they are *impartial grammatical standards* that demand our unflagging obedience.

Richard Chenevix Trench, the dean of Westminster, archbishop of Dublin, and friend of Tennyson, was a literary man who like his contemporary Harrison was primarily concerned with the historical development of the English language. But Trench finds little in the area of usage to object to. He sees no difference between the written language of England and America, and very little difference in speech. Trench does argue against the spelling reform because it would tend to obliterate etymology and because pronunciation changes so often that spelling would have to change just as frequently to keep up with it. In *English Past and Present* (New York, 1855), Trench says that phonetic spelling would lessen the conservative power of the written word: "Whatever was spoken would have also to be written, let it be never so barbarous, never so great a departure from the true form of the word" (p. 180). In fact Trench is so conservative a speller he rejects the established *whole* for *hole* and *island* for *iland* because they are based on false analogy and incorrect derivation. In his concern for correctness, which for Trench seems to involve the historical forces at work on language rather than the rational principles sought by Harrison, Trench calls for the creation of a dictionary that is a true record of the language, one that includes not just the "good" words but all words. The lexicographer, according to Trench, is a historian, not a critic of language, and he should not be concerned with setting a standard for English.[18]

The Alford-Moon Controversy

In the 1860s a major usage controversy erupted between Henry Alford, dean of Canterbury and editor of the Greek New Testament, and George Washington Moon, a religious poet and novelist, who was the London-born son of American parents and a Fellow of the Royal Society of Literature. In 1863 Alford published a series of essays in the journal *Good Words*, entitled "A Plea for the Queen's English." The next year these were collected and issued as a book, *The Queen's English*. Like all commentators on usage, Alford ran the risk of exposing his prose as well as his ideas to public criticism, and Moon, seeking to discredit Dean Alford, responded with *A Defense of the Queen's English* (1863), republished the following year under a new title, *The Dean's English*, to ensure that no one could misinterpret Moon's position as being favorable to Alford. The work of both men was popular in England and America, and interest in the controversy is reflected in the numerous testimonials of support that accompany later editions of their books.

Henry Alford is a tame purist, as purists go. His willingness to accept actual usage rather than prescriptive rules is no doubt what got him into trouble, but Alford's anti-American streak was added provocation for Moon, who combed *The Queen's English* line by line to point out solecisms, contradictions, misstatements, and anything else he could find that would allow him to accuse Alford of incompetence. Alford reacts graciously in print, silently correcting some of the phrases Moon objects to, but generally maintaining his original positions.

For Alford, the phrase *the Queen's English* is simply a way of indicating the relationship between language and country. He has no nostalgia for the older Saxon forms of English; rather, he is a believer in linguistic and cultural progress: "There was a day when [the language] was as rough as the primitive inhabitants."[19] As language is capable of progress, it is also capable of decay, and Alford feels that the English language has deteriorated in America, that it has become full of reckless exaggeration and contempt for congruity, just like the American character.

Alford defends customary usage at the expense of rule. Objecting to the respelling of words that end in *-our* he says, "It is only the maintenance of our national custom and usage for which a reasonable man can plead" (p. 12). Alford cannot explain why *show* has come to be spelled *shew*, but he recognizes that once the spelling has become established, it is useless to attempt to change it: "We seem bound to follow usage, and not rashly to endeavour to reform it" (p. 36). He does object to certain vagaries of spelling, for example the unwarranted doubling of consonants as in *benefitted* and *lett*, or the back-formation of a singular *mean* from *means*, but on the whole Alford rejects the principles of the spelling reform movement. He feels that the users of language cannot be swayed by the emphasis of that movement on the practicality and rationality of their reforms: "*Our* object is not expeditious writing only, nor is it easy spelling, nor uniformity in expressing the same sounds" (p. 16). For Alford, rules are appropriate only when custom is various, but even so, such rules ought to be determined by actual usage. For example, he finds the variation between final *-ise* and *-ize* to present an open question: here, "usage varies, but has not pronounced positively in any case" (p. 36).

In discussing grammatical constructions Alford also emphasizes his reliance on usage, noting that he is more concerned with the explanation of usage than with its censure. He distinguishes between the more relaxed constraints on spoken language and the harsher ones on writing, and he generously accepts variants and extended uses, supporting his judgments with reference to the extension of the second person plural pronoun *you* to the singular as well in violation of the so-called rule of concord. Alford's stated position on usage is liberal, but it is also somewhat misleading. He does not write to demonstrate that any and all language is acceptable, and in many cases he is eager to pass judgment on a language question. Like many usage commentators in the nineteenth century, Alford objects to the use of feminized substantives such as *authoress*, *poetess*, *pilgrimess*, or *portress*, feeling that most occupational names are common to both sexes: "It savours of pedantry to attempt by adding the feminine termination, to make a difference" (p. 89). Although he suggests that the masculine form be used when both sexes are included, Alford is careful to point out that the strictures he presents are tentative: "I do not of course mean to advocate absolute strictness in this or any other usage. Accuracy is one thing, punctiliousness is another. The one should be always observed, the other always avoided" (p. 94).

Replying to George Washington Moon's complaint that he ignores the rules of grammar, Alford says that there are in language "many things which follow no rule but that of custom, and of which it is very difficult to give any reasonable account. I mention this to show how inadequate the laws of ordinary grammar are to regulate or even to describe our practice'' (p. 191). This insight into the fallibility of contemporary grammars is repeated more strongly in Alford's assessment of the role of education in language decay. Alford, like many writers on usage, finds fault with grammarians and grammar lessons. He attributes "very much of the degenerate English of our day" to school instruction in which the Bible and Shakespeare are held up as examples of faulty usage. Here we see the bias of Alford the clergyman who uses the King James version to settle disagreements over the pronunciation of initial *h*'s. Of the universal rules promulgated by the school grammars, Alford advises, "All I would say . . . to my younger readers is, the less you know of them, the less you turn your words right or left to observe them, the better" (p. 126). According to Alford, school grammar rules must always be subordinated to the demands of style: "Very often we cannot have exactness and smoothness together. Wherever this is the case, the harsher method of constructing the sentence is, in colloquial English, abandoned, even at the risk of exactness and school rules" (p. 131). Defending such purist bugbears as *than me* and *It is me*, Alford comes down hard on the side of descriptive grammar: "We must show an equal regardlessness of what ordinarily passes for grammar, if we would give a correct account of the prevalent usages of our language" (p. 146). Another school rule that Alford is willing to bend is the one which states that related parts of a sentence should be placed as close as possible to one another. Alford observes that we change the position of phrases in a sentence for emphasis, not through carelessness, "because the writer was intent on expressing his meaning in good manly English, and was not anxious as to the faults which carping and captious critics might find with his style" (p. 120).

Alford's negative attitude toward the imposition of linguistic behavior by schools and critics has been stressed because it provoked a strong reaction, as such attitudes invariably do, from the advocates of formal grammatical regulation of the language. But Alford's practice does not always match his theory. Certainly some of his judgments are not at all severe. For example, in discussing *ain't* Alford is gentle by modern standards. Alford opposes *ain't*, even though it is often used by educated persons, partly because it is proscribed (here he bows to a traditional rule) and also because it is ill-formed. As a contraction, it bears no resemblance to *am not* or *are not*, and therefore he claims it may not be used legitimately to replace these phrases (p. 88). Supporting usage with an appeal to nationality, Alford finds the distinction between *last* (referring to two or more) and *latter* (referring to two only), "a mere arbitrary regulation laid down by persons who know little and care little about [the laws of thought]" (p. 98). Other opinions are more traditional and heavy-handed. In the very next breath he finds fault with the expressions *a superior man* and *a very inferior person* because the comparative adjectives are used without expressed objects of comparison. Of this practice he says, "With all its convenience, and all the defence which can be set up for it, this way of speaking is odious; and if followed out as precedent, cannot but vulgarize and deteriorate our language" (p. 100).

Alford again throws usage to the winds when he rejects the adjective *talented* because it does not derive, as all past participles should, from a verb *to talent* and because it is a newspaper word. And he argues in favor of maintaining a distinction between the indicative and subjunctive moods on the grounds that "the rule is not one belonging to English only, but to the conditions of thought" (p. 195). Alford defends *shall / will* distinctions in English as instinctual rather than rule-based, and argues, from his obviously inaccurate observation of usage, that split infinitives cannot and do not occur: "Surely this is a practice entirely unknown to English speakers and writers. It seems to me, that we ever regard the *to* of the infinitive as inseparable from its verb" (p. 171).

Most of Alford's pronouncements hinge not on usage or rationality (what he calls the laws of thought) but on personal preference. And, like the school grammarians he theoretically objects to, he often makes judgments without providing an explanation for his decisions. Alford disapproves of *write me*—he seems to disapprove of elliptical forms in general—preferring *write to me*, with the preposition expressed, despite the fact that, historically speaking, the latter is an innovation. He does not care for *to experience* as a verb or for the newfangled passive, *is being done* (a commonly objected to replacement for the older passive *is doing: the book is writing*, compared with the present-day English *is being written*). He recommends avoiding such constructions; but, conceding the influence of custom, rather than applauding it, he recognizes that it is probably a vain effort to protest against them.

Alford also objects to using the relative personal pronoun in connection with *one* (that is, *one . . . his*; in cases such as this, the personal pronoun was often considered a relative because it "related" to an antecedent), preferring *one . . . one's*. Personal preference also comes to the fore in the Dean's criticism of a sexual imbalance in the language. Of the popular use of *female* for *woman*, Alford says, "Why should a *woman* be degraded from her position as a rational being, and be expressed by a word which might belong to any animal tribe, and which, in our version of the Bible, is never used except of animals, or of the abstract, the sex in general? Why not call a man a 'male,' if a woman is to be a 'female?'" (p. 227). He also objects to inflated diction: "We constantly read of the '*Hebrew persuasion*,' or the '*Jewish persuasion*.' I expect soon to see the term widened still more, and a man of colour described as '*an individual of the negro persuasion*'" (p. 232). *Reliable*, another example of inflation, is for Alford hardly a legitimate word; *trustworthy* is sufficient to express its meaning.

Perhaps the most intriguing of Dean Alford's personal preferences—revealing an even more acute sense of formality in language than many of the most hard-core prescriptivists—are his objections to the use, in public, of "unmeaning and ridiculous familiar nicknames or terms of endearment" and to the use of baby talk to infants and small children. Alford's sense of decorum leads him to condemn such language when it is used in the private world as well as in the public one. Even from the boudoir, "if there be real good sense present, all that is childish and ridiculous will be banished" (pp. 241–42).

Although he often ignores or contradicts his own advice, Alford concludes his rambling discussion of English usage by urging his readers to practice simplicity and straightforwardness of language: "Write much as you would speak; speak as you think." He counsels us to avoid singularity in word choice and in pronunciation, and to avoid slang. Finally, and perhaps ironically, Alford undercuts much of what he himself has just done, cautioning us against the continual correction of other people's language and adding:

> Grammarians and rhetoricians may set bounds to language: but usage will break over in spite of them. And I have ventured to think that he may do some service who, instead of standing and protesting where this has been the case, observes, and points out to others, the existing phenomena, and the probable account to be given of them. [P. 256]

Reacting sharply to Dean Alford's ideas on language, George Washington Moon published *The Dean's English*, a series of letters to Dean Alford that criticize his usage. According to Moon, it is with great writers, not grammarians, that responsibility for the language rests. He chooses as his personal authorities, however, Campbell (*Philosophy of Rhetoric*), Kames (*Elements of Criticism*), and Blair (*Lectures on Rhetoric and Belles Lettres*), three men who are primarily commentators on usage rather than littérateurs. Like Alford, Moon is suspicious of grammarians. He stresses the fact that grammar follows usage, citing Campbell's opinion that grammar does not legislate language. According to Campbell, the grammarian is the digester of the law, a critic whose job it is to facilitate the learning of English by foreigners and to "render natives more perfect in the knowledge of it."[20] Moon's aversion to grammar is more clearly expressed in *The Bad English of Lindley Murray and Other Writers on the English Language* (London 1868): "Of all the tasks of our school days, perhaps none was more repugnant to any of us, than the study of grammar; . . . we questioned whether it was worth while going through so much to learn so little" (p. 1). Moon's experience of grammar in school was pure torture. He imagines "the almost malicious pleasure which Lindley Murray felt as he wrote, 'a verb is a word which signifies *to be, to do*, or *to suffer*.'" Yet we can imagine the pleasure Moon now feels in correcting the corrector: "In the very volume in which he laid down his rules, he frequently expressed himself ungrammatically" (p. 2). Moon accuses Murray of errors in concord, tense, mood, and adverb placement. For example, Murray prescribes *each . . . his* but writes *each . . . their*. In taking to task grammarians and critics of usage, Moon shows himself as a more strict and more literal-minded prescriber of language than either Alford or Murray.

Moon does not approve of Dean Alford's usage. He does not think Alford is a good writer, and he does not hesitate to challenge Alford's ability to direct the writing of others: "So far were you from being competent to teach others English composition, that you had need yourself to study its first principles" (*Dean's English*, p. 44). But the examples Moon chooses to criticize often do not seem in need of revision. For instance, Moon would change Alford's "Sometimes the editors of our papers fall, from their ignorance, into absurd mistakes" to "Sometimes our editors, in consequence of their ignorance, fall into absurd mistakes" (pp. 9–10). Moon unjustly accuses Alford of unclear pronoun reference and of using adjectives instead of adverbs. He finds, for example, that Alford has written "a paragraph of less than ten lines, yet so ambiguously worded that you may ring as many changes on it as on a peal of bells" (p. 69), yet the paragraph in question, though full of pronouns, is perfectly clear. Moon objects to the Dean's reference to Queen Victoria as a *female*, adding, "I am sure that all who desire your welfare will join me in hoping that Her Majesty will not see your book" (pp. 114–15), and he attacks Alford's anti-Americanism. Moon points out that, although Alford objects to the dropping of *u*'s in words ending in *-our*, a volume of the Dean's poetry, published in England, exhibits the proscribed spellings in words such as *favor* and *savor*. Moon defends American usage as superior to the British: "You sneer at 'Americanisms', but you would never find an educated American who would venture to say, '*It is me*', for 'It is I'; or, 'It is him', for 'It is he'; or 'different to', for 'different from.' And nowhere are the use and the omission of the 'h' as an aspirate, so clearly distinguished as in the United States" (pp. 53–54).

Moon is a stickler for what he feels to be accuracy of construction, and he insists that such accuracy should have precedence over the less important stylistic demands of emphasis. He would change the comparatives in Alford's "If with your inferiors speak no *coarser* than usual; if with your superiors, no *finer*" to *no more coarsely* and *no more finely*. To this Alford replies in equally misguided fashion that *no more* cannot be used here because it is the equivalent of *never again*. In one of his more lucid readings, Moon admits that the phrase can indeed mean *never again*, but that it certainly cannot mean it in this instance (pp. 92–93). Responding to Alford's statement that *ain't* is used by educated persons, Moon says, "I suppose you mean, educated at college, where the study of English is altogether ignored" (p. 107).

Moon cites D'Orsey's *A Plea for the Study of English* and the *Report of Her Majesty's Commissioners Appointed to Inquire into the Management of Certain Colleges and Schools* (1864) as indications of the poverty of native language instruction in Great Britain. According to Moon, one result of such lack of instruction will be the eventual decay of the language. Moon regards ellipsis as evidence of such decay, and he takes Alford to task for his use of *treat* instead of *treat of*, as in "a matter treated in my former paper" (p. 108). Moon fears that "the consequence of too free an indulgence in the elliptical form of expression, would probably be that (in the language of every-day life, at any rate,) all connective words would gradually disappear from use," and that human languages would eventually be replaced by animal noises such as *quack! quack!* and *bow wow!* (pp. 109–10).

Moon objects to Lindley Murray's excessive use of ellipsis (for example, Murray writes *a house and orchard* instead of *a house and an orchard*), but paradoxically he also complains of Murray's wordiness. He also criticizes the usage of the scholar George P. Marsh: "It is not scholarly to begin a sentence with the conjunction *and*" (*Bad English*, p. 95). And he finds errors in subject-verb agreement, the use of *shall* and *will*, misplaced *both* and *only*, and lack of parallel construction in Edward S. Gould's usage book, *Good English*. Gould, in turn, attacked Moon's language in the pages of the *New York Round Table*, and Moon defends himself against Gould and other critics by pointing out his own conformity with the grammatical rules set down by Goold Brown, forgetting for the moment his earlier denunciation of grammarians and their effects.

Gould's *Good English*

Edward S. Gould's *Good English; or, Popular Errors in Language* was published in 1867, although many of the journalist's comments appeared earlier in the New York *Evening Post*. Gould felt that while English had improved a bit in the past twenty-five years, it had deteriorated even more, "through the heedlessness of those who should be its conservators, and the recklessness of those who have been, and are, its corrupters."[21] Gould's concern is largely with misuse and innovation in vocabulary, and he places the blame for this aspect of the deterioration of English on the partially-educated. According to Gould, it is only the educated man who can originate a new word or discover a new sense. The ignorant man counterfeits words. And the partially educated man picks up this counterfeit as real, spreading it until ultimately even the best writers use it in their work.

Gould feels that usage must be subordinated to regulation. Successful communication is simply not enough. Some people mistakenly "think the purposes of language are fulfilled, when a speaker or writer has made himself understood." But, Gould argues, everyone must admit that syntax is subject to grammatical rules such as concord of number and person, "and, if he does admit such necessity, he must further admit that no amount of usage can supersede it" (p. 4). Gould himself does not enumerate the rules that ought to govern usage, although he does accuse newspaper writers and authors of what he calls "sensation novels" of doing the most mischief in destroying the English vocabulary by introducing *spurious words*. He defines such words as those "fabricated by ignorant people, and afterward adopted by people of education." Gould denies the validity of such innovations in what has come to be a traditional refusal to grant neologisms the status of *words*: "In the strict sense, such things are not *words*—certainly not English words—at all" (p. 11). One example of an innovation which Gould refuses to recognize as a word is *jeopardize*. Gould and others who resisted the nineteenth-century neologism (which has now become quite standard) insist that the correct and only permissible verb must be *jeopard*.

According to Gould, in order to qualify as a legitimate word an expression must be necessary, be justified by analogy, and be created by someone who is educated. The term *leniency* fails all three tests for Gould, who states simply and unabashedly, "The thing meant to be expressed by the word is *lenity*, and lenity is English" (p. 15). *Lenity* is English, we are told, in all seriousness, because it derives from the Latin *lenitas* and because it is found in Johnson's *Dictionary*. Unfortunately both Webster and Worcester list *leniency* in their dictionaries, but Gould does not find the two great American lexicographers to be of sufficient authority to sanction the term as a word. *Underhanded*, which like *leniency* is now considered perfectly acceptable English, is discredited by Gould because he feels a participial termination cannot be given to an adjective (p. 19). While all words that he rejects are ultimately rejected solely on the weight of his own authority and opinion, sometimes Gould does not even go through the motions of rationalizing their dismissal. In the case of *standpoint* he simply closes his eyes to the fact of its existence: "'Stand-point' does not mean point of view for two good reasons, one of which suffices; namely, it does not mean anything" (p. 26).

Gould very often insists on the literal interpretation of words, denying them any extended sense. *Paraphernalia*, originally referring to the possessions of a bride exclusive of her dowry, should not, according to Gould, be used outside of its strict legal sense. Similarly he would restrict *predicate* to its etymological sense of 'saying, affirming, declaring'. Its use to mean 'to found', as in *predicate an argument on*, is found to be inappropriately admitted by Webster, and provides Gould with evidence that the lexicographer is an enemy of the language: "Who can hope to stay the progress of corruption in language, when the very men who should be its guardians actually help on the corruption?" (pp. 39–40). *Journal* for Gould can only mean a 'daily publication', and *you are mistaken* should only signify 'you are misjudged by someone else'. The proper form should be *you mistake*. Critics are often wistful about their inability to make language conform to their ideals, and Gould grudgingly accepts the misuse of *mistaken*: "Neither its formation nor its use can be disturbed. The word is too firmly rooted in the language, to be subject to serious criticism" (p. 69).

In addition to dealing with language itself, Gould finds time to criticize his fellow language critics. Claiming not to have read Moon's commentary on Alford, he tabulates errors he finds in the Dean's book. Gould also discredits Webster's orthographic reforms, equating them with the attempts to change the name of the United States of America to reflect more accurately its discoverer or its deliverer: both are proposed with unimpeachable reasoning but with no effect. Gould is highly critical of Webster's sanctioning of illegitimate words and of his spelling reforms: "In his capacity as lexicographer, he had no right to go behind the certificate of the good writers both in England and the United States" (p. 160). Taking a characteristically pessimistic view of the effects of language reformers other than himself, Gould finds that Webster's efforts to correct the spelling of many of our words did more harm than good: "Before Webster commenced his tinkering, the spelling of those two hundred words, however irregular to his apprehension, was more uniform than probably it ever will be again" (p. 165).

9 Grammar and Good Taste: Part 2

Richard Grant White, Armchair Linguist

One of the best-known usage commentators of the nineteenth century was Richard Grant White. His *Words and Their Uses* (1870) is a compilation of articles that appeared in *The Galaxy* during 1868 and 1869, and the normative view of language that it exhibits provoked a response by Sanskrit scholar Fitzedward Hall, *Recent Exemplifications of False Philology* (1872). White, who studied medicine and law before settling on a career as a critic of music, art, and literature, and who published a variorum edition of the works of Shakespeare, readily admits that he is no linguist. Displaying the characteristic distrust that the armchair observer of language holds for the language professional, he describes the competition in an unflattering light: "A real philologist is a man who, horsed upon Grimm's law, chases the evasive syllable over umlauts and ablauts into the faintly echoing recesses of the Himalayas." Although he does occasionally delve into the history of the language, White's concerns are more those of the gentleman than the scientist: "The points from which I have regarded words are in general rather those of taste and reason than of history."[1] In pursuing his goal, the preservation of the English language from the forces of decay, White adopts the common stand of the nineteenth- and twentieth-century usage critic. Assuming that the constituted authorities, be they littérateurs or philologists, have failed as guardians of the language, White bands his followers together into a vigilante group, "a sort of linguistic detective police," to expose error wherever it can be found. The responses to White's call for popular action were enthusiastic, as are those to similar calls that still occur today in the press, an indication that there are a significant number of ready and willing Americans who consider it their patriotic duty to inform on the linguistic vagaries of their friends and relatives.

The Law of Reason

The sole criterion for acceptability in language, according to White, is reason. He sees language as continually struggling to mold itself according to the law of reason, an unending struggle toward an ever-receding goal. White claims that

> in the development of language . . . reason always wins against formal grammar or illogical usage, and that the 'authority' of eminent writers, conforming to, or forming, the usage of their day, while it does absolve from the charge of solecism those who follow such example, does not completely justify or establish a use of words inconsistent with reason, or out of the direction of the normal growth of language. . . . In language, as in morals, there is a higher law than mere usage. [P. iii]

The law of reason is seen by White to lie behind the law of language growth, while usage for him remains at best an imperfect representation of a linguistic ideal. Foreseeing objections from those who take authoritative usage as their standard, White claims that such people are so wrong-headed they simply cannot be argued with. He compares the relationship between those who rely on reason and those who look to authority in language to the relationship between Protestants and Papists (White apparently connects reason with Protestantism), asserting bluntly, "We do not approach each other near enough for collision" (pp. iii–iv). Arguing that reason has always won out over grammar when the two have been in conflict, White claims, "There is a misuse of words which can be justified by no authority, however great, by no usage, however general" (p. 24).

White feels that writers have no innate superiority when it comes to language use (an opinion which the frequent stiffness of his own style confirms): "I cannot see why the endowment of the creative genius should, or that it does, insure to its possessor a greater certainty of correctness in the use of language than may go with the possession of inferior powers." In the very next breath White separates his work from the linguistic self-improvement handbooks, assuring his readers that his book will not help them in their writing, for good style comes "only through native ability and general culture" (pp. v–vi). Then, advising us that the study of language must be pursued for its own sake, White paradoxically claims that his work can help us in the regulation of our own language use.

Down with Grammar

In regulating language, White will have nothing to do with grammar. Dedicating his book to James Russell Lowell, White condemns grammatical instruction in the schools: "I have as little faith as I believe you have in the worth of a school-bred language. Strong, clear, healthy, living speech springs, like most strong, living things, from the soil, and grows according to the law of life within its seed" (p. 2). This organic metaphor is not to be taken too far: White assures us that language, like a plant, requires its share of pruning and training for health. White's suspicion of school grammar is grounded in his personal experience. He tells us, "The first punishment I remember having received was for a failure to get a lesson in English grammar." This punishment, described in a scene that could have served as a model for Joyce's *Portrait of the Artist*, was inflicted on an uncomprehending five year old who would live to remember the irrational torture and fear of original sin associated with grammar education:

> I found myself standing in an upper chamber of a gloomy brick house, book in hand,—it was a thin volume, with a tea-green paper cover and a red roan back,—before an awful being, who put questions to me, which, for all that I could understand of them, might as well have been couched in Coptic or in Sanskrit; . . . when asked about governing, I answered, "I don't know," and when about agreeing, "I can't tell," until at last, in despair, I said nothing, and choked down my tears, wondering, in a dazed, dumb fashion, whether all this was part and parcel of that total depravity of the human heart of which I heard so much; . . . the being—to whom I apply no harsh epithet, for, poor man, he thought he was doing God service—said to me, in a terrible voice, "You are a stupid, idle boy, sir, and have neglected your task. I shall punish you. Hold out your hand." I put it out half way, like a machine with a hitch in its gearing. "Farther, sir." I advanced it an inch or two, when he seized the tips of my fingers, bent them back so as to throw the palm well up, and then, with a mahogany rule, much bevelled on one side, and having a large, malignant ink-spot near the end,—an instrument which seemed to me to weigh about forty pounds, and to be a fit implement for a part of that eternal torture to which I had been led to believe that I, for my inborn depravity, was doomed,—he proceeded to reduce my little hand, only just well in gristle, as nearly to a jelly as was thought, on the whole, to be beneficial to a small boy at that stage of the world's progress. [Pp. 274–75]

As a result of this torture, the adult White has no use for grammar: "That I am unversed in the rules of English grammar (so called), I am not ashamed to confess" (p. 276). He feels that English is a grammarless tongue, and that this is the basis for its superiority, citing Sir Philip Sidney's claim, in the "Apologie for Poetrie," that English "is so voyd of those cumbersome differences of Cases, Genders, Moodes, and Tenses, which I think was a peece of the Tower of Babilon's curse, that a man should be put to schoole to learne his mother tongue" (p. v). According to White, it was only after English had become grammarless that it was supplied with a Latin model totally unrelated to it, and from this heterogeneous union of English words and Latin grammar "sprang that hybrid monster known as English grammar, before whose fruitless loins we have sacrificed, for nearly three hundred years, our children and the strangers within our gates" (p. 279).

White feels that the grammatical rules found in books leave much to be desired: "Some are absurd, and the most are superfluous." His own quite serious list of syntax rules reveals his attitude:

> The verb needs not, and generally does not, agree with its nom-
> inative case in number and person:
> Pronouns do not agree with their antecedent nouns in person,
> number, and gender:
> Active verbs do not govern the objective case, or any other:
> Prepositions do not govern the objective case, or any other:
> One verb does not govern another in the infinitive mood:
> Nor is the infinitive a mood, nor is it governed by substantive,
> adjective, or participle:
> Conjunctions need not connect the same moods and tenses of
> verbs. [Pp. 295–96]

White summed up his idea of syntax concisely: "In English, words are formed into sentences by the operation of an invisible power, which is like magnetism" (pp. 297–98). He states that "nearly all of our so-called English grammar is mere make-believe grammar." Children in school "are required to cite a rule which they cannot understand, as the law of a relation which does not exist" (p. 304). He claims that it is easier to understand the Apocalypse than Lindley Murray's tenth law, which states, rather cryptically, "One substantive governs another sig-nifying a different thing in the possessive case" (pp. 323–24).

White has as little use for dictionary makers as he has for grammarians. He objects to the inclusion of etymologies in dictionaries because such information is useful only to specialists, and he faults dictionaries for the multiplicity of their definitions. White claims that metaphorical uses and compounds are included simply for the purpose of swelling the number of words. His most serious complaint is that these books are not designed for the use of native speakers: "One great vice of our dictionaries, as of our grammars, is, that they are planned and written as if for men who know nothing of their own language" (p. 384).

The Danger of a Little Learning

Despite his outright rejection of formal grammar, White feels the need to protect the language against the forces of decay represented by a tendency to slang, colloquialism, and vulgarity. His main concern is with the health of American diction—with words and their uses—and he agrees with the linguist and lexicographer William Dwight Whitney in regarding diction as a particularly American problem, "a besetting sin," which we have a moral duty to overcome: "The mental tone of a community may be vitiated by a yielding to the use of loose, coarse, low, and frivolous phraseology" (p. 5). White recognizes that language is a natural phenomenon that develops of its own accord, but, when it is threatened by decay, he cannot ignore the call to arms: "Language is generally formed by indirect and unconscious effort; but when a language is subjected to the constant action of such degrading influences as those which threaten ours, it may be well to introduce into its development a little consciousness."

Like Dean Alford and Edward Gould, White sees not the ignorant but the partly-learned as the most serious threat to English: "Language is rarely corrupted, and is often enriched, by the simple, unpretending, ignorant man, who takes no thought of his parts of speech. It is from the man who knows just enough to be anxious to square his sentences by the line and plummet of grammar and dictionary that his mother tongue suffers most grievous injury" (p. 6). White speaks of "that unconscious, intuitive use of idiom which gives life and strength to the simple speech of very humble people" (p. 45), but in the long run it is not these people that concern him or many of the other language commentators who celebrate the speech of the common folk. White's book is not pitched to the partly-learned, the linguistically insecure, as a rule for them to square their language with. White does not directly accuse his readers of language incompetence, unlike the writers of usage guides which consist mainly of lists of common errors specifically designed to help those most likely to be committing them. Rather, he invites his readers to join him on a crusade. Taking a middle course between pedants and coarse libertines, White uses metaphors of the eradication of disease and sin to describe the effects of his efforts to regulate American English: "Although I do not expect to purge away corruption, I do hope to arrest it in some measure by giving hints that help toward wholesomeness" and that may work to "prevent evil in the future" (p. 7). For him, careless and incorrect usage is dishonest, and we must all strive against it, "almost as if it were a question of morals" (p. 18).

British and American English

White has been criticized for anglophilia in matters of language and literature. He does have an unflattering view of those American aspirations which he feels are expressions of an unwarranted separatism: "When that new 'American' thing, so eagerly sought, and hitherto so vainly, does appear, if it ever do appear, it will not be a language, or even a literature" (p. 8). But White does defend American usage, claiming that middle-rate British writers are, if anything, more open to attack than their American counterparts. He feels that the British are more prone to "free and easy deviations from correct English speech" (p. 57), but in a mixed company of British and Americans there would be little to distinguish the speech of the two nationalities except a few local slang expressions. The standard for both countries is and ought to be the same, and, accusing British writers of "slovenly grammar," White concludes by reaffirming the validity of American English: "Of the mother tongue no purer form is known to the Old England than to the New" (p. 56).

White admits that language is formed by consent and custom, that usage can establish a de facto rule, and he also admits that "no man, no number of men, however great, can of purpose change one monosyllable" of a tongue. But he also takes issue with Robert G. Latham's version of Pope's "Whatever is, is right," arguing that "in language, as in all other human affairs, that which is may be wrong" (p. 15). One area of correction where White is particularly optimistic involves misused words. He feels that "a neglect to preserve any well-drawn distinction in words between thoughts or things is, just so far, a return toward barbarism in language," and he cites primitive language and the speech of children as examples of language that is too impoverished to make such distinctions. The British, White feels, are especially guilty here, although he also criticizes the Irish, for example their use of *adopt* in the sense, *be adopted* (pp. 82–85).

Some Specific Objections

White decries the use of *aggravate* for *irritate* (a sense that is now common, though still objected to), and he faults the London Society for the Prevention of Cruelty to Animals for apparently excluding humans from the term *animal*. He opposes *balance* for *remainder* (another sense much fought against in the nineteenth century that is now more than tolerated), and suggests *violoncello* as more correct than *violincello*, using etymology rather than reason to support his contention. A *couple*, for White, is not simply any pair, but "a pair united," and *convene* is misused even in the Constitution of the United States for *convoke*. *Dirt*, for White, means *filth*; it cannot mean 'earth'. And *divine*, as a noun (for 'priest, clergyman'), though of long usage and high authority, is found to be fantastic, extravagant, and at variance with (an unstated) reason (p. 107). *Dress* is another term that White finds grossly misused. It should not refer only to gowns, but to all items of apparel, even undergarments.

A good many of the misused words that White highlights are now standard. We may even suspect that some of them were already standard in White's day. Linguistic complaints are loudest when language seems most threatening, and the reactions of the few ultraconservative self-appointed guardians of language against particular forms suggest that the forms are already being used by enough people as to have become automatic and neutral. One continual cry of the vigilantes is that we are unaware of the errors we are committing. The language guardians frequently admit that their protests are in certain cases vain, although the fact that they object anyway indicates that they are the last to abandon hope. *Executed* in the sense 'put to death' was opposed by a number of commentators in the nineteenth century. White objects to it too, at the same time admitting that the meaning has become well entrenched. In his comment his defeatism about all efforts at reform becomes apparent: of *executed*, he says, "There is little hope of its reformation, except in case of that rare occurrence in the history of language, a vigorous and persistent effort on the part of the best speakers and writers and professional teachers" (p. 111).

White finds that *editorial* is "an unpleasant Americanism for *leader*." He feels that *get* should not be used for simple possession. *Humanitarian* does not mean 'humane person' but someone "who denies the godhead of Jesus Christ, and insists upon his human nature." White sees the popularization of this word as self-congratulatory, "the result of an effort by certain people to elevate and appropriate to themselves a common feeling by giving it a grand and peculiar name" (p. 127). *Ice-water* and *ice-cream* should in fact be *iced-water* and *iced-cream*, for *ice cream* must mean 'cream made from ice', and that is impossible. But some words White defends. To him, the term *Jew* is simply a racial designation, not the singling out of a person's religion: "What offence could be reasonably taken at this designation, it would be difficult to discover" (p. 131).

White's note on *marry* may or may not reveal something of his personal situation with respect to the female sex, but it certainly shows a pedantic strain that is matched by few of his reform-minded colleagues. White claims "to marry is to give, or to be given, to a husband, *mari*":

> Properly speaking, a man is not married to a woman, or married with her; nor are a man and a woman married with each other. The woman is married to the man. It is her name that is lost in his, not his in hers; she becomes a member of his family, not he of hers; it is her life that is merged, or supposed to be merged, in his, not his in hers; she follows his fortunes, and takes his station, not he hers. And thus, manifestly, she has been attached to him by a legal bond, not he to her; except, indeed, as all attachment is necessarily mutual. But, nevertheless, we do not speak of tying a ship to a boat, but a boat to a ship. And so long, at least, as man is the larger, the stronger, the more individually important, as long as woman generally lives in her husband's house and bears his name,—still more should she not bear his name,—it is the woman who is married to the man. [p. 140]

In marriage, then, a woman may only serve as the subject of the passive for White. This grammatical bias is found again when White speaks of the term *widow woman*. To White it is redundant, a pleonasm; *widow* is the proper term. He adds that *widow* is one of the few English words where the feminine is the basic form: "But finely formed and touching as the original feminine word is, it was inevitable that the preposterousness of forming upon it a masculine counterpart should produce monstrosity," that is, the term *widower* (p. 174).

White objects to the use of *obnoxious* to mean 'offensive'; to *railroad* instead of *railway*; and to *depot* for *station* (*depot* should only be used for 'warehouse'). He finds *real estate* to be "a compound that has no proper place in the language of every-day life, where it is merely a pretentious intruder from the technical province of law" (p. 150). Pretension bothers White as much as any form of language misuse, and he objects strongly to euphemisms. He prefers *woman* to *female* (a case made earlier by Alford, although White does not acknowledge the Dean's influence). And in a remarkably modern outburst he opposes the use of *limb* for *leg*, a word regarded in the nineteenth century as potentially indecent: "It is the occasion and the purpose of speech that make it modest or immodest, not the thing spoken of, or the giving it its proper name" (pp. 181–82).

Like most usage commentators, White deals with a category of words that he feels are illegitimate, and that ought to be denied wordhood. Curiously, he finds himself compelled to invent a term to describe them: they are *words-no-words*, "usurpers, interlopers, or vulgar pretenders; some are deformed creatures . . . in many cases the consequence of a misapprehension or whimsical perversion of some real word" (p. 201). Some of his *words-no-words* we recognize now to be back-formations, for example *intercess* from *intercession*. Others are adjectives used as nouns, such as *locals* for *local reporters*. White disapproves of *donate*, formed upon *donation*, "itself not among our best words." He finds *enthused* a Southern vogue word, calling it ridiculous. If we need a word at all, he would have it be *enthusiasmed*, modeled on the French verb, *enthousiasmer* (p. 208).

Although he approves of borrowings, White also regrets them, for they are often ill formed. He finds *telegram* "both superfluous and incorrectly formed" and argues that *photographer* ought to be *photographist*. His opinion of neologists is not high: "If those who have given us *petroleum* for *rock-oil* had had the making of our language in past times, our evergreens would have been called sempervirids." Borrowings can also indicate to White a weakness in our language. He defends its native word building capacity and reveals an implicit sympathy with the Saxonist movement:

> The language is full of words compounded of two or more simple ones, and which are used without a thought of their being themselves other than simple words—*chestnut, walnut, acorn, household* . . . and the like. The power to form such words is an element of wealth and strength in a language; and every word got up for the occasion out of the Latin or the Greek lexicon, when a possible English compound would serve the same purpose, is a standing but unjust reproach to the language—a false imputation of both weakness and inflexibility. The English *out-take* is much better than the Latin compound by which it has been supplanted—*except*. And why should we call our bank-side towns *riparian*? In dropping *wanhope* we have thrown away a word for which *despair* is not an equivalent; and the place of *truth-like*, or *true-seeming* would be

poorly filled by the word which some very elegant people are seeking to foist upon us—*vraisemblable*. [P. 216]

White objects to the progressive passive, *is being done*, a neology which he claims is only eighty years old and which is meeting with resistance by the unlettered. He compares it to nonstandard Southern *done gone* and *gone done*: "The Southern provincial use of *do* and *go* is capable of formulation into tenses, which, if it were not for the prejudice in favor of other—in the present delicate condition of the country, I will not say better—usage, might claim the attention, and even the adhesion, of people like those who adopt *is being done*—who shun an idiom as they would be thought to shun a sin, and who must be correct, or die." To this he adds a mock conjugation of *do* with *go* as its auxiliary, concluding, "I *gwine gone done* is as reasonable a part of the verb *to do* as *I shall* or *will have done*" (pp. 350–52). The ruin of English threatened by *is being done* "comes of laying presumptuous hands upon idioms, those sacred mysteries of language" (p. 363).

Reason and Usage

In the final chapter of *Words and Their Uses* White again takes up the question of usage. He describes the connection between usage and reason in more detail: "Usage does not act arbitrarily. It is guided, almost governed, by a union of the forces of precedent and reason" (p. 395). He accepts the force of usage when there is no alternative: "Owing to the peculiar function of language as the only means of communication between man and man, whatever is, must be accepted, in a certain degree at least. A writer or speaker cannot be justly censured, as for a personal fault, because he uses words and phrases which are current in his day" (p. 412). Such a statement, of course, undercuts to some extent White's own judgments on the English language, but White had always admitted the force of usage in language. His conservatism in resisting change, or the tampering with "sacred" idioms, and his acceptance of innovation, when it is appropriate, soften his apparent rigidity when it comes to matters of reason. His main objections in the area of usage are to what he perceives as mistakes made by a certain segment of American society: the partly-learned, those "who must be correct, or die." It is not clear that the errors White cites are those actually made by the partly-learned, but it is significant that White senses (as did Alford before him) the linguistic insecurity of certain social groups, and their consequent tendency toward hypercorrection, an insecurity most recently described and quantified in the twentieth century by the sociolinguist William Labov.

Even though usage is a force to be reckoned with, reason is for White the highest of linguistic laws. When language can conform itself to the dictates of reason, it is made better. Once reason prevails, its effects cannot easily be reversed. According to White, the decline of the Anglo-Saxon double negative is "chiefly owing to a deliberate conformity to the requirements of logic, which in the process of time was inevitable, and which, once attained, will never be abandoned until language comes to be informed by the rule of unreason" (p. 415). The blind faith White places in reason prevents him from seeing the English language more clearly and from noticing the inconsistencies in his own comments. In fact, reason plays a small part in the corrections White proposes—although it is true that usage plays one that is even smaller. Fitzedward Hall is not far from the truth when he rails against "vernacular philology" in the hands of "criticasters" like White, accusing them of ipsedixitism and a disregard for calm statement or argument.[2]

Reaction to the Armchair Philologist

Hall's criticisms of White are anything but calm. Although he claims that the sole rational criterion of grammaticalness is "general consent" and he cites authority, analogy, and historical precedent to back up his own opinions, Hall's fanaticism blinds him to the fact that his method is virtually identical to White's. Despite White's explicit aversion to school grammar and his insistence that English is a grammarless tongue, Hall considers White and writers like him to be grammarians, self-appointed high priests of language: "Any 'strict grammar' for which a basis is claimed apart from usage must be a species of theology, of which prophets by divine designation alone possess the key" (p. 66). Only rational philology is a legitimate enterprise, and Hall accuses White's work of standing in relation to philology as alchemy does to chemistry. (In fact, contemporary linguists still employ the term *grammarian* in a negative sense.)

Hall calls White unscientific and antihistorical, despite the fact that White, in his discussion of pronouns, argues from a historical and philological perspective. He accuses White of acting solely on the principle of whim, and he criticizes him for treating "English much in the manner of a tailor who, instead of making new coats after the measure of his customers, should pare down his customers to fit coats ready-made" (p. 85). But Hall does the same thing, time after time. Like White, Hall objects to *telegram* as an "obnoxious vocable." He argues that the compound in question must derive from the Greek *tele-* and *grapho-*, and shows that *telegraph* is the appropriate form for the sender, the instrument, and the message. Hall then suggests *telegrapheme* as a suitable term to distinguish the message from the other meanings of the word. Referring to White, Hall warns of "the contagion of his numberless crotchets and crudities," but, in his item-by-item treatment of White's suggestions for improving English, Hall proves as crotchety and crude as his subject, engaging in flights of rhetoric, convoluted syntax, and hyperlatinate diction. As White misleadingly bases his judgments on reason, Hall's vain exercise in overkill and his crabby tone barely mask his own attempts to convince us that his whimsical, ipsedixitist judgments are really based on empirical science.

Every-day English

In *Every-day English* (Boston, 1880), a collection of essays written by Richard Grant White that had originally appeared in the *New York Times* and *The Galaxy*, White reaffirms his opinion that the English language has no grammar. He feels that the English people managed to rid themselves of the complexities of grammar as they became civilized, and he goes so far as to suggest that English has no true parts of speech, pointing to the fact that almost all our nouns may be used as verbs, our pronouns as adjectives, and so forth. As he did in *Words and Their Uses*, White sidesteps Hall and other critics of his work. Responding to attacks on his own use of language, he argues that his own linguistic errors need not limit his effectiveness as a teacher: "That a physician cannot heal himself is no ground for belief that his advice may not profit others" (p. xv).

White renews his attack on American schools for their encouragement of vulgarity and pomposity. He expresses disdain for an inordinate concern with correctness of pronunciation. And, as he had earlier dismissed grammar, he now dismisses spelling and spelling reform: "I have not the highest respect for spelling: I don't take it to heart" (p. xix). In *Every-day English* White has become a pronounced anglophile. He feels that the English must set the standards for the language because they spoke it first: "It is manifestly to England that we are to go if we would find that which is emphatically and unquestionably English." Anything differing from the usage of polite English society might as well be a different language: "In so far as it deviates from the language of the most cultivated society in England it fails to be English" (p. 89).

Although he claims to be unconcerned with pronunciation, White finds that Americans, particularly women, exhibit an inferior quality of voice. Resurrecting the stereotype of the bookishness of American English, White sees spelling pronunciation as an American disease, attributable to common school teaching. His portrait of an American speaker reveals our national linguistic insecurity:

> In regard to the pronunciation and enunciation of words, the striking defect of common "American" speech is again due to constraint, to conscious effort. The "average American" tries to pronounce too distinctly. He is conscious about his syllables, and seems to talk with the spelling-book before his eyes. He is in constant fear of the "dictionary," that Juggernaut of speech. [P. 97]

Much of *Every-day English* is concerned with a history and criticism of the spelling reform movement, but White does manage to include some additional usage comments in the last few chapters. He objects to the use of *can* for *may*, and *talk* for *speak*. *Every once in a while* is labeled nonsense: "In this phrase, *every* qualifies all that comes after it; and what is a *once in a while*?" (p. 410). According to White, the correct phrase should be either *once in every little while*, or *once in a little while*. Two other words that now have an unshakable position in English, *scientist* and *physicist*, are regarded by White as intolerable, unlovely, and improper in their formation. He suggests *sciencist* or the even less likely *scientialist* as proper synonyms for *scientific man*. White acknowledges that *physicist* has already proved its permanence, but he feels obliged to point out its etymological inappropriateness: "We should make the word *physics-ist*" (p. 470). White again shows sympathy for the work of the Saxonists. Although he urges no immediate reformation of English, he expresses regret at the passing of *leech* and *leechcraft* from the language, and their replacement by *physician* and *medicine*: "We might learn in this respect much from the Germans, who within the last half century have turned many Latin and Greek words out of their language, even in their scientific vocabulary, to replace them by Teutonic words, simple and compound; the gain whereby to their language in strength, significance, and symmetry has been great, and no less in nationality of character" (p. 471).

White concludes his study on a pessimistic note. Although he seeks to improve the English language through his commentaries, the force of books and reason have little hope of success. The half-educated will continue to pollute our tongue, for good English is a matter of birth, and language improvement cannot be a self-conscious process:

As I have before said, they who speak the best English are they who take no thought as to their speech, either as to the words they use, or as to their way of using them. The mastery of their mother tongue has come to them from association, from social and intellectual training, and from an acquaintance with the writings of the best authors. For this way of learning to speak and write English well there is no substitute; although intelligent endeavor may do somewhat in later years to supply the lack of these advantages in early life. Even then, however, the same end must be obtained by substantially the same means. [Pp. 502–03]

Usage Handbooks: Common Errors Corrected

Despite the elitist position taken by men like Henry Alford, Edward S. Gould, and Richard Grant White that good grammar and good taste were more the products of birth than education, concise handbooks of correct English had become very popular in America by the mid-nineteenth century. These are usually slim volumes that catalogue and correct mistakes in pronunciation and idiom without lengthy explanations, and without appeals to reason, usage, philology, or even taste. They are designed for a readership conscious of its linguistic shortcomings and hopeful that these shortcomings may be neutralized in a few easy lessons. In 1856 Walton Burgess published *Five Hundred Mistakes of Daily Occurrence in Speaking, Pronouncing, and Writing the English Language, Corrected.* The author states that his book "was prepared to meet the wants of persons—numbered by *multitudes* in even the most intelligent and refined communities—who from deficiency of education, or from carelessness of manner, are in the habit of misusing many of the most common words of the English language, distorting its grammatical forms, destroying its beauty, and corrupting its purity."[3] Appealing directly to the linguistic insecurity of the undereducated "man in the street," who does not want to be mistaken for a newcomer to America, rather than the more literary audience of White and his colleagues, Burgess lists five hundred items to be corrected, in random order. His is the true *ipse dixit* authority, for he never goes beyond the simple statement of correct and incorrect.

Burgess's advice concerns the familiar as well as the unfamiliar, and many of his suggestions continue to be made by today's usage reformers. He deals with all aspects of language use: spelling, pronunciation, grammar, diction, and style, handing down his decisions with little or no discussion. For example, his readers are told not to say *fizzled out,* but *proved a failure*. They should avoid *I reckon* when they mean to say *I think*, and they should say *I left*, not *I made tracks*. *Pay over* is proper, *fork over* is not. *Learn* cannot mean *teach*. *Sewed* should not be used for *sewn*. And *between you and I* must be *between you and me*. *Combatants* should be accented on the first syllable; *warrior* has two syllables, not three; *chimney* is not to be pronounced *chimley* or *chimbley*; and *creek* should be rhymed with *brick*.

According to Burgess, *lit* is obsolete; only *lighted* is correct. *Dry* must not be used to mean *thirsty*; *strength* should never be pronounced *strenth*; and *first of all* and *last of all* should simply be *first* and *last*. A *new pair of shoes* is more properly *a pair of new shoes*. Superfluous *r*'s, giving such mispronunciation as *drawring* and *sawr*, must be avoided. *Catsup*, not *ketchup*, is correct. And we should always say *Is Mr. Smith within?* rather than *Is Mr. Smith in?* The name *United Kingdom* is certainly incorrect; it should be *United Kingdoms* instead. After all, Burgess reminds us, "Who ever speaks of the United State of America?" And again, according to Burgess, "*to peff*, meaning *to cough faintly* (like a sheep), is hardly a useable word."

Burgess states in his preface that grammar books, where we might ordinarily expect to find such information as he is providing, are both difficult to read and ineffective in correcting error. He avoids grammatical terminology because he assumes his readers will not be familiar with it and, perhaps, because he feels it will frighten his audience away. Burgess's main concern is with correcting errors in speech, although he does occasionally comment on the written language. His book is designed to prevent his readers from making errors that will embarrass them: he hopes "the work shall be the means of saving one sensitive man from a confusion of blushes, in the presence of a company before which he desired to preserve his equanimity" (p. v). Assuring his readers that they do not have to be highly intelligent in order to be able to speak well, Burgess repeats that his purpose is "to insure persons who often have a good thing to say, from the confusion and mortification of improperly saying it" (p. 7). Noting that his list is by no means complete, Burgess plays on both the xenophobia and the assimilationist desires of his audience by reminding them that their incorrect use of English will make others suspect them of being uncivilized foreigners. Concluding his introduction, he tells us that his book is simply a first step for the partly-educated, that class of society whose usage is ridiculed by the learned Dean Alford and Mr. White. Burgess, whose motto is "Never too late to learn," expresses the hope that his work will inspire "some who are unfortunately deficient in education, to seek so much additional knowledge as shall enable them at least to converse in a dialect which is within the compass of the language of their country, and free them from the imputation of belonging to another tribe of men, speaking another tongue" (pp. 16–17).

Like Pulling Teeth

Another book of this sort is *Every-day Errors of Speech*, published in 1871 by L. P. Meredith, a dentist who learned the trade from his father, and who was perhaps better known as the author of *The Teeth and How to Save Them*. Meredith is mainly concerned with correct pronunciation, and he aims his book at those of fair or excellent education, warning that if the errors he notes are not eradicated, "it will not be many years before our orthoepic standard will be overthrown as it was in England some years ago."[4] Meredith tells us, for example, to pronounce *blouse* as *blowz*, not *blowss*; to say *burst*, not *bust*; to avoid r-less *February* and *partridge*. The fact that the pronunciation *blowss* is now standard, that *bust* has become an accepted word, and that the first *r* in February seems in danger of extinction shows the powerlessness of books like this to alter usage. Meredith's book also contains a few usage comments: he objects to *Let's us go* and *Let's him and me go* as being redundant, and he disapproves of *says* (pronounced *sez*) when used to refer to the past (that is, the historical present). The rest of Meredith's work is taken up with lists of correct pronunciations of names and medical terms, and exercises in correct usage designed as party games.

Harlan H. Ballard's *Handbook of Blunders* (Boston, 1886) is another example of this correctionist genre. Ballard was a science teacher with a concern for public speaking, and his list of errors, alphabetically arranged, reminds us that *balance* cannot mean *remainder*; that the use of the term *pants* for *trousers* is to be avoided; that a *negro* is not a *darkey* or a *black*; that *creole* has no implication of admixture of African blood; that there is no verb *to diagram*; that *catholic* should not be used for *Roman Catholic*; that *the blues* is a colloquial expression for *low spirits*; and that *biscuit*, which he treats as a mass noun, is often incorrectly used for *roll*: "Biscuit are hard, and we commonly call them crackers."

Slips of Speech

John Bechtel was a compiler, editing collections of mythology, Sunday-school readings, temperance lectures, and books on spelling and pronunciation. His handbook of common language errors, *Slips of Speech*

(Philadelphia, 1903), affirms the need for rules in language: "Grammarians and rhetoricians . . . set forth the laws and principles governing speech, and formulate rules whereby we may follow the true, and avoid the false" (p. 3). But Bechtel is only giving lip service to the rule makers. He recommends his own book because the longer tomes of the learned and the voluminous textbooks of the schools are generally ignored by the public. He criticizes school grammar as meaningless, dull memorization, and claims that students generally burn their grammar books when school has ended. Bechtel is mainly concerned with the development of taste in his readers, a task that can only be accomplished by reading the best literature. He emphasizes a connection between speech and thought that is commonly assumed by the language reformers of the present: "Looseness of style in speaking and writing may nearly always be traced to indistinctness and feebleness in the grasp of the subject" (p. 8).

Bechtel advises his readers to avoid poetic terms when discussing homely ideas, and to avoid foreign terms, hackneyed phrases, and fad words. In addition to emphasizing the importance of a style appropriate to the subject, Bechtel cautions his readers to avoid what he calls very vulgar vulgarisms: "No one who has any regard for purity of diction and the proprieties of cultivated society will be guilty of such expressions as *yaller* for yellow, *feller* for fellow, . . . *yarbs* for herbs, *taters* for potatoes, . . . *bile* for boil, *hain't* for ain't or isn't, . . . *teeny* for tiny, *fooling you* for deceiving you, *them* for those, *shut up* for be quiet, . . . *lots of books* for many books, . . . *gents* for gentlemen" (pp. 13–14).

Bechtel presents the list of objectionable expressions compiled by William Cullen Bryant when he was editor of the *New York Evening Post*, a list which forbids the use of trite or pretentious expressions, for example *above* and *over* (for *more than*), *aspirant*, *authoress*, *humbug*, *en route*, *lengthy* (for *long*), *decease* as a verb, *leniency* (for *lenity*), *poetess*, *ovation*, *progress* (for *advance*), *juvenile* (for *boy*), *taboo*, *talented*, *jeopardize*, *donate*, and so on. Bechtel proclaims the usage of the best writers and speakers as his standard, provided that they have obeyed the genius of the language: "An author's diction is pure when he uses such words only as belong to the idiom of the language" (p. 19). But Bechtel never justifies his linguistic judgments by referring to respected authors, or to the idiom of the language. Like the writers of other handbooks, he avoids explanations as much as possible.

Bechtel also stoutly rejects slang. For him slang is an indication of linguistic disease and it calls up images of social poverty and decay. Slang, like the chicken pox, is highly contagious, and "it is severest, too, where the sanitary conditions are most favorable to its development" (p. 22). In addition to Bryant's list, Bechtel has proscriptions of his own to record. Like other commentators, he maintains that *mutual* cannot mean *common* in reference to a friend (citing the novel, *Our Mutual Friend*, Bechtel comments, "Dickens's strong point was not grammar"). And he feels that we should avoid expressions such as *I love cherries* because "love is an emotion of the heart, and not of the palate" (pp. 28–29). For Bechtel, *prejudice* must always be negative, never neutral or positive; *got* should not be overused; *little bit, dry* (for *thirsty*), and *different than* should be avoided. He defends the American use of *drive* and *ride* as synonyms, and he rejects certain uses of *fire*: "To *fire a stone, fire him out of the house, fire him out of our employ*, may be graphic ways of presenting the thought, but good writers never use them and good speakers should avoid them" (pp. 78–79).

Bechtel is uncomfortable with contractions, admitting *ain't, weren't, mightn't*, and *oughtn't* with caution, while excluding *shalln't* and *willn't*. *Ain't* is permitted with the stipulation that it is inelegant and that it must never be used with the third person singular. *Haint* and *taint* are excluded as "indicative of an entire lack of culture" while *aren't* is said not to have found much favor among writers or critics of the language. Bechtel is also extremely offended (as was Dean Alford) by expressions of family intimacy:

> The use of such words as *dad, daddy, mam, mammy, the old man, the old woman*, when applied to parents, not only indicates a lack of refinement, but shows positive disrespect. . . . After the first lispings of childhood the words *papa* and *mama*, properly accented, should be insisted on by parents, and at the age of twelve or fifteen the words *father* and *mother* should be substituted and ever after used, as showing a proper respect on the part of children. [Pp. 97–98]

Ambrose Bierce: The Devil's Grammarian

Before disappearing mysteriously in Mexico in 1914, Ambrose Bierce, author of *The Devil's Dictionary*, also compiled a popular usage guide called *Write It Right, a Little Blacklist of Literary Faults* (1909). Like his predecessors, Bierce rejects all authority but his own. He is particularly critical of dictionary makers: "Few words have more than one literal and serviceable meaning, however many metaphorical, derivative, related, or even unrelated, meanings lexicographers may think it worth while to gather from all sorts and conditions of men, with which to bloat their absurd and misleading dictionaries." Bierce rejects the usage of both the learned and the unlearned, the "narrow etymons of the mere scholar and loose locutions of the ignorant."[5] But he accepts the notion that style and taste are personal matters, and that his blacklisting of misused words cannot be categorical: "Excepting in the case of capital offenders—expressions ancestrally vulgar or irreclaimably degenerate—absolute proscription is possible as to serious composition only. . . . In neither taste nor precision is any man's practice a court of last appeal, for writers all, both great and small, are habitual sinners against the light" (pp. 6–7).

Bierce's alphabetical list of blunders is concise, and there are few comments about preferred terms. But when explanations do occur they reveal both Bierce's wit and his stand on usage matters. Bierce rejects *apt* when it is used to mean 'likely', saying, "Even the dictionary-makers cannot persuade a person of discriminating taste to accept it as synonymous with likely." His comment on *locate* further shows his opinions of lexicography: "Some dictionaries give locate as an intransitive verb, . . . but—well, dictionaries are funny." Bierce describes *lengthy* as "no better than breadthy, or thicknessy" and *banquet* as "a good enough word in its place, but its place is the dictionary. Say, dinner." Bierce is also picky about passive forms. He tells his readers, "Do not say, 'I am afraid it will rain.' Say, I fear it will rain." Of the phrase, *You are mistaken* he says, "For whom? Say, You mistake." In the case of *given*, he is insistent: " 'The soldier was given a rifle.' What was given is the rifle, not the soldier. 'The house was given a coat (coating) of paint.' Nothing can be 'given' anything."

Just as some phrases cannot be said, some words simply do not exist for Bierce. He informs us that "there is no such word as illy, for ill itself is an adverb," despite the fact that *illy* is recorded by the *Oxford English Dictionary* as being used as early as 1547. Though the *OED* marks *illy* as now chiefly dialectal, it cites uses of the word by Carew, Jefferson, Southey, Lowell, Washington Irving, and Thomas Hardy.

A word can have only one meaning, and since Bierce defines *laundry* as "a place where clothing is washed, this word cannot mean, also, clothing sent there to be washed." Of *would-be* we are told, "The word doubtless supplies a want, but we can better endure the want than the word." *Donate* is said to be "good American, but not good English," and *electrocution* is "no less than disgusting, and the thing meant by it is felt to be altogether too good for the word's inventor." On *commit suicide* Bierce takes a stand against back-formations as well as against what he perceives to be the overuse of *commit* and *get*: "For married we do not say, 'committed matrimony.' Unfortunately most of us do say, 'got married,' which is almost as bad. For lack of a suitable verb we just sometimes say committed this or that, as in the instance of bigamy, for the verb to bigam is a blessing that is still in store for us."

Henry James: Advice to Young Ladies

In an address entitled "The Question of Our Speech," given to the graduating class at Bryn Mawr College in 1905, novelist Henry James advises his audience of young ladies to cultivate good speech. James takes for granted the notion of a mutually agreed-upon standard English that needs no further definition: "A virtual consensus of the educated, of any gathered group, in regard to the *speech* that, among the idioms and articulations of the globe, they profess to make use of, may well strike us, in a given case, as a natural, an inevitable assumption" necessary for the "imparting of a coherent culture."[6] James finds fault with American speech because it does not have a "tone-standard," by which term he seems to mean "a clear criterion of the best usage and example . . . avoiding vulgarity, arriving at lucidity, pleasantness, charm" (p. 16). The absence of a concern with tone is seen as a fundamental of American society: "Against a care for tone, it would very much appear, the elements of life in this country, as at present conditioned, violently and increasingly militate" (p. 13). This threat from within could, if we are not careful, lead to the total destruction of the English language as we know it. Although James's concern for tone primarily has to do with pronunciation, he extends his views occasionally to a consideration of general usage: "There are plenty of influences round about us that make for an imperfect disengagement of the human side of vocal sound, that make for the confused, the ugly, the flat, the thin, the mean, the helpless, that reduce articulation to an easy and ignoble minimum, and so keep it as little distinct as possible from the grunting, the squealing, the barking or the roaring of animals" (p. 16).

Despite this danger, James is optimistic that more Americans will learn to speak well and minimize the evil by influencing each other to improve usage. Like most language guardians, James regards the scientific study of language with suspicion. He sees linguistic relativism as one of the strongest forces of aggression and corruption, "the forces assembled to make you believe that no form of speech is provably better than another, and that just this matter of 'care' is an affront to the majesty of sovereign ignorance" (p. 18). Our syllables, vowels, and consonants, the way we say things, are of primary importance: "I mean speaking with consideration for the forms and shades of our language . . . the innumerable differentiated, discriminated units of sound and sense that lend themselves to audible production, to enunciation, to intonation" (pp. 19–20). James warns his audience against the dangers of what he sees as the scientific concern for data rather than style: "You must be prepared for much vociferous demonstration of the plea that the way we say things—the way we 'say' in general—has as little importance as possible." But language is not a question of rational proof but one of faith: "Let the demonstration proceed, let the demonstration abound, let it be as vociferous as it will, if you only meanwhile hug the closer the faith I thus commend to you" (p. 22).

By the phrase "speaking badly" James means "speaking as millions and millions of supposedly educated, supposedly civilized persons— that is the point—of both sexes, in our great country, habitually, persistently, imperturbably, and I think for the most part all unwittingly, speak." The characterization of vast numbers of American speakers as uncivilized because their English is not to his taste is a normal attitude for a language guardian like James to take. He feels that bad speech produces in us the same effect as bad manners or any other breach of social decorum: "Speaking badly is speaking with that want of attention to speech that we should blush to see any other of our personal functions compromised by—any other controllable motion, or voluntary act, of our lives." In short—and in a rare burst of preciseness for James—he declares that bad speech is as dangerous as walking, dressing, and eating in the dark, where we "run the chance of breaking our legs, of misarranging our clothes, of besmearing our persons" (pp. 23–24).

While Elias Molee complained that English was deficient in vowel sounds, James faults American youth for not pronouncing their consonants. Their speech is "a mere helpless slobber of disconnected vowel noises—the weakest and cheapest attempt at human expression." *Yes* becomes, in their speech, "the abject 'Yeh-eh' (the ugliness of the drawl is not easy to represent) which . . . makes its nearest approach to deviating into the decency of a final consonant when it becomes a still more questionable 'Yeh-ep'" (pp. 25–27). Intrusive *r*, that is, an *r* that is pronounced but that does not appear in writing, also bothers James, who complains that supposedly cultivated people speak of "vanilla-r-ice-cream, of California-r-oranges, of Cuba-r, . . . of the idea-r-of." Such behavior "illustrates our loss, much to be regretted, alas, of the power to emulate the clearness of the vowel-cutting, an art as delicate in its way as gem-cutting" (pp. 27–28). James does not approve of the intrusive *s* in *somewheres-else* and *a good ways-on*; or the flatly drawling "gawd and dawg, sawft and lawft, gawne and lawst and frawst;" or the *e* converted to *u*, "which is itself unaccompanied with any dignity of intention" as in *vurry*, *Amurrica*, and *tullegram* (pp. 30–31).

For James, the forces shaping what he refers to as the *vox Americana* are the same ones that shape our national character. The English, French, and Italians are held up as examples of nations where speech is trained and regulated, while the Americans neglect it: "The *vox Americana* . . . is for the spectator . . . one of the stumbling blocks of our continent. . . . It has been, among the organs of the schooled and news-papered races, perceptibly the most abandoned to its fate" (pp. 33–34). The situation is as bad for usage as it is for speech: "No language, so far back as our acquaintance with history goes, has known any such ordeal, any such stress and strain, as was to await the English in this huge new community" (p. 38). James portrays the English language as a damsel in distress, a captive in the New World: "Taken on the whole by surprise it may doubtless be said to have behaved as well as unfriended heroine ever behaved in dire predicament—refusing, that is, to be frightened quite to death, looking about for a *modus vivendi*, consenting to live, preparing to wait on developments." He also notes that American English has been orphaned and made subject to the uncontrolled assault of the common schools and the newspapers: "Our transported maiden . . . our medium of utterance, was to be disjoined from all the associations, the other presences, that had attended her. . . . It is the high modernism of the conditions now surrounding, on this continent, the practice of our language that makes of this chapter in its history a new thing under the sun" (pp. 39–40).

James portrays the forces of linguistic corruption as virtual ravishers of the English that has been abandoned on our shores: "To the American common school, to the American newspaper, and to the American Dutchman and Dago, as the voice of the people describes them, we have simply handed over our property—not exactly bound hand and foot, I admit, like Andromeda awaiting her Perseus, but at least dis-tracted, dishevelled, despoiled, divested of that beautiful and becoming drapery of native atmosphere and circumstances which had, from far back, made, on its behalf, for practical protection, for a due tenderness of interest" (p. 41). James sees the immigrants to America as being left free to do anything, "but the thing they may best do is play, to their heart's content, with the English language." The schools and the news-papers add to the overall effect by diffusing, vulgarizing, and simplify-ing; and, in the absence of vigilance and criticism, "the forms of civility, with the forms of speech most setting the example, drift out to sea" (pp. 42–44).

A true guardian of the language, James objects to the triple threat of school, press, and immigrant, but it is his disdain for immigrants that takes over toward the end of his lecture. He resents the feeling immi-grants apparently have that, "from the moment of their arrival, they have just as much property in our speech as we have, and just as good a right to do what they choose with it." They not only usurp the rights of those who have come before, they show a tasteless concern for price. Our language "strikes them as an excellent bargain: durable, tough, cheap" (pp. 45–46). James repeats his assertion that carelessness in speech makes men no better than animals, and he implies that the new-comers to our shores are both careless and animalistic. James admits that language is a living organism, but this is not a concession to de-scriptive linguistic theory, for he insists that without conservatism as its most important force, the language organism will not survive. James feels that conservatism is as necessary in language as it is in marriage. Without it we would be as beasts, "who prosper as well without a vo-cabulary as without a marriage service." He continues, "It is easier to overlook any question of speech than to trouble about it, but then it is also easier to snort or neigh, to growl or to 'meaow', than to articulate and intonate" (p. 47).

Given all that is wrong with American society and American English, James advises his listeners to seek models of good speech to emulate. Here and there an articulate individual, a torchbearer, a guardian of the sacred flame will emerge. James invites the young women of Bryn Mawr to follow this model and to sacrifice themselves in the cause of good usage. Although James implicitly adopts the role of high priest of language, he does not offer to place himself in any danger: "Perhaps, at last . . . you may, sounding the clearer notes of intercourse as only women can, become yourselves models and missionaries, perhaps a little even martyrs, of the good cause" (p. 52).

The Critique of Purism

Sterling A. Leonard, a historian of the purist movement in the eighteenth and nineteenth centuries, saw fit to parody the efforts of writers like Richard Grant White and Ambrose Bierce (Bierce, in his *Devil's Dictionary*, had parodied the lexicographers that he so strongly disapproved of) in "A Purist Glossary," which appeared in the *Saturday Review of Literature* in 1929. Using the argument from history, that newfangled forms are not as valid as their ancestors, together with an extraneous reference to logic, Leonard shows that *climbed* "is an error of the illiterate, based on the analogy of the weak verbs which infest our language. The correct preterite is *clomb*, which has the force of history and logic back of it."[7] Arguing that *let* must only be used in its original meaning, Leonard appeals to our fear of appearing uneducated: "Only an ignorant barbarian would use this word in any sense but that of *prevent.*" *Prevent*, however, cannot be used in the customary sense. It must fall victim to the argument from etymology, which states that a word can mean no more than the sum of the meanings of its parts: "Whoever knows Latin is aware that this word means *go before*. Its use to mean *hinder* is a late and utterly baseless innovation which those who have at heart the welfare of the English language will resist earnestly."

The argument from etymology, popular among purists, is shown to be invalid without a careful consideration of decorum and social class as well. Of the word *delirious* we are told, "The fact that this word is of Latin extraction should not blind us to its low slang origin. Its meaning, as is evident to any Latinist, is no different from that of the current vulgarism, 'off his trolley.' It will be avoided by all who value the dignity of the language." (The word *delirious* derives from *de*, 'out of' or 'away from', and *lira*, 'track, furrow', and is used in the sense of 'mad, crazy' by Cicero and Horace.) Leonard pretends to approve of the efforts of men like Elias Molee to restore lost distinctions in English. Of *sitten* and *slidden* he says, "The enormous value of having past participles different from the preterite forms of verbs, difficult as it is to preserve in English, should lead us to keep every possible differentiation."

Using the *ipse dixit* approach, in which words speak for themselves, Leonard asserts the true meaning of *restive*. Richard Grant White had stubbornly allowed only one meaning for the word: "Restive means standing stubbornly still, not frisky, as some people seem to think it does" (*Words and Their Uses*, p. 152). Leonard, on the other hand, interprets the word literally, restoring its original sense, and insisting that "the most ignorant person should be able to see that this word means *in a state of rest*, and is abominably misused in the exactly opposite sense." The argument from literality, so important to Ambrose Bierce, is the cause for Leonard's rejection of the phrase *light a pipe*: "This expression is patently absurd, as anybody would know who had ever had the misfortune to have his pipe burn through. We light the tobacco, not the pipe." Leonard manages to turn the arguments of the usage critics on their heads in an imitation of their style so exact that some readers might be tempted to take his suggestions seriously were they not accompanied by an article in which Leonard makes his position on the subject plain. The stand taken by Leonard and other enlightened students of the language, however, has not changed matters much in the twentieth century, and the guides to correctness flourish as Americans continue to seek authorities in matters of usage to soothe their sense of linguistic insecurity. The popular press frequently contains hints on language etiquette and sarcastic commentaries on the current state of language affairs. Improper usage, new words and phrases, and slang and other modish expressions still come under fire in such recent works as Edwin Newman's *Strictly Speaking* (1974) and *A Civil Tongue* (1976), William and Mary Morris's *Harper Dictionary of Contemporary Usage* (1975), Arn and Charlene Tibbetts's *What's Happening to American English?* (1978), and the collection of essays edited by Leonard Michaels and Christopher Ricks, *The State of the Language* (1980).

   Nineteenth-century commentators crystallized the usage book genre that had been begun by Vaugelas in the seventeenth. Their conception of improper usage as immoral, criminal, and diseased reflects an attitude toward language shared by grammarians as well. But usage critics generally remain suspicious of formal grammar largely because they consider it a school subject, and they tend to blame American schools for what they regard as the deterioration of the American language. There have been many usage works written in the twentieth century, and there have been many attempts to reform the American language in more specific ways. It would easily require another full-length study to chart the history of twentieth-century language reform and the complex and often uneasy relationship it has maintained with modern theoretical linguistics. In the next chapter we will examine some representative usage works, concentrating not so much on the points of usage discussed as on the attitudes toward improper language use that are revealed by them. Most of the controversies dealt with in contemporary commentaries concern points specific to present-day English. But some usage questions that have concerned grammarians and language commentators since the eighteenth century do crop up: subject-verb agreement, number and gender concord, the use of *who* and *whom*. Arguments still occur over the relative merits of usage and reason as criteria for linguistic judgment. And the role of etymology, the merits of tampering with other people's words, the fixing of standard spellings and pronunciations, the influence of literature upon good usage, and the merits of British versus American English are still topics that are hotly debated. Fear is still strong that English will decay and disintegrate into a series of animalistic grunts and groans if preventive measures are not immediately taken. Many of the forms of English that drive commentators to distraction are already so firmly established in the language that there is little chance they will be driven out. Finally, usage critics, like their colleagues the spelling reformers and the grammarians, remain inconsistent, contradicting themselves and committing the very offenses that inspire their contempt.

10 Watching Our Grammar

In his poem "To a Waterfowl," Donald Hall describes a situation that most English teachers will find only too familiar. He speaks of men that he meets on airplanes,

> Who close their briefcases and ask, "What are *you* in?"
> I look in their eyes, I tell them I am in poetry,
>
> and their eyes fill with anxiety, and with little tears.
> "Oh, yeah?" they say, developing an interest in clouds.
> "My wife, she likes that sort of thing? Hah-hah?
> I guess maybe I'd better watch my grammar, huh?"
> I leave them in airports, watching their grammar.[1]

But although the English teacher is characterized in American folklore as a Miss Fidditch or a Miss Thistlebottom, an unattractive grammar monger whose only pleasure in life is to point out the language faults of others, the usage critics of today, like their counterparts in the past, are as often as not linguistic amateurs. Edwin Newman, author of two popular works which predict the death of English, *Strictly Speaking* (1974) and *A Civil Tongue* (1976), is a television newscaster and "critic-at-large." William Safire, author of *On Language* (1980), was a speech-writer and political analyst before he compiled a political dictionary and began his series of language columns in the *New York Times Magazine*. Philip Howard, who holds a record with three recent books on the decline of our tongue, *New Words for Old* (1977), *Weasel Words* (1978), and *Words Fail Me* (1980), is a journalist writing for the *Times* of London. And Jim Quinn, whose *American Tongue and Cheek* (1980) is that rare book of usage criticism, a plea for language as it is, not as it should be, is a poet, satirist, and food columnist. John Simon, author of *Paradigms Lost* (1980), and well-known critic of the arts, goes so far as to argue that a nonspecialist is best qualified to conduct an inquiry into language abuse. Simon distrusts structural and transformational linguistics and feels that his ignorance in these areas is an asset in his work: "The fact that I had long since given up being a teacher of English and had never been a scholar of linguistics was actually an advantage. After all, when you are inquiring into a scandal in the automotive industry, it is best not to appoint Henry Ford as investigator."[2]

Of course the teaching profession is well represented in the genre of usage criticism, although for some reason, perhaps because Americans distrust the English teacher who is always watching their grammar, or because we judge writers like actors, according to a star system, their books tend to carry less weight with the general public. Richard Mitchell, the "Underground Grammarian" and author of *Less Than Words Can Say* (1978), teaches at Glassboro State College in New Jersey. *What's Happening to American English?* is jointly written by Arn Tibbetts, professor of English at the University of Illinois, and Charlene Tibbetts, an English teacher at the University High School. Harvard's Dwight Bolinger, who wrote *Language—The Loaded Weapon* (1980), is one of the few professional linguists to enter the discussions of present-day language abuse (among teachers of English in general and those who write on usage in particular, even a small degree of formal linguistic training is still the exception rather than the rule).

Linguistic Insecurity Today

As we have seen, language reform in America is nothing new. It has been with us since colonial times, and despite its past failures, it is as strong today as ever. A look at the work of some contemporary usage critics reveals that little has changed in the area of language commentary since the nineteenth century. Like the purists of the past, today's reformers play on our sense of linguistic insecurity, the feeling that many Americans have that their language is somehow not quite up to snuff, that it is out of control, riddled with errors, or simply unskillful and gauche. It is a feeling of guilt that is sometimes conscious, but more often not, an uneasy sense that our commas, both literally and metaphorically, come in all the wrong places. Linguistic insecurity drives otherwise ordinary people to watch their grammar in the presence of English teachers. On the other hand, it turns English teachers, who are often woefully untrained in philology, into unwilling language experts forced to rely on their subjective judgments to arbitrate the language disputes of everyday life. Linguistic insecurity drives students in college-level descriptive grammar courses to demand that they be taught a description not of what the language is, but of what it ought to be, that they be told where to put their commas. It fuels the fire of the university back-to-basics programs and it inflames the defenders of our language against such barbarities as *chairperson* and *finalize*, which seem always ways at the gates. At one extreme it produces hypercorrections that alter the course of the language; at the other it produces a devastating, though usually temporary, state of silence that inhibits communication between individuals and groups.

Two major forces in our culture cooperate to produce linguistic insecurity: the ranking of social and geographical dialects as superior and inferior, and an educational system based on a doctrine of correctness and purity in language that invariably conflicts with the observable facts of English usage. Linguistic insecurity may very well be a sociolinguistic given for many Americans. It is induced by formal language study in the schools—the ascertaining of standards, the writing of grammars, the instruction in English for speakers of English—and by the self-appointed language elite that has emerged in every age to defend standards and to regulate the language behavior of others. These are the gatekeepers of language, and their attitudes are sometimes liberal, sometimes conservative, often contradictory, and invariably prescriptive. These experts variously appeal to and reject reason, custom, authority, taste, morality, and their own personal vision. They defend the language by mounting attacks on its speakers. And they do not concern themselves so much with keeping the enemy out—particularly at the present time—for they are firmly convinced that the barbarians are those already inside. So we find them, sitting at their gates, constantly watching our grammar.

The Paradigm Regained

John Simon is perhaps the most conservative of contemporary language guardians, aligning himself—no doubt unconsciously, for he mentions the work of no critic earlier than Wilson Follett, author of *Modern American Usage* (1966)—with the tradition, the paradigm of usage criticism established over the centuries by his predecessors. Simon strongly feels that language does not belong to the illiterate. By *illiterate* he means not those who are unable to read and write but those whose level of culture or refinement is not sufficiently elevated. Like many writers before him, Simon calls for the creation of an academy to regulate Anglo-American English. He admits that language changes, and that some changes may be desirable, but Simon rejects all innovations that derive from error. Like Bishop Lowth, Simon dismisses the argument from literary authority. Just because Shakespeare or Milton uses a phrase does not mean that we may do so, for even the best of writers make mistakes. The argument from history is also invalid, for Shakespeare and his contemporaries wrote at a time when the language was, according to Simon, still in its formative stage. It is only in the present that our language has become sufficiently standardized and codified that "we now have the means to slow down changes in language considerably, if not to stop them altogether" (p. 39).

Like the spelling reformers, the gatekeepers and grammarians are invariably inconsistent. Some, for example, seek to improve the language with borrowed words, others to reform the language by purging it of foreign impurities. Close examination will show that the guardians often violate their own prescriptions. Addison, arguing in the eighteenth century against the loss of the unstressed vowel in *drown'd*, *walk'd*, and *arriv'd*, which he says "has very much disfigured the Tongue, and turn'd a tenth part of our smoothest Words into so many Clusters of Consonants,"[3] himself disfigures *turn'd*. Usage critics run the risk of having their own words attacked by others. The nineteenth century saw George Washington Moon and Fitzedward Hall cannibalize the prose of Henry Alford and Richard Grant White. More recently Simon, in his essay "Guarding the Guardians" (*Paradigms*, pp. 44–48), feels called upon to expose what he regards as inappropriate usage on the part of his fellow language custodians, Arn and Charlene Tibbetts, Edwin Newman, Donna Woolfolk Cross, author of *Word Abuse* (1979), and Jacques Barzun, whose *Simple and Direct* (1975) Simon praises highly.

But there is no safety in attack, for Simon himself can be tripped up. For example, he faults the Tibbettses' elliptical phrase, *to either the author's thesis or conclusion*, requiring instead *to either the author's thesis or his conclusions* (and adding a gratuitous plural to the original *conclusion*), but he then goes on to defend ellipsis when he recommends *most important*, which is "the elliptical form of 'what is most important,'" over the increasingly common unelliptical adverbial *most importantly*.

The Great Permitters

Like John Simon, William Safire, language columnist for the *New York Times Magazine*, claims no specific linguistic credentials—in fact Safire does not even claim a college degree. He acts as a usage authority because he is "a working writer. . . . with an interest in the implements of my craft."[4] While Simon, operating in the tradition of usage critics, arrogates virtually all authority to himself, Safire is willing to share decision making with the other "Great Permitters," the makers and defenders of language rules, among whom he numbers Henry Fowler, author of *Modern English Usage* (1926), Bergen Evans, who with Cornelia Evans wrote *A Dictionary of Contemporary American Usage* (1957), Theodore Bernstein, author of a number of usage books including *Miss Thistlebottom's Hobgoblins* (1973), and Jacques Barzun. And in a strikingly democratic move for a usage critic, Safire includes his readers among the rule makers and defenders: "We are the people who care; we've registered for the linguistic primary. Our interest is our power" (p. xii).

Safire rejects the authority of usage if it is to mean the usage of the average person, whom he jocularly refers to as "Norma Loquendi," for he feels that the average is too low. He cites the Danish linguist Otto Jespersen's argument that "the investigator as a user of language has the same right as others to influence the language where he can, and he ought to be able by virtue of his greater knowledge to do this with greater insight and greater effect than those who have no linguistic training" (p. xiii). This is the stand of the modern scientific language planner, although Jespersen, who spoke as a scientist, probably did more to describe the English language than he did to influence its direction (see, for example, his monumental seven-volume *A Modern English Grammar on Historical Principles*, 1909–49). But Safire, an avowed amateur in language matters, prefers the role of activist to that of descriptive scientist. He sees himself as a conservative advocating rules that will promote clarity. Safire claims to be not a "traditional" conservative, one who issues categorical imperatives to be obeyed by all, but a "libertarian" who places linguistic responsibility with the individual rather than with a constituted authority.

In short, in matters of usage Safire wants to "let thinking people decide for themselves" (p. xiii), and he encourages the efforts of his band of "Lexicographic Irregulars"—a phrase reminiscent of Richard Grant White's "linguistic detective police"—correspondents whose comments and complaints he regularly airs in his columns and in his book. Although he has stated that the average level of language use is inadequate, Safire is one of the few usage critics openly to oppose "people who like to put less-educated people down—Language Snobs, who give good usage a bad name" (p. xv). Echoing the nineteenth-century usage guides, Safire sees language improvement, like learning how to dress correctly, as a form of self-improvement. In his optimism, he sees it as one of the few areas of modern life "where personal action has effect—we can stand fast against the tide of solecisms that enshrines ignorance and fight the inflation of modifiers that demeans meaning" (p. xv). But Safire's libertarianism gives way to a more traditional authoritarian stance when he gets down to discussing specific issues. And despite Safire's optimism, the power that the individual may exercise over his own life, when reduced to a question of choosing the better of alternative linguistic forms, does not seem likely to lessen any twentieth-century sense of despair: "The sense of powerlessness that has been bothering so many intellectuals . . . should stop at the edge of language. There, in classroom and home, some personal muscle can be flexed: 'Different from' is preferable to 'different than,' because 'from' separates more strongly than 'than'" (p. xv). We may be tempted to ask, if 'from' really separates more strongly than 'than,' why not say 'from' separates more strongly *from* 'than?'

Will America Be the Death of English?

Edwin Newman, whose writing is representative of contemporary language attitudes, is a direct descendant of such usage commentators as Vaugelas, Robert Baker, and Richard Grant White. In *Strictly Speaking* (1974) he asks the question, "Will America be the death of English?" and not surprisingly his answer turns out to be yes. Newman clearly believes that our language has become as decayed and impoverished as our natural resources and social institutions. He traces this imagined decay, in part, to the cult of youth, the cult of change, and the war in Vietnam, which "conferred a kind of blessing on youth and inexperience and not being in the establishment." He feels that these social and historical conditions led to "a wholesale breakdown in the enforcement of rules, and in the rules of language more than most. . . . Correct and relatively conventional language was widely abandoned by those in revolt."[5] Actually Newman does not cite examples of the language of revolutionaries or the young, but he does liberally recount the howlers of conservatives, aristocrats, and the middle-aged and middle-classed. The implication, however, is always that corruption has come from below, that the linguistic and nonlinguistic Watergates were caused by inside agitators.

Newman attacks language that he doesn't like by ridiculing it, and some of his examples are amusing: his *cake du jour* and *potatoes o'grattan* are reminiscent of the increasingly popular American menu item, *roast beef with au jus*. But some of his ridicule is poorly directed. A five-page list of college presidents whose first, last, and middle names are interchangeable, for example, Lloyd Drexell Vincent (of Angelo State University, San Angelo, Texas), makes at best a weak point, since college presidents, like most Americans, do not usually choose their own names. Rejecting the historical record of English, Newman also attacks language that he has decided is improper. He says, for example, "You may convince that. You may convince of. You may not convince to" (p. 35)—unaware that the *Oxford English Dictionary* shows examples of this form occurring as early as the sixteenth century. Newman, like William Safire, also objects to *different than*, a great infuriator of contemporary purists (purists of the past had objected to *different to*). Interestingly, the citation in Webster's *Third New International Dictionary* for *different than* is taken from the writing of Nathan Pusey who, among other things, was a college president (Harvard) whose first and last names could not be interchanged.

Newman's second book on language, *A Civil Tongue*, is not tinged with the bitterness of his earlier work: the general comments on the nature of language are toned down, but still revealing. Newman reiterates his notion that language is an aspect of human behavior that must be subject to regulation: "The alternative to a code of conduct is, if not chaos, certainly confusion and embarrassment, and language is conduct."[6] Newman has retreated from a severely purist stance to one that is enlightened but still despotic. He defines a civil tongue as one "not bogged down in jargon, not puffed up with false dignity." And he personifies its self-correction mechanism as benevolent but firm: "It treats errors in spelling and usage with a decent tolerance but does not take them lightly" (p. 6). In a grand gesture, Newman declares himself unopposed to language change, but only because the language is already in such bad shape today (p. 4).

The Usage Panel: An Enlightened Despotism

A more representative survey of current language attitudes is found in the *Harper Dictionary of Contemporary Usage*, edited by William and Mary Morris, with the help of "a panel of 136 distinguished consultants on usage."[7] This panel, similar in idea and composition to the one used for the *American Heritage Dictionary* (1969) edited by William

Morris, is a novelty in usage commentaries, although it has a precedent in Sterling A. Leonard's *Current English Usage* (1932). In Leonard's study a panel of 229 judges, including linguists, editors, authors, businessmen, and 130 English and speech teachers, was asked to decide whether each of 230 expressions was literary, formally correct English; colloquial, but well-bred, standard English; or popular, illiterate usage.[8]

The *Harper Dictionary* panel, composed of popular writers, editors, television journalists, lawyers, and a few professors, votes on such ticklish cases as the acceptability of *hopefully* as a sentence adverbial. So-called dangling *hopefully*, in the sense 'it is to be hoped' rather than the simple adverbial 'in a hopeful manner' is found in such examples as "Hopefully the Dodgers will win the double-header," and, although the panelists do not acknowledge this, it is similar to other English sentence adverbials (*certainly, assuredly*) and is the exact equivalent of the German *höffentlich*. *Hopefully* is a hot issue in usage today; exchanges on the subject have appeared in the *Times Literary Supplement* of London and Edwin Newman has treated it as well. The Harper panelists are asked to take a yes / no stand on each usage question, and to comment as well. Fifty-eight percent of them disapprove of the use of dangling *hopefully* in speech, seventy-six percent disapprove of it in writing. Most usage questions are decided in a similarly negative manner, although not surprisingly the panel accepts variation more readily in speech than in writing.

The pseudodemocratic arbitration system of the *Harper Dictionary* is an attempt to illustrate the process of decision making in matters of English and thereby to demystify it and give readers a feeling of participation in the process of linguistic self-determination. The panelists rarely take a unanimous stand on the questions that are put to them, and readers always have the option of siding with the minority view. To do so, however, would place readers in an awkward position. If the premise of majority rule is to be valid, those of us desiring to imitate the language of the literate must reject not only the stigmatized form in question but also reject those *a priori* distinguished literati on the usage panel who backed a loser. If only landslides are to be decisive, as in the case of the almost universal disapproval of *critique* as a verb, we are asked to embrace linguistic norms that, like their political analogues, may stay in power only till the next election. While two of the panelists note that *critique* fills the gap being created as *criticize* comes more and more to mean 'find fault with,' eleven others openly or implicitly pretend such a shift is not taking place.

The force of committee rule is further undercut by an editorial statement on *Franglais*, "the importation into French of English and American terms." According to the Morrises, the efforts of groups of French linguists and politicians to solve this problem were predictably unsuccessful, "for the processes of linguistic change are not often much affected by the actions of committees, no matter how earnest they are or how pure their motives." Ironically, the editors do not connect their comment on efforts to eradicate Franglais with their own group efforts to improve the English language.

Flowers of Evil

The *Harper Dictionary* panelists reveal a set of extreme and varied attitudes toward favored and disfavored styles of discourse. For example, positive responses by the panel to questioned forms are usually neutral in tone. Acceptance by the panel of *hectic* in the sense 'characterized by excitement' rather than the original 'flushed, feverish' reveals an awareness of the role of popular usage in the process of semantic change. Many panelists admit that they are unaware of the original meaning of the word, and all agree that the new sense is universal. For example, *New York Times* music critic Harold Schonberg says, "Yes [I use it this way], and so does everybody else," and editor A. B. C. Whipple agrees, "Yes. It really has become generally used in this new sense." Sometimes the panelists' positive responses are downright enthusiastic. Writer Isaac Asimov says, when asked if he uses *hectic* in its modern sense, "Sure!" And journalist Robert Sherill does not hesitate to approve of the verb *defenestrate* 'to throw out of a window': "God, yes! We really need that!" Occasionally the comments of the panelists indicate an acceptance of the linguistic status quo. Charles Kuralt, a television news correspondent, says of *hectic*, "I wasn't even aware of the medical connotations. Words *do* change in meaning."

Many of the panelists are confident that they live in a perfectible world, and they indicate their willingness to work unselfishly to bring about a linguistic Eden. Asked about the difference between *disinterested* and *uninterested*, panelist Asimov replies, "I'm very proud of knowing the distinction and insist on correcting others freely." Panelist Edwin Newman, taking the position that *unique* is an absolute that cannot be qualified by words such as *more, most,* or *rather*, informs us, "I deliver unwelcome lectures on the subject to colleagues." Only a few of the panelists despair of eating the cake, let alone having it. Discussing whether *decimate* can be held to its original meaning of "every tenth man," Peter Prescott, writer and book reviewer, feels powerless in the face of language change: "Who really tries to correct other people's speech? All we can do is close our eyes and nod."

The panelists affirm the need for vigilance, yet despite their zeal they are anxious to avoid the negative stereotype of the language pedant. Novelist Herman Wouk, strongly rejecting the modern, generalized sense of *dilemma* as 'acute problem' adds, "I lack the grammarian's frenzy." And Peter Prescott, voting against the majority of the panel who would allow *foremost* to apply to more than one person or thing, maintains a purist stand while rejecting the negative purist label: "I don't think you have to be a purist here; superlatives as comparatives denote illiteracy." Educator Elvis Stahr, Jr., accepting *boast* as a transitive verb, reveals that the Argus-eyed gatekeepers are only human after all: "This one grew up on me (and the language) while I wasn't watching."

The nice-guy attitude of panelists often disappears when they consider what they feel to be serious or threatening misuses of language. Some errors are seen as evidence of general cultural decay. They are certainly weeds in the garden of paradise, if not flowers of evil. Novelist Ben Lucien Burman exclaims that the use of *gift* as a verb "is one of the reasons America is in such terrible shape today!" And Metropolitan Opera Assistant Manager Francis Robinson feels that the use of the verb *finalize* is "another reason the country is going to hell." But the evils of bad usage are generally seen to be more personal than national, and some panelists admit their own failings in a flurry of self-flagellation. We find comments such as novelist Robert Crichton's all too human observation of the difference between *farther* (physical distance) and *further* (degree or quantity) "Yes [I observe it], but I slip." Other panelists come out with such confessions as "Yes I use it, slob that I am"; "I'm a hypocrite! I probably use either"; "I count myself a traditionalist—and am amazed at my inconsistency"; and, "I'm afraid my standards are impure and utterly subjective."

Interestingly, the panelists recognize and even celebrate their own fallibility. They often admit to using a form and apologize for that use at the same time. For example, the panel favors by three to one the observation of a distinction between *less*, for degree and *fewer* for quantity. Novelist and historian Thomas Fleming says, "It makes me feel guilty to admit [not observing the distinction]," and of dangling *hopefully* he admits, "Mea culpa—I can see myself writing it—but it's wrong." There is however no indication given by Fleming that he cannot live with this guilt. Isaac Asimov admits his failure in this area of usage but senses he must make an effort to reform: "I do not observe the distinction but I should, now that it has been explained to me." And Francis Robinson is even more positive: he admits not maintaining a distinction between *less* and *fewer*, adding, "But I will from now on!" Columnist Shana Alexander, who feels that perfectibility begins at home, explicitly sums up the panel's feelings of personal fallibility: "One function of these ballots is to spruce up the language habits of your panelists." Perhaps the extreme case is to be found in journalist and historian John Brooks's mock-serious comment on dangling *hopefully*, couched in terms of confession and contrition: "To my shame I once wrote it before I learned to hate it." But Brooks tempers the gloom, adding hopefully, "and there may be a lesson in that."

While many of the panelists are happy to put their language under the correction of their colleagues, they are clearly more comfortable when they themselves are the dictators of usage. Their comments on disfavored language may be neutrally phrased. Reporter David Schoenbrunn says of *thank you much*, "I would not use it but it does not offend me." But generally the negative comments of the panelists are not as restrained or as analytical as their positive comments are. Language offenders have been viewed traditionally as nonhuman, or at least as physiologically or morally incapable of using language, but ironically some of the panel's own comments on stigmatized forms are nonverbal: for example, "!!"—or the more emphatic "!!!" Sometimes comments are vocalized as primitive animalistic or humanoid responses: "UGH!" "Yeech!" or "PFUI," indicating a reaction that is visceral rather than intellectual.

It is also traditional to regard disfavored language as ugly. The editors of the *Harper Dictionary*, explaining *nonce words*, words whose existence is temporary or ephemeral, illustrate with two terms from linguistics that are now fairly well established, *glottochronology* and *lexicostatistics,* offering the gratuitous comment, "At least we hope they are *nonce* words. They are much too ugly to survive." We may often feel relieved that the editors are only judging words, not human beings. Erich Segal is one of the few panelists who rejects the role of linguaesthetician. In his comment on *thank you much* he says, "Are we discussing what is 'beautiful' or what we consider to be 'correct'? I don't think we should adjudicate the beauty or ugliness of a phrase. Our task is tough enough." Segal is no wild-eyed descriptivist, however. Like the other panelists, he clearly feels that truth and beauty are linguistic universals. His position is simply that beauty is too hard to legislate.

We also find traditionally caustic, mocking, or trivializing responses by the panel to certain usage items, particularly those concerning sex reference (a distinct contrast, by the way, to the affirmative stand on sex-neutral language taken by the editors of the *Harper Dictionary*). Many of the panelists simply cannot resist making trivializing jokes. A question on maintaining distinctions between *groom* and *bridegroom* brings the following response from journalist Lester Kinsolving: "Do anywhere near as many men handle horses as handle brides?" Vermont Royster, editor emeritus of *The Wall Street Journal*, comments, "What is the difference between handling women and horses?" And reporter John A. Barbour says, "Horses, wife, why quibble?" In discussing the term *Ms.*, several panelists believe that it is useful when marital status is unknown, thereby substituting a pragmatic function for the original political one, that of removing attention from marital status altogether. Other panelists consider *Ms.* a sop, unfortunately the fate of much sex-neutralizing language, and typically they use it only to refer to women who they think expect it. It is one thing to bend a word to suit one's purpose, but quite another to scorn it by ignoring it, as mystery writer Rex Stout does in his comment on *Ms.*, "Certainly [I use it]. It means 'manuscript,'" or by punning, as in journalist Pinckney Keel's reply, "I find that most ladies prefer *Miss* or *Mrs.*, not a near Ms."

In addition to sex, violence plays an important part in the Harper panel's negative responses. Couched in metaphors of evil, there is a strong temptation for us to read the panelists' comments literally. Some examples of improper usage are themselves seen as acts of violence. Joseph A. Brandt, an editor and educator, sees the improper use of *decimate* as "raping the language." But more often the panelists are stirred to violence of their own. Editor Bill Vaughan says of the phrase *I could care less*, "No! No! Kill! Kill!" Panelists also employ metaphors of disease, criminality, and social decay in their comments. Bad language can have the power of a twenty-four-hour virus. For example, writer Judith Viorst says of the common suffix *-wise*, "I love splitting infinitives, for instance, but 'performancewise' gives me pains in my stomach." And Harold Taylor, writer and former college president, says of dangling *hopefully*, "This is one that makes me physically ill." Bad language also provokes the panelists to insult. Elvis Stahr, Jr., says of the use of *nauseous* for *nauseated*, "If someone says 'I feel nauseous' I'll reply, 'You sound it.'" And it can inspire contempt: Isaac Asimov says of the increasingly common *I could care less*, "I don't know people stupid enough to say this."

Panelists are eager to treat language that they do not approve of as crime crying out for punishment. They see their roles as figurative legislators or judges, and they seem to be dealing with felonies, not misdemeanors. Charles Kuralt says of the use of *like* for *as*, "The ad writer who dreamed up the Winston commercial should be jailed." And journalist and critic John K. Hutchens takes a sterner view of things: "I propose that it be made a federal offense to use *fun* as an adjective. Twenty years for the first offense; life sentence for second offenders." Hutchens also proposes twenty-year sentences for anyone saying *emote*. There is clearly no room for due process when it comes to capital crimes: Thomas Fleming says of dangling *hopefully*, "Its adherents should be lynched."

In dealing with language literally too horrible for words, the panelists and editors, exhibiting incredible acts of will, revert to hard-core and at times paradoxical know-nothingism. The editors calmly tell us that "the words *grievious* and *grieviously* simply do not exist, although they turn up all too often in popular speech." And Elvis Stahr, Jr., makes a similar contradiction when he contends that "*irregardless* is not only a nonword . . . it is wasteful of breath." Writer Anthony Burgess, echoing Ambrose Bierce, seems to feel that a word cannot have more than one meaning. He says of *alibi*, "It can't mean one thing in Latin and law and another in nonlegal English," a sharp contrast to former Supreme Court Justice William O. Douglas's approval of the use of the term to mean any excuse at all.

Historian Laurence Lafore combines a vague feeling for language theory with a severe moral and aesthetic judgment: "Acceptance as standard usage is, I judge, a matter of time. To use words like 'finalize' is merely to be inelegant and to uglify the language." Furthermore, the panelists do not hesitate to reject the historical record of the language when it goes against their own sense of what is right. Herman Wouk says of the use of *gift* as a verb, "It disgusts me, and I'm sorry there's an accidental justification in OED."

Despite their often adamant stands, the panelists are aware that language has a social function, and that it is sometimes difficult to correct language without going too far and disrupting communication completely. In a blatant concession to sociolinguistic reality, the panelists recognize, no doubt unwittingly, that there is a force affecting them that is more powerful than prescriptivism. Many of them read the apparently coordinate usage question posed by the editors, "Would you correct a friend or pupil who used [*dilemma*] in this more generalized application?" as a request to choose either A or B, and they respond as Vermont

Royster does by making the distinction, "Pupil yes, friend, no, for I would lose too many of them!" They are sure of their opinions on language, but only sure enough to flaunt them where they hold the cards. The gatekeepers of contemporary American usage reveal a curious mixture of hate and fear toward our language and its users (although they are democratic enough to judge their own faults as well as those of others), a mixture that may well prove disconcerting to readers of the *Harper Dictionary*. Except for a few cases where absolutes are legislated, the reader is kept off-balance by the division of panel opinion. This state of confusion masquerading as authority can only increase the level of insecurity of many of those who consult the *Harper Dictionary*, causing them to over-correct their own language in an attempt to do what they think they are being told is right. And the changes in the shape of the language that must result from such over-correction will only help to keep the linguistic gatekeepers in business.

Conclusion

The early planners and reformers of American English whose work has been discussed in these pages have left one common legacy for their twentieth-century counterparts to ponder: an overwhelming lack of success. Their history of failure has proved to be no deterrent. Whether conservative or radical, the language planners, some ignorant of past attempts at reform, others optimistic in spite of the failure of those attempts, continue their efforts to alter our English.

The movement for spelling reform seems finally to have breathed a dying gasp. The Chicago *Tribune*, after fifty years of attempting to influence our spelling, announced just a few years ago that it was abandoning such simplified forms as *thru*, *tho*, and *thoro*, although it retains forms like *epilog*, *synagog*, *dialog*, and *catalog*. Spelling variation still exists, and it is tacitly approved by our dictionaries. Even the highly prescriptive *American Heritage Dictionary* prints *axe* alongside *ax*, and *grey* alongside *gray*, and approves *catalog* for *catalogue*, though only when it refers to library use. But spelling simplification remains with us despite the relaxation of organized reform efforts. We find it, for example, in highway information signs (*thru*, *thruway*, *slo*, *xing*), in entertainment listings in newspapers and magazines (*nite*, *show biz*), in names of businesses (*Kwik-Kopy*, *Sunriz Restaurant*), and in product names (*lite* beer and *lite* cigarettes have paved the way for *lite* salt, *lite* syrup, *lite* bread, *lite* fruit, and a variety of other *lite* inventions including a proposed but as yet unmarketed *lite* dog food). At the University of Illinois a sign at the entrance to the offices of the School of Humanities, located in the same building as the Department of English, states the prophetic warning: "No Thru Way to English."

Questions of usage remain a source of controversy in educational circles and in the popular press as attempts to standardize, sex-neutralize, or de-hyperbolize our language continue. British spellings, or what are supposed to look like British spellings, are used to add a touch of class in advertising and naming (*olde*, *colour*), and the spelling *theatre*, marked since the eighteenth century as the British version of American *theater*, is commonly found in both academic and commercial use (both the *American Heritage Dictionary* and *Webster's New Collegiate Dictionary*, 8th edition [1974] give both spellings without comment), and many of our shopping malls are called shopping *centres*. French also retains its influence on American English. In addition to its appearance on menus (although an American *entree* is quite different from one in a continental restaurant, as hungry tourists in France are often disappointed to discover), a touch of French is used to make goods more attractive to potential buyers. The version of the Renault 5 that is sold in America is called *Le Car*, and purchasers of this automobile may find that they are required to repeat the article when they tell their friends that they bought a *Le Car* or that the *Le Car* gets, or does not get, good mileage. Americans can also find *Le Shoe* and *Les Jeans* (the latter a re-borrowing of a word that the French originally borrowed from us, and that we originally borrowed from the Italian), a ceiling-mounted cooling device called *Le Fan*, shopping bags labeled *Junque*, and curtains made of luxurious-sounding genuine imported French *tergal* (which is in blunt, hellenized English, *dacron polyester*). But the outcry against British and French invasions of our language has been muted, no doubt because the balance of trade has been reversed: American English is now exporting more than it takes in.

Two major concerns of the reformers of American English in the 1970s have been Standard English and sex-neutral terminology. Attempts by educators and language guardians to institutionalize Standard English in speech and writing are hampered by the same obstacles that faced the proponents of Federal English: lack of an authoritative and consensual definition of Standard English; lack of effective enforcement procedures; a general feeling among the populace that it's the other guy whose language is not standard (such a feeling, while apparently paradoxical, does not in fact conflict with feelings of linguistic insecurity, which are usually associated with specific formal speaking or writing situations rather than general language competence); and the existence of competing regional and social language standards. Similarly, attempts to neutralize what has been perceived as the inherent sexism of the English language have met with only partial success. The term *Ms.*, which offers a feminine honorific that is neutral with respect to marital status and is therefore equivalent to the masculine term, *Mr.*, seemed for a time to be gaining ground. There are indications now that the use of the term may be declining, and that when it is used it often serves either as a replacement for *Miss* (that is, it is not used in reference to married women), or it is directed toward individuals who the user feels may prefer the term. In either case, semantic neutrality is compromised. The sex-neutral neologism *chairperson* has met with stiff resistance since its appearance in the early 1970s. Purists warn that *personhole cover* will replace *manhole cover*, and they imply that our traditional family structure will disintegrate as a result. They insist that the English language is not to be tampered with by sex-neutralizers, although the same purists offer to put the English language right every chance they themselves get. But more powerful than the arguments of purists is the linguistic inertia which must be overcome by logically or politically inspired changes, be they of spelling, grammar, idiom, or lexicon, no matter how desirable they may be.

The martyrdom that Henry James proposes for the young women of Bryn Mawr is neither sweet nor glorious. As James suggests, the martyrs in the struggle for good grammar and good taste are not the reformers, either the cranks and quacks on the fringes of English philology or the more linguistically sophisticated language planners, but the reformed, those speakers and writers of English who, out of an abiding sense of their own linguistic inadequacy, must "be correct or die"; those who, from internal or external pressure, seek to conform their spelling, grammar, and usage to the elusive norms of a mythical Standard English. These martyrs become confused in their usage. Aiming at correctness they produce language that the language guardians still judge to be inappropriate. Or they become bitter, or mute. In some cases— this apparently happened with Richard Grant White—they join the ranks of language critics, and the cycle of linguistic reform begins again.

Notes

Chapter 1

1 Joan Rubin and Björn H. Jernudd, eds., *Can Language Be Planned?* (Honolulu: University of Hawaii Press, 1971), p. xvi.
2 H. C. G. von Jagemann, "Philology and Purism," *PMLA* 15 (1900): 93–95.
3 Charles C. Fries, *The Teaching of the English Language* (New York: Thomas Nelson and Sons, 1927), p. 52.
4 Henry Cecil Wyld, *English Philology in English Universities* (Oxford: Clarendon Press, 1921), p. 10.

Chapter 2

1 Samuel Daniel, *Musophilus*, in *Complete Works*, ed. Rev. Alexander B. Grosart (London, 1885), 1:255.
2 Cited by Allen Walker Read in "British Recognition of American Speech in the Eighteenth Century," *Dialect Notes* 6 (1933): 322.
3 "Account of the College and Academy of Philadelphia," *American Magazine* (Supp., 1758): 631.
4 "To the Literati of America," *Royal American Magazine* (January 1774): 6–7.
5 Sarah H. J. Simpson, "The Federal Procession in the City of New York," *New York Historical Society Quarterly Bulletin* 9 (July 1925): 43.
6 William Dunlap, *History of the American Theatre* (London, 1833), 1:164–65.
7 Basil Hall, *Travels in North America* (Edinburgh, 1829), cited in *American Social History as Recorded by British Travelers*, ed. Allan Nevins (New York, 1923), pp. 157–58.
8 Allen Walker Read, "The Philological Society of New York, 1788," *American Speech* 9 (1934): 133.
9 Marquis de Chastellux, *Travels in North America* (London, 1787), 2:265–66.
10 *Quarterly Review* 10 (1814): 528.
11 Charles Jared Ingersoll, *Remarks on the Review of Inchiquin's Letters* (Boston, 1815), pp. 138–39.
12 Herbert Croft, *A Letter from Germany, to the Princess Royal of England; on the English and German Languages* (Hamburg, 1797), p. 8n.

13 Charles Astor Bristed, "The English Language in America," in *Cambridge Essays, 1855* (London, 1856), 1:75–76.

14 James P. Herron, *American Grammar: Adapted to the National Language of the United States* (Columbus, Ohio, 1859), pp. iv–v.

15 *Secret Journals of the Acts and Proceedings of Congress* (Boston, 1820), 2:95–96.

16 For a discussion of attitudes toward New World languages other than English, see Stephen J. Greenblatt's "Learning How to Curse: Aspects of Linguistic Colonialism in the Sixteenth Century," in *First Images of America: The Impact of the New World on the Old*, ed. Fredi Chiapelli, Michael J. B. Allen, and Robert L. Benson (Berkeley: University of California Press, 1976), 2:561–80. For reactions to American English, see Allen Walker Read's "British Recognition of American Speech in the Eighteenth Century," *Dialect Notes* 6 (1933): 313–34.

17 Capt. Frederick Marryat, *A Diary in America* (London, 1829), 1st ser., 2:230.

18 Fernand Baldensperger, "Une prédiction inédite sur l'avenir de la langue des Etats-Unis (Roland de la Platière, 1789)," *Modern Philology* 15 (1917): 91–92.

19 John Adams, "To the President of Congress" (September 5, 1780), in his *Works*, ed. Charles Francis Adams (Boston, 1852), 8:249–51.

20 John Adams, "To Edmund Jennings" (September 23, 1780), *Works*, 9:510.

21 Charles Jared Ingersoll, *Inchiquin, the Jesuit's Letters, during a Late Residence in the United States* (New York, 1810), pp. 105–06n.

22 Brander Matthews, *Parts of Speech* (New York: Scribner's, 1901), p. 32.

23 The *gall nut*, found in some species of oak, from which ink and other dyes were made.

24 Read, "The Philological Society," pp. 133–34.

25 *Letters of Noah Webster*, ed. Harry Warfel (New York: Library Publishers, 1953), p. 4.

26 For discussions of language reform in Britain in the eighteenth century see Sterling A. Leonard, *The Doctrine of Correctness in English Usage, 1700–1800*, University of Wisconsin Studies in Language and Literature 25 (Madison: University of Wisconsin Press, 1929).

27 Noah Webster, *Sketches of American Policy* (1785), ed. Harry R. Warfel (New York: Scholar's Facsimiles and Reprints, 1937), p. 47. Warfel notes that Madison refused to give Webster's essay any special importance.

28 John Pickering, *A Vocabulary, or Collection of Words and Phrases Which Have Been Supposed to Be Peculiar to the United States of America. To Which Is Prefixed an Essay on the Present State of the English Language in the United States* (Boston, 1816), p. 11.

29 James Fenimore Cooper, *Notions of the Americans: Picked Up by a Travelling Bachelor* (Philadelphia, 1828), 1:62.

30 James Fenimore Cooper, *The American Democrat* (Cooperstown, N.Y., 1838), p. 118.

31 Isabella Lucy Bird Bishop, *The Englishwoman in America* (London, 1848; rpt., Madison: University of Wisconsin Press, 1966), p. 323.

32 Jonathan Boucher, *Glossary of Archaic and Provincial Words* (London, 1832), p. xxiii.

33 John Woods, *Two Years' Residence in the Settlement on the English Prairie* (London, 1822), cited in Paul M. Angle, *Prairie State: Impressions of Illinois 1673–1967 by Travelers and Other Observers* (Chicago: University of Chicago Press, 1968), p. 82.

34 Royall Tyler, *The Yankey in London* (New York, 1809), 1:106–07.

35 John Foster's *Life of Dickens* (London, 1872–74), bk. 3, chaps. 5 and 6; cited in *American Social History as Recorded by British Travelers*, ed. Allan Nevins (New York, 1923), p. 270.

36 Charles Augustus Murray, *Travels in North America* (London, 1839), 2:363.

37 Benjamin Franklin, *Complete Works*, ed. John Bigelow (New York, 1887), 2:233–34.

38 E. T. Coke, *A Subaltern's Furlough* (New York, 1833), 1:155.

39 "Hints on Language, 9," *Godey's Lady's Book* 84 (1872): 381.

40 Frances M. Trollope, *The Domestic Manners of the Americans* (London, 1832; rpt., Barre, Mass.: Imprint Society, 1969), p. 257.

41 Charles Henry Wilson, *The Wanderer in America* (Thirsk, 1822), pp. 33–34.

42 Review of Webster's *An American Dictionary of the English Language* (1859) and Joseph Worcester's *A Dictionary of the English Language* (1860), *Atlantic Monthly* 5 (May 1860): 631–37.

43 Samuel Lorenzo Knapp, *Lectures on American Literature* (New York, 1829), p. 9.

44 "Americanism," *Encyclopedia Americana* (New York, 1834), 1:211; "English Language," 4:516.

45 Jacob A. Cummings, *The Pronouncing Spelling Book* (Boston, 1819), p. 10.

46 Philip Howard, *New Words for Old* (New York: Oxford University Press, 1977), p. xii.

47 James K. Paulding, *The United States and England: Being a Reply to the Criticism on Inchiquin's Letters Contained in the Quarterly Review for January, 1814* (New York, 1815), p. 8.

48 Shirley Brice Heath, "A National Language Academy? Debate in the New Nation," *Linguistics* 189 (1977): 9.

49 Washington Jay McCormick, *A bill to define the national and official language of the Government and people of the United States of America, including the Territories and dependencies thereof*, H.R. 14136; introduced February 1, 1923.

50 "Language by Legislation," *The Nation* 116 (April 11, 1923): 408.

51 H. L. Mencken, *The American Language*, 4th ed. (New York: Knopf, 1936), pp. 82–83.

Chapter 3

1 Noah Webster, *Letters*, ed. Harry R. Warfel (New York: Library Publishers, 1953), p. 296.

2 Noah Webster, *A Grammatical Institute of the English Language (Part 1)* (Hartford, 1783), p. 15; referred to hereafter as *The American Speller*.

3 Noah Webster, *Dissertations on the English Language* (Boston, 1789), p. 36.

4 Joseph E. Worcester, *A Dictionary of the English Language* (Boston, 1860), p. xxii.

5 Noah Webster, *An American Dictionary of the English Language* (New York, 1838), introduction, n.p.

6 "To the Friends of Literature" (New Haven, 1807).

7 "The Columbian Language," *New-England Palladium* 18, no. 27 (October 2, 1801): 1. This usage of *Miss* is noted in the *OED* and in Richard H. Thornton's *Glossary of Americanisms* (1912; rpt. New York: Ungar, 1962).

8 Advertisement, dated February 17, 1875; in the Webster Collection, New York Public Library.

9 Several autograph versions of this piece are in the Webster Collection.

10 Noah Webster, *The Elementary Spelling Book* (Concord, N.H., 1840), pp. 5–6.

11 Letter to the editor of the *Westminister Review*, dated April 11, 1831; Webster Collection.

12 Noah Webster, *A Compendious Dictionary of the English Language* (Hartford, 1806; rpt., New York: Crown, 1970), p. xvi.

13 Benjamin Franklin, *Works*, ed. Jared Sparks (Boston, 1840), 10:412–19.

14 Lyman Cobb, *A Critical Review of the Orthography of Dr. Webster's Series of Books for Systematick Instruction in the English Language* (New York, 1831), p. ii.

Chapter 4

1 Robert Ross, *The New American Spelling Book* (New Haven, 1785), pp. 116–19.

2 Thomas Sheridan, *A Course of Lectures on Elocution* (London, 1762), pp. 221–62.

3 *The Papers of Benjamin Franklin*, vol. 15, ed. William B. Willcox (New Haven, 1972), p. 177.

4 J. G. Chambers, "The Elements of Orthography," *The Universal Asylum and Columbian Magazine* (July 1791): 35.

5 For more detailed information see the article by Raoul N. Smith, "The Philosophical Alphabet of Jonathan Fisher," *American Speech* 50 (1975): 36–49.

6 William Thornton, *Cadmus: or, a Treatise on the Elements of Written Language* (Philadelphia, 1793), pp. v–vii.

7 James Ewing, *The Columbian Alphabet, Being an Attempt to New Model the English Alphabet* (Trenton, N.J., 1798).

8 James Carrol, *The American Criterion of the English Language* (New London, Conn., 1795), p. iii.

9 Michael H. Barton, *Something New* (Boston, June 30, 1830), p. 11.

10 Amasa D. Sproat, *An Endeavor Towards a Universal Alphabet* (Chillicothe, Ohio, 1857), p. vi.

11 Rev. Ezekiel Rich, "New Project for Reforming the English Alphabet and Orthography" (U.S. Serials 442, Document 126: February 19, 1844), p. 6.

12 N. E. Dawson, "Reformed Alphabet and Orthography" (U.S. Serials 1815: February 5, 1878), p. 15.

13 Francis A. March, *The Spelling Reform* (Washington, D.C., 1893), p. 33.

14 Charles S. Voorhees, "A Bill to Provide for an Amended Orthography" (H.R. 7779, introduced February 27, 1888).

15 G. H. McKnight, "The Movement for Simplified Spelling in America," *Germanisch-Romanische Monatsschrift* 2 (1910): 595.

16 Joseph Medill, "Essay on Spelling," in *Our Accursed Spelling*, ed. E. O. Vaile (Chicago, 1901), p. 59.

17 *A Century of Tribune Editorials* (Chicago: The Tribune Co., 1947), pp. 146–47.

18 "Simplified Spelling and the Universities," *Circulars of the Simplified Spelling Board*, 8 (October 20, 1906), p. 4.

19 Theodore Roosevelt, Letter to Charles A. Stillings (August 27, 1906), in *Simplified Spelling* (Washington, D.C.: Office of the Public Printer, 1906), pp. 5–6.

20 Samuel Clemens, "Simplified Spelling," in *Letters from the Earth*, ed. Bernard DeVoto (New York: Fawcett World Library, 1967), pp. 131–33.

21 Samuel Clemens, "A Simplified Alphabet," in *Mark Twain's Works* (New York: Harper and Bros., 1929), 26: 257.

22 Thomas R. Lounsbury, *English Spelling and Spelling Reform* (New York: Harper and Bros., 1909), p. 6.

23 H. L. Mencken, *The American Language*, 4th ed. (New York: Knopf, 1936), pp. 403–04.

24 "Thru's Through and So Is Tho," Editorial, *Chicago Tribune* (September 29, 1975), sec. 2, p. 2.

Chapter 5

1 Arn and Charlene Tibbetts, *What's Happening to American English?* (New York: Charles Scribner's Sons, 1978), pp. 167–69.

2 Allen Walker Read, "American Projects for an Academy to Regulate Speech," *PMLA* 51 (1936): 1141–79; Shirley Brice Heath, "A National Language Academy? Debate in the New Nation," *Linguistics* 189 (1977): 9–43.

3 *Academy Papers; Addresses on Language Problems by Members of the American Academy of Arts and Letters* (New York: Charles Scribner's Sons, 1925), p. v.

4 *Society for Pure English, Tract No. 1* (Oxford: The Clarendon Press, 1919), p. 6.

5 Joel Barlow, *Prospectus of a National Institution to Be Established in the United States* (Washington City, 1806), p. 19.

6 William S. Cardell, "Circular Letter from the Secretary of the American

Academy of Language and Belles Lettres," *The Port Folio* 5th ser. 11 (June 1821): 398–99.

7 *The Writings of Thomas Jefferson*, ed. Andrew A. Lipscomb (Washington, D.C., 1903), 13:340–46.

8 James Madison, *Letters and Other Writings* (Philadelphia, 1865), 3:172–73.

9 William S. Cardell, *Philosophic Grammar of the English Language* (Philadelphia, 1827), p. xi.

10 American Academy of Language and Belles Lettres, *Circular No. III* (New York, 1822), pp. 28–29. Described by Cardell as imperfect and not for publication, the circular breaks off at the end of page 40, in mid-sentence. The copy referred to here is in the collections of the New York Public Library.

11 Edward Everett, "Circulars Addressed to the American Members of the American Academy of Language and Belles Lettres. By the Corresponding Secretary," *North American Review* 14 (1822): 352.

12 Allen Walker Read, "Edward Everett's Attitude Towards American English," *New England Quarterly* 12 (1939): 114.

13 Walt Whitman, "The American Primer," *Atlantic Monthly* 93 (1904): 461–64.

Chapter 6

1 John Locke, *Some Thoughts Concerning Education* (London, 1705), pp. 290–91.

2 Benjamin Franklin, "Sketch of an English School," in *Works*, ed. Jared Sparks (Boston, 1840), 2:132.

3 Benjamin Franklin, "Proposals Relating to the Education of Youth in Pennsylvania," in *The Papers of Benjamin Franklin*, ed. L. W. Labaree (New Haven: Yale University Press, 1961), 3:404.

4 Rollo Laverne Lyman, *English Grammar in American Schools before 1850*, Dept. of the Interior, Bureau of Education Bulletin 1921, no. 12 (Washington, Government Printing Office, 1922), p. 70.

5 Connie C. Eble, "Etiquette Books as Linguistic Authority," in *The Second LACUS Forum, 1975*, ed. Peter A. Reich (Columbia, S.C.: Hornbeam, 1976), pp. 468–75.

6 W. B. Fowle, "Preventive Discipline, No. 12," *Common School Journal* 11 (1849): 257–60.

7 Thomas Dilworth, *A New Guide to the English Tongue* (1793), ed. Charlotte Downey (Delmar, N.Y.: Scholars' Facsimiles and Reprints, 1978), p. 87.

8 Sterling A. Leonard, *The Doctrine of Correctness in English Usage, 1700–1800*, University of Wisconsin Studies in Language and Literature, no. 25. (Madison, 1929), p. 275.

Chapter 7

1 Robert Lowth, *A Short Introduction to English Grammar* (Philadelphia, 1775; rpt. Delmar, N.Y.: Scholars' Facsimiles and Reprints, 1979), p. iii.

2 Robert Lowth, *A Short Introduction to English Grammar* (London, 1762), p. 1.
3 Lindley Murray, *An English Grammar*, 2d ed. (New York, 1814), 1:vii.
4 Personal communication.
5 Samuel Kirkham, *English Grammar in Familiar Lectures*, 11th ed. (New York, 1829), pp. 9–11.
6 Samuel Kirkham, *English Grammar in Familiar Lectures*, 3d ed. (Cincinnati, 1826), pp. 13–14.
7 Noah Webster, "Advertisement to the Philosophical and Practical Grammar," in *An American Dictionary of the English Language* (New York, 1828), n.p.
8 Charles C. Fries, "Rules of the Common School Grammars," *PMLA* 42 (1927):221; Robert C. Pooley, *Grammar and Usage in Textbooks on English*, University of Wisconsin Bureau of Education Research Bulletin no. 14 (Madison, 1933), p. 12. See also, Ferdinand B. Gruen, *English Grammar in American High Schools since 1900* (Washington, D.C.: Catholic University of America, 1934).

Chapter 8

1 Claude Favre de Vaugelas, *Remarqves sur la langve françoise* (Paris, 1659), p. a,i,v (my own translation).
2 Renée Balibar, "Le rôle de l'intervention politique dans la création du français comme langue nationale sous la Révolution française," *Equivalences* 8 (1977): 22 (my own translation).
3 For a discussion of variations in French usage see Lewis C. Harmer, *Uncertainties in French Grammar* (Cambridge: Cambridge University Press, 1979).
4 Sterling A. Leonard, "Educational Quackery," *Saturday Review of Literature* 5 (March 23, 1929): 806.
5 "Understanding of Plain English Grammar Sought by Adults," *Christian Science Monitor* (October 14, 1926): 11.
6 Horace Walpole, "Original Letter on the Improvement of the English Language," *Monthly Magazine* 6 (1798): 117–18.
7 Thomas Cooke, *Tales, Epistles, Odes, Fables . . . To Which Are Added Proposals for Perfecting the English Language* (London, 1729): 204–11.
8 Jonathan Swift, "A Discourse to Prove the Antiquity of the English Tongue," in *The Prose Works of Jonathan Swift*, ed. Herbert Davis (Oxford: Blackwell, 1957), 4:229–39.
9 Jonathan Swift, "A Proposal for Correcting, Improving, and Ascertaining the English Tongue," in *The Prose Works*, ed. Davis, 4:9.
10 John Oldmixon, *Reflections on Dr. Swift's Letter to the Earl of Oxford about the English Tongue* (London, 1712; rpt. Menston: Scolar Press, 1970), p. 3.
11 Archibald Campbell, *Lexiphanes, A Dialogue . . . Being an Attempt to Restore the English Tongue in Its Ancient Purity* (1767; 3d ed. London, 1783), pp. xxii–xxiii.

12 Robert Baker, *Reflections on the English Language* (London, 1770; rpt. Menston: Scolar Press, 1968), pp. 111–12.

13 William Mitford, *An Inquiry into the Principles of Harmony in Language* 2d ed. (London, 1804), pp. 376–406, passim.

14 Archibald Ballantine, "Wardour-Street English," *Living Age* 179 (1888): 502–03. A more complete account of Saxonism from the sixteenth century to the present can be found in Dennis E. Baron's *Going Native: The Regeneration of Saxon English, Publication of the American Dialect Society*, no. 69 (1982).

15 Charles Louis Dessoulavy, *Word-Book of the English Tongue* (London: George Routledge, 1917), p. v; *singers* is Dessoulavy's Saxonism for *poets*.

16 For a history of proposals for common gender English pronouns, see Dennis E. Baron, "The Epicene Pronoun: The Word that Failed," *American Speech* 56 (1981): 83–97.

17 Dugald Stewart, "Dissertation First," *Encyclopaedia Britannica* (7th ed., 1842; rpt. in 8th ed., Boston, 1860) 1:229–30n.

18 Richard Chenevix Trench, *On Some Deficiencies in Our English Dictionaries* (London, 1860), p. 4.

19 Henry Alford, *The Queen's English* (London, 1864), p. 3.

20 George Washington Moon, *The Dean's English*, 4th ed. (New York, 1865), p. 6.

21 Edward S. Gould, *Good English; or, Popular Errors in Language* (New York, 1867), p. 1.

Chapter 9

1 Richard Grant White, *Words and Their Uses* (1870; 19th ed., Boston, 1891), p. ii.

2 Fitzedward Hall, *Recent Exemplifications of False Philology* (New York, 1872), pp. 1–2. Hall's own philology was attacked by Ralph O. Williams. That controversy is recapitulated in Williams's *Some Questions of Good English* (New York, 1897).

3 Walton Burgess, *Five Hundred Mistakes of Daily Occurrence in Speaking, Pronouncing, and Writing the English Language, Corrected* (New York, 1856), p. iii.

4 L. P. Meredith, *Every-day Errors of Speech* (Philadelphia, 1875), p. iv.

5 Ambrose Bierce, *Write It Right; A Little Blacklist of Literary Faults* (New York: Walter Neale, 1909), p. 5.

6 Henry James, *The Question of Our Speech* (Boston: Houghton Mifflin, 1905), p. 6.

7 Sterling A. Leonard, "A Purist Glossary," *Saturday Review of Literature* 5 (March 23, 1929): 806.

Chapter 10

1 Donald Hall, "To a Waterfowl," *American Poetry Review* 2 (November/December 1973): 1.

2 John Simon, *Paradigms Lost* (New York: Clarkson Potter, 1980), p. x.

3 Joseph Addison, *The Spectator* 135 (London, August 4, 1711).

4 William Safire, *On Language* (New York: Times Books, 1980), p. xii.

5 Edwin Newman, *Strictly Speaking* (Indianapolis: Bobbs-Merrill, 1974), p. 11.

6 Edwin Newman, *A Civil Tongue* (Indianapolis: Bobbs-Merrill, 1976), p. 4.

7 William Morris and Mary Morris, eds., *The Harper Dictionary of Contemporary Usage* (New York: Harper and Row, 1975).

8 Sterling A. Leonard, *Current English Usage* (Chicago: National Council of Teachers of English, 1932).

Index